This book is due

Reading Ireland

MANCHESTER
1824

Manchester University Press

Politics, culture and society in early modern Britain

General editors

PROFESSOR ANN HUGHES

DR ANTHONY MILTON

PROFESSOR PETER LAKE

This important series publishes monographs that take a fresh and challenging look at the interactions between politics, culture and society in Britain between 1500 and the mid-eighteenth century. It counteracts the fragmentation of current historiography through encouraging a variety of approaches which attempt to redefine the political, social and cultural worlds, and to explore their interconnection in a flexible and creative fashion. All the volumes in the series question and transcend traditional inter-disciplinary boundaries, such as those between political history and literary studies, social history and divinity, urban history and anthropology. They contribute to a broader understanding of crucial developments in early modern Britain.

Reading Ireland

Print, reading and social change
in early modern Ireland

RAYMOND GILLESPIE

Manchester
University Press

Manchester and New York

distributed exclusively in the USA by Palgrave

Published by Manchester University Press
Oxford Road, Manchester MI3 9NR, UK
and Room 400, 175 Fifth Avenue, New York, NY 10010, USA
www.manchesteruniversitypress.co.uk

Distributed exclusively in the USA by
Palgrave, 175 Fifth Avenue, New York, NY 10010, USA

Distributed exclusively in Canada by
UBC Press, University of British Columbia, 2029 West Mall,
Vancouver, BC, Canada V6T 1z2

British Library Cataloguing-in-Publication Data
A catalogue record for this book is available from the British Library

Library of Congress Cataloging-in-Publication Data applied for

ISBN 0 7190 5527 x *hardback*
EAN 978 0 7190 5527 0

First published 2005

14 13 12 11 10 09 08 07 06 05   10 9 8 7 6 5 4 3 2 1

Typeset in Scala with Pastonchi display
by Koinonia Ltd, Manchester

Printed in Great Britain
by CPI, Bath

Contents

Preface

To some extent the task of writing a book about the past is rather like trying to formulate a response to Archimedes' problem of how to find a place to stand in order to move the earth. Finding such a place to observe, even without moving, the world of early modern Ireland is not an easy task. Traditionally our understanding of that world has been filtered through the lenses of war, plantation and colonisation. More recent work has placed the historian at other vantage points, offering new perspectives from the localities, the world of death and burial and that of popular religious ideas. This book uses yet another vantage point, developed elsewhere, to observe early modern Ireland from a different perspective. In other contexts the history of books has proved to be an important focal point around which ideas about social, cultural and political change can cluster and be tested. The work of Roger Chartier, Robert Darnton, David Hall, D.R. Woolf and D.F. McKenzie, among others, has served to release the history of the book from being simply a bibliographical exercise, describing the material form of printed books, to one which sets the book in its cultural, economic and social context. In particular, by understanding how communities involved with the world of print, as producers, distributors and readers, put printed artefacts to use in daily life, it is possible to reconstruct something of the social and cultural topographies of those worlds. That is the task and the approach to the past that this book attempts for early modern Ireland.

Much of the evidence on which this book draws, and particularly the evidence of the books themselves, is well known. Nineteenth- and early twentieth-century bibliographers, such as E. McClintock Dix, Richard Best, R.J. Hayes, W.K. Sessions and most recently Tony Sweeney, have done much fundamental work in identifying surviving imprints and in cataloguing the output of the Irish presses. More recently Mary Pollard's monumental *Dictionary of members of the Dublin book trade, 1550–1800* (London, 2000) has allowed us to put some flesh on the stark imprints by charting the careers of printers and booksellers. The way I have used that evidence is, I think, rather different from that in which bibliographers have proceeded although there are clearly overlaps and the first part of this book, in Chapters 2, 3 and 4, is heavily dependent on the pioneering work of others. My perspective differs also from the way in which intellectual historians have approached print, searching for evidence of formal sets of propositions about God, the physical world or the life of the mind. In the main I am not concerned with the history of ideas at a high social level or the world of the university or of learned society. Rather this is a book about the social and cultural history of books throughout society. To do this I have examined books not simply for their physical make up or the ideas they contain, although both of these are important attributes of the printed word, but rather in an attempt to understand how books, and the world of print generally, were used in early modern Ireland. This process of using books I have termed reading, and it lies at the centre of Part III in Chapters 5 to 7. As such, reading is not a simple decoding of symbols on a page which separated the formally literate from the illiterate, a cleavage which some have seen as underpinning much of the social differentiation in early-modern societies. Recent research, however, has highlighted the fact that those two worlds are not mutually exclusive. Those who were technically 'illiterate' could use books, and other documents, in that they understood how, if necessary, to manipulate them in particular social contexts. In that sense the world of reading and writing serves to shape, and to be shaped by, the experiences of the everyday world. As Carlo Ginzburg's portrait of Menocchio, the miller from Friuli, in *The cheese and the worms* (1980) demonstrates, reading is a complex issue in which readers deploy different strategies in understanding the printed word, and in doing so restore agency to the reader.

This book has been written over a long period of time. It is, in some sense, a successor to an earlier book, *Devoted people: belief and religion in early modern Ireland* (Manchester, 1997). That book was concerned about what it meant to be religious in early modern Ireland and argued for the importance of experience, rather than formally expressed doctrine or institutions, in shaping the religious worlds. Some of those questions are revisited in Chapter 6 below. However, this book is an attempt to broaden the argument of *Devoted people* and ask what it was like to live with a wider range of experiences in early modern Ireland. As such it is a book about meanings, or how contemporaries constructed the world around them and were, in turn, shaped by those constructions. I use the world of print as the focus, and reading as a way of understanding how people constructed print, in which many were involved, to begin to formulate answers to the problem of reconstructing the experience of the early modern Irish world. Inevitably, as I have discussed other aspects of early modern Irish society in articles and conference papers I have considered various aspects of the role print may have had in those diverse worlds. Thus some of what I have to say here is already published, and textual critics will have no difficulty in tracing it. In particular I have drawn on two earlier articles on 'The circulation of print in seventeenth-century Ireland' in *Studia Hibernica* no. 29 (1995–97), pp. 31–58, and 'Reading the Bible in seventeenth-century Ireland' in Bernadette Cunningham and Máire Kennedy (eds), *The experience of reading: Irish historical perspectives* (Dublin, 1999), pp. 10–38. Nevertheless, I am confident that enough that is new has crept in to justify the purchase price of this volume.

This is a survey of the world of reading and writing over a period of two hundred years. It is not a subject which has attracted much attention from historians hitherto and hence the secondary literature is limited. I have been forced back into the jungle of primary sources in an endeavour to find patterns in the making and using of print. The scattered nature of that evidence means that I have had to draw on the knowledge and good will of two groups of people. The first is the librarians and archivists who have charge of the material cited in the notes and bibliography. Without exception, in a time of overstretched resources, they have been unfailingly helpful and without the patience and kindness this book could not have been written. The second group is those who have provided me with references or have sent me on new and profitable trails by their suggestions. In particular I would like to thank Toby Barnard, Jimmy Kelly, Brian Mac Cuarta, Giles Mandlebrote, Maighréad Ní Mhurchadha and Tony Sweeney. In addition Toby Barnard read the entire text and, in the manner of an eighteenth-century landlord, improved it a great deal. The remaining blemishes are the result of my wilfulness rather than his generous chiding. In other practical ways I am indebted to John McLoughlin and Virginia Davis whose kindness made a good deal of the research possible. Like *Devoted people* this book is published by Manchester University Press which is made manifest in history editor Alison Welsby. In this case she, and the press, have had their patience severely tried by a wayward author who has insisted on being diverted down the byways of history instead of getting on with the business in hand. I trust that their faith has finally been translated into good works. More than any others two people are responsible for what follows. The first is Penny Woods, librarian of the Russell Library in NUI Maynooth, who in 1994 offered me the chance to talk at a conference organised by the Rare Books Group of the Library Association of Ireland on the book trade outside the pale. My resolute refusal of the invitation was met by an equally, though probably misguided, resolute insistence that I was the only person who could do this. The result was that a vague interest in the history of books, which most historians possess, was crystallised into a concrete research project with which I have lived, intermittently, for the last ten years. Over that period I have been encouraged, criticised, given much practical help and distracted by Bernadette Cunningham, who has made this book possible in ways which are too numerous to mention. While both Penny and Bernie deserve many thanks neither is to blame for what follows.

As with most explorations into early modern Ireland the nature of the evidence and the historiography dictates that there will be lacunae in this analysis, and unanswered questions remain. The nature of the evidence means that not enough has been said about the detail of the geography of book availability, which is clearly an important question in assessing the social and cultural impact of print. Given the space available I have not been able to say much about language change, which is also clearly an important area, but recent work in this area by Pat Palmer and Vincent Carey has made this a less pressing, though far from resolved, problem to which I hope to return. If this book serves to provoke others to try to resolve some of these problems, or indeed others, then it will have achieved at least one of its aims.

Note on the text

In order to make the text as accessible as possible the spelling of quotations has been modernised and punctuation added to make the meaning more comprehensible. Titles of early modern printed books have been modernised and limited publication details have been given. Full details will be found in the CD Rom version of the *English short title catalogue, 1473–1800* (3rd edn, London, 2003). All dates have been given in Old Style except that the year has been taken to begin on 1 January. In the notes, references have been given in their most accessible form and where adequate editions of texts or reprints of early-modern printed works exist these have been used. Calendars of documents are cited when the calendar entry provides enough information to illustrate the argument. In the footnotes references are given in full when a work is cited for the first time in a chapter and it is subsequently abbreviated in that chapter. Document collections are not described in the notes but descriptions are included in the bibliography although genuinely miscellaneous collections have not been so described.

Abbreviations

The following abbreviations have been used in the notes:

B.L.	British Library, London
Bodl.	Bodleian Library, Oxford
Cal.S. P. dom	*Calendar of State Papers, Domestic*
Cal. S. P. Ire.	*Calendar of State Papers relating to Ireland*
H.M.C.	Historical Manuscripts Commission
N.A.	National Archives, Dublin
N.L.I.	National Library of Ireland, Dublin
N.L.W.	National Library of Wales, Aberystwyth
P.R.O.	The National Archives, Public Record Office, London
P.R.O.N.I.	Public Record Office of Northern Ireland, Belfast
R.C.B.	Representative Church Body Library, Dublin
T.C.D.	Trinity College, Dublin

Part I

The conditions of print

Chapter 1

The social meaning of print

Historians have not been slow to appreciate the importance of print in early modern European history. The success of seismic shifts in religious and intellectual life in the sixteenth and seventeenth centuries has been, at least in part, attributed to the invention and diffusion of printing across Europe in this period. In the view of one of the first modern accounts of the history of the book, 'the printed book was one of the most effective means of mastery over the whole world'.[1] For some early modern people also print was an important force in shaping their lives and the world around them. The English Protestant martyrologist John Foxe regarded print as a providential gift from God which allowed the shackles of Rome to be shaken off and the true light of the Gospel to dawn.[2] How print actually worked in the early modern world is now less clear than it may have appeared to Foxe and his contemporaries. For some modern historians, such as Elizabeth Eisentein, the 'print revolution' was about the process of printing, especially the increasing of output of works, the standardisation of texts and the preservation of documents. However the technology of print which such explanations emphasise was not, of itself, an agent of change in Ireland. In economic terms, the technology of print was of limited significance in sixteenth- and seventeenth-century Ireland, employing no more than a handful of individuals on a full-time basis. For those who imported printed material it remained a small part of the cargoes in the holds of their ships. Rather it is only when the products of the printing press are embedded in a social, religious and political context that their significance becomes clear. From this perspective the revolution which print engendered is a more complex affair, operating over a longer time-scale and as much concerned with the reception of the printed word as about its production.[3] Reading as much as printing is central to this approach, yet reading, like writing or printing, was not a neutral process. Texts, whether manuscript or print, were read in particular contexts. Churches, for instance, instructed their followers how to read the Bible, and lawyers and politicians thought they knew how statutes could best be read. These social, political, economic, institutional and cultural frames which surrounded both reading and printing provide a point of departure in understanding the world of print in early modern Ireland.

I

In 1689 the Cork Williamite and future lord chancellor of Ireland Richard Cox, passing his exile from Jacobite-controlled Ireland in London, wrote a history of his native country. He concluded his address to the reader in the second part of the history, which dealt with the events nearest his own time, by observing 'when these windings and revolutions will end God almighty knows'.[4] Later historians have followed Cox's lead in describing early modern Ireland as an age of dramatic, indeed revolutionary, change. It was, according to T.W. Moody's introduction to the third volume of the *New history of Ireland*, 'above all an age of disruption ... more catastrophic and far-reaching than anything Ireland had experienced since the Anglo-Norman invasion of the twelfth century or was to experience again till the great famine, the land war and the struggle for national independence'.[5] Some would go further and, like Cox, characterise the events of the sixteenth and seventeenth centuries as a revolution. Roy Foster, for instance, has characterised the eighteenth-century Irish experience as owing 'everything to the fundamental and protracted revolution of the seventeenth century'.[6]

Evidence for this sense of early modern Ireland as a revolutionary age is not wanting. In some respects it shared in processes that can be traced in outline across early modern Europe. The centralisation of authority in Dublin after the end of the Nine Years' War in 1603 and the undermining of powerful local magnates such as Hugh O'Neill, earl of Tyrone, for example, reflect trends at work elsewhere in Europe also. The state increasingly monopolised violence and the machinery of war at the expense of local nobilities. Similarly the economic transformation of Ireland, with the rise of a market economy and the greater commercialisation of economic life, echoed a broader European process. In religious terms too, the progress of the Reformation and Counter-Reformation in Ireland needs to be seen in a European context, if only to emphasise some of the aberrant features of the Irish experience.

In other areas the development of Irish society in the sixteenth and seventeenth centuries was unique. The composition of the Irish social and political elite underwent a dramatic shift in the years between 1580 and 1700. The Irish peerage summoned to the parliament of 1585 was drawn from five Gaelic or Gaelicised families and twenty Old English landed families, the descendants of the medieval Anglo-Norman settlers. By the end of the seventeenth century, of the fifty-nine elite families who were summoned to the House of Lords thirty-nine (or about two-thirds) were drawn from New English settler families who had arrived in the country in the half century before 1641. A further five were from settler families of post-1641 origin. Old English families had thirteen representatives while just two were of native Irish extraction. The changing composition of this parliament reflects a major transfer of power from one social group to another.[7] Underpinning this transfer of political influence was a dramatic shift in the pattern of Irish landownership as land passed from Catholic to Protestant landowners through both formal plantation and informal colonisation. However, the traditional estimates of the fall in the proportion of Irish land held by Catholics from 61 per cent in 1641 to 22 per cent in 1688 and by 1703, after the Williamite land settlement, to 15 per cent may be too sweeping.[8] The simple equations of Protestant with settler, and Catholic with native are far from being perfect. At least some new settlers, such as the Hamilton family, earls of Abercorn in Ulster or the Browne family, Lords Altamont in Mayo, were Catholic. Again some of the former Catholic families, such as the Butlers, earls of Ormond, converted to Protestantism. Yet the shift in landholding patterns is striking enough to delineate, at least in outline, the decline of one elite and its replacement by another.

Such patterns of change are the stuff of history but they are rarely as simple as they appear at first glance. Only occasionally is it possible to see anything which might even resemble a single, coherent revolution. Irish Catholics may have lost land but in many cases they retained considerable social prestige. As Archbishop Oliver Plunkett noted in Ulster during the 1670s, many of the 'ancient vassals' who were now reduced to the rank of tenants to new settlers 'are more or less so well disposed to their former overlords that they always give them some contribution'.[9] It may have been easy to effect a change in land ownership but social attitudes proved more difficult to alter. In the sphere of religion, too, it is possible to map out the institutional revolution that took place in early modern Ireland. However, the effects of these developments on religious belief are much more problematical because the laity shaped their own ideas about God for day to day use in the world.[10] Changes in the various spheres of human existence happened at differential rates. Some areas of experience, such as belief or social attitudes, shifted only slowly while other aspects, such as economic status or institutional change, responded more quickly to external stimuli.[11] To this already complex situation it is necessary to add a consideration of regional variation in the distribution of power and wealth. Such variations in power and wealth help to explain why Ulster, where the social and political vacuum which followed the 1607 flight to Europe of the northern earls allowed a major social engineering project to be carried out, was so different to Longford where local native families devised survival strategies to minimise the impact of plantation.[12] All of this suggests that early modern Ireland did not undergo a single revolution but rather a series of interlinked revolutions moving at varying speeds. Their differential progress in different parts of the country may go some way to explaining not only the highly localised nature of early modern Irish society but also why large-scale movements, such as the Reformation, comprising a series of linked revolutions in institutions and beliefs, had the character that they did.

For the historian, this understanding of early modern Ireland gives rise to the problem of observing these various, overlapping revolutions in action. This book uses the perspective of the world of print as a vantage point from which to observe the shifts in early modern Irish society. To do this it exploits two important attributes of print. First, the printed word had a material form and hence by examining how it was created, traded and owned as a commodity it is possible to chart some of the economic changes that took place in early modern Ireland as a traditional exchange economy gave way to a more commercial one. However print as a commodity had a greater signi-ficance than simply revealing the workings of the marketplace since print, especially in the form of books, was an important marker of status for its owners in this new commercial world. The accumulation of a library by a gentleman, even if none of the books was read, was an important sign of a person's social and economic position. Thus the rise of the world of print provides an insight into social change as Ireland moved from a Gaelic polity, which relied on oral traditions to preserve and spread ideas, to a more Anglicised one, in which books conveyed thoughts but also allowed their owner to display in physical form his real or imagined erudition. The second important attribute of print was that it had the potential to transmit ideas. Those ideas did not exist in a vacuum but rather were appropriated by those who came into contact with them through the process of reading. In practice, reading was a technique which deployed a much wider range of skills than simply the technical mastery required to decode letter forms. How people understood the printed texts with which they came into contact was a complex process as they absorbed the ideas they found on the page and applied them to their own worlds. Chapters 3 and 4 of this book exploit the first attribute of print, its existence as commodity, to chart some of the revolutions that took place in the supply of books in the early modern period. Chapters 5 to 7 deal with the second attribute of print by attempting to construct how contem-poraries used the books they had bought, borrowed, stolen or heard others read aloud. In so doing these chapters chart something of the ways in which the inhabitants of early modern Ireland perceived their world and how that world was shaped by its representation in print. The expansion of print was contingent on one other important variable that needs to be examined. Print depended on a world in which the social rules for writing were well established. Chapter 2 deals with the significant shift in the social context that took place in early modern Ireland which enabled writing to become an accepted part of that world. It was that revolution which allowed the other linked revolutions that accompanied print to flourish. The remainder of this first chapter will deal with another aspect of the social context of print, its social meaning, and with what contemporaries thought of the material and intellectual commodity that printing with movable type brought to Ireland.

II

There was a wide range of attitudes towards the printed word in early modern Ireland. Some of those who came into contact with print were enthusiastic about it. Thomas Gent, the York printer who was born in Dublin and served his unhappy apprenticeship to Patrick Campbell in the city, declared in his early eighteenth-century verse autobiography

> Printing is sure a fine and curious art
> Esteemed by princes, great and mighty men
> Because the things obscure it doth impart
> More quick than numbers e'er could do by pen;
> So cheap withal – what manuscripts contain
> As saves the world of time with little pain.[13]

The late seventeenth-century Presbyterian minister of Benburb, County Tyrone, John Kennedy, would have agreed, declaring in his notebook that the invention of printing led to 'knowledge [being] greatly increased in men's minds'. In particular, he noted that printing had put the Bible into widespread circulation 'and every one applied to find out the meaning of the original' and communicate it to others rather than have that knowledge confined to clergy.[14] From a different confessional position Thomas Bourke, the printer to the Catholic Confederation of the 1640s, also extolled the power of print in a preface to one of his printed works. Of books, he claimed,

> without the print many either lie hidden in obscure angles or are moth eaten in old desks or hutches or finally buried in perpetual oblivion. I might therefore say much of the incomparable good and benefit that doth redound to the Commonwealth by the print of which the Catholics of this kingdom were deprived since the revolt from the true religion, which was not the less of their sufferings, or the meanest prejudice done to their learned men ... But now it hath pleased God after so long pressures and afflictions to dispose so of the affairs of the Catholics of this kingdom necessitated to take arms ... that among other blessings they also have a print, I am confident that the studies and brave works of learned men shall shortly come to light for the public good ... wherefore gentle reader, with this my labour in the press confident that to thine use I will shortly publish other learned works which hitherto, through the iniquity of former times lay lurking in darkness.[15]

From yet a third perspective, that of Gaelic Ireland, print also appeared attractive. By the early seventeenth century the preserving power of print was viewed by some as a way of capturing the history and culture of a traditional world that appeared under threat. In 1642 Rory O'More, one of those who had planned the rising of the previous year, in a fit of enthusiasm for the study of Irish history wished that 'those learned and religious fathers in Louvain did come over in haste with their monuments and with an Irish and Latin print'.[16] Certainly by the beginning of the eighteenth century one native Irish scribe was so entranced by the world of print that he scribbled two long notes on its history in the margins of a manuscript he was writing.[17]

Others were less certain of the benefits of print. For some, print, with its ability to circulate ideas widely, could be a source of disruption. As Dean George Rust declared in a preface to a funeral sermon in 1663, 'I am well aware how indiscreet it is to expose that to the eye which was intended but for the ear'.[18] In the field of politics many contemporaries were well aware of the problems which print could cause. When the secretary of the Kilkenny Confederation, Richard Bellings, came to write his memoirs in the 1670s he refused to allow them to be printed, despite many rumours that they would be, because he feared the divisions which the unrestricted circulation of the work would create. Instead they seem to have circulated widely in the more traditional and restrictive form of manuscript.[19] Again the desire to minimise widespread conflict may lie behind the duke of Ormond's unwillingness to enter into a printed debate with the earl of Anglesea in the 1680s.[20] In religion too, fear of fracturing local, delicately balanced relations may well be one factor in explaining the near absence of locally printed works of religious controversy in early modern Ireland. While in England the presses produced several hundred controversial works in the reign of James I alone, the Irish press produced almost none. One explanation for such difference may lie in the fact that those who wished to attack Catholicism had to do so without creating tensions with the Catholic majority in Ireland. Thus, controlled discussion and circulation of manuscript tracts rather than the shotgun effect of print were the preferred options. It may also help to explain the care which Bishop King took to manage the controversy which he generated with the Presbyterians in the 1690s by attempting to restrict circulation of his printed tracts.[21]

The power to disrupt, some felt, was the result of the anonymous property of print, appearing cold on a page, which it was argued was more durable and reliable and so some gave more credit to it than rumour. One pamphleteer of the 1640s, for instance, complained of the fabulous pamphlets printed about the rising in Ireland which were 'making credulous people to believe such things as are contrived from their [the pamphleteers'] hellish brains'.[22] Again during the political crises of the popish plot in the early 1680s the Irish chief governor, the duke of Ormond, complained of allegations being made that his sympathies lay with Catholics, 'yet if it get into a narrative thousands will swallow it as truth and against this there is no [de]fence. The credulous that trust in print will never leave or consider whether it be material or no.'[23] Whatever about the individual words of print, the printed book, used as a prop in argument, could also carry authority which could be used to reinforce spoken messages. The physical power of the printed book to persuade people, particularly those who could not read it, in a way that oral recitation would not is suggested by the events surrounding a gathering in a house in Dublin in November 1641. One man, George Hackett, 'drew a little book which the examinant [Bartholomew Lennon] knewest was an almanac and there read the names of divers persons which the said Hackett said were the principal rebels'. Hackett, according to his own deposition, was able to sign his name while most of the others were not. He was clearly using the book as a prop in his performance to convince others to whom the contents of the book would be seen as mysterious. The book probably did not contain any such list of names since none of the surviving almanacs does but it was sufficient that his audience believed it might.[24] A rather similar performance occurred in early 1642 in Tipperary during the seige of a castle when one of the besiegers took an unspecified book from his pocket and swore that if those holding the castle came out they would be released.[25] Again the book as prop helped convince.

The enthusiasm, albeit guarded at times, which contemporaries expressed for the printed word did not sweep all before it. Print was seen as being appropriate to particular circumstances. As the duke of Ormond commented of one work in 1678, 'it is too long to pass to many hands in any other way than by printing and that I do not think it or the subject worth'.[26] Print settled down as another means of communication alongside speech and the written word of the manuscript. What began as speech often made its way into manuscript and subsequently into print.[27] Sermons, for example, might move through all three media. According to Henry Jones, the bishop of Meath, one of his sermons which was printed in 1676 'at first was intended but for that honourable auditory [at Christ Church cathedral, Dublin]' but

> being awakened by an imperfect copy taken while it was in speaking which I understood to have been dispersed I know not how far and might be (I feared) to the prejudice of the truth and to the advantage of adversaries I therefore conceded to the revising and publishing thereof for avoiding those inconveniences declaring this and none other to be what I own.

To fit into the new medium of print 'something also is added for further enlargement which might better pass (I conceive) in writing than speaking'.[28] Again what began in print might well end up in speech. The Protestant polemicist Barnaby Rich claimed that after the publication of his *New description of Ireland* in 1610 he happened to be at the house of a Dublin alderman 'where a woman began to pick quarrels both at me and my work, belying and slandering both it and me and with such false and untrue reports that a number of those that had never seen the book itself believed all to be true that she reported'. Rich was ostracised on the basis of reports of his book rather than the printed work itself although as he observed 'the book is extant to be seen and to answer for itself'.[29]

In many respects oral communication continued to dominate the world of early modern Ireland. The tradition of story telling, for example, remained strong although by the end of the seventeenth century many traditional tales had been committed to manuscript form for recitation.[30] In some contexts oral forms were preferred to written ones. As one Irish scribe wrote in the margin of a manuscript he was working on in 1679, 'A blessing on the souls of good reciters that used to be who could speak this to me and not weary me [by having to write it down]'.[31] Face to face communication could achieve things that writing could not. As Oliver Plunkett, the archbishop of Armagh, observed of one of his Franciscan adversaries during a dispute, 'I shall write to Coppinger ... but a man to man conversation would accomplish a great deal more than an impersonal letter and I would say many things to him face to face which I do not think it suitable to put on paper ... he would be able to show my letter and boast about it'.[32] Furthermore written documents could be forged, a point which religious controversialists made great play of with Catholic writers claiming that Protestants had inserted material into the Bible or the Church Fathers.[33] Documents could also be lost and because of this could be deemed less reliable than oral testimony provided by an individual whose trustworthiness was recognised. The reliability of such memory could be tested against the wider communal memory and with reference to the standing of the witness in the community. This may help to explain why in property boundary disputes the oral evidence of 'old men' was often preferred to written descriptions of boundaries, since boundary markers could be moved or destroyed and documents could be altered. Even in the 1660s when Drogheda corporation had maps of their property they still fretted that the 'ancient men' who knew the property boundaries would die because then the real boundaries of the corporation's property would be uncertain.[34] To this end rituals enacted to remember property and jurisdictional boundaries were an important aid to memory. In the case of Drogheda the corporation reinstituted the riding of the franchises so that the boundary of the town's authority would be remembered. In a 1639 case involving the Christ Church cathedral property of Astagob in County Dublin, for which deeds certainly existed, a number of witnesses described an elaborate ritual in which five or six men perambulated the meres of the property. In one case Nicholas Crenan, a man in his late fifties in 1639, described how 'he was whipped at the Hoar stone [a boundary marker] upon mereing of the said land with the other boys of his parish when he was ten years of age'. Others described being whipped at another part of the mereing 'to the end that he might take notice of the mereing aforesaid'.[35] Memory and oral testimony were clearly more important than the written document in such contexts. They also had the advantage of simplicity since the record of the past was only as old as the memory of the oldest living person and hence could easily be reshaped to remove potential conflicts between past and present.

Many in early modern Ireland were inclined to rely on oral evidence to understand the world and its past. Others, particularly of a scholarly tradition, which placed its faith in writing, increasingly turned to manuscript records for their evidence about the Irish past and tended to trust such texts over the oral tradition.[36] In doing so they tended to remake the Irish past in the image of the present, as having been a literate world in which documents were important. The antiquarian Conall Mac Geoghegan, for instance, preparing his translation of the Annals of Clonmacnoise in 1627, recreated the past in an acceptable, literate form. He stressed the importance of the written word for those in Ireland's past and equated civility with literacy and books arguing that the Viking wars meant that the Irish 'were grown rude and altogether illiterate' and more recent loss of books had led to ignorance.[37] Those of the Gaelic learned class in early seventeenth-century Ireland repeatedly deferred to manuscripts as sources of authority. In the poetic dispute known as the 'Contention of the bards', at the beginning of the seventeenth century, the contenders referred each other to manuscripts as proofs of their arguments. As one participant in the debate argued, 'let him who would challenge me rub it out from the books'.[38] In some cases the list of manuscripts was very specific and many of the same works, which clearly held considerable authority, were used by both historians and poets writing about the Irish past in the seventeenth century.[39] It would be wrong to assume that such manuscript volumes existed in isolation. They were subject to interpretation from within the oral tradition because the literate standards of documentation could not be uniformly or readily applied in every case since literate ways of transacting business developed only slowly. Contradictions between the oral and written interpretations of the past sometimes needed to be resolved. In the poetic 'Contention' the manuscript tradition was juxtaposed with the oral tradition of poetry, and the Old English historian of the 1630s, Geoffrey Keating, also referred his readers to the oral tradition of poetry on which he based some of his interpretations. Such a method of presenting evidence was modelled on much older historical texts.[40]

Much of what was written in Irish in the sixteenth and seventeenth centuries remained in manuscript. The limited market for works requiring Irish type meant that it was uneconomic to print such texts unless a large subvention was forthcoming from church or state which, with a few exceptions, it was not. Significant capital investment in paper, the largest cost in book production, and storage for books which did not sell quickly was simply not possible in an undercapitalised business. As a result works in Irish tended to be published scribally. Geoffrey Keating's *Foras feasa ar Éirinn*, for instance, circulated widely in seventeenth-century Ireland in manuscript form.[41] Such scribal publication was not confined to Irish-language works. For English-language texts also scribal publication was an approved way of circulating information in certain social contexts. Manuscripts of the works of literary coteries, such as that which existed around Katherine Philips in Dublin in the 1660s, certainly circulated widely among intended audiences.[42]

Rigid demarcations between the worlds of manuscript and print are not possible. Contemporaries distinguished only slowly between the two forms of communication. The earl of Kildare in the 1520s did not differentiate between manuscripts and printed works when he listed his books.[43] Differentiation appeared first in institutional collections and the early library catalogues of Trinity College, Dublin, did not include manuscripts because they were listed separately. By the 1620s, when the library of Limerick cathedral was listed, there too manuscripts and printed books were carefully distinguished.[44] However, printed books and manuscripts circulated in the same worlds. While the distribution of printed books improved greatly in the seventeenth century there were some who could not obtain their own personal copy of works which they wanted, particularly in the case of illegally imported Catholic works. One Franciscan, Connor MacParlane, for instance copied a printed devotional tract, available in Dublin in the 1680s, into his own commonplace book and also complied a theological miscellany for his own use.[45] Again by the end of the seventeenth century a professional scribe had put Bonaventure Ó Eodhasa's *An teagasc Críosdaidhe*, printed in Louvain in 1611, into manuscript again, and in Dublin, Cavan and Fermanagh printed catechisms were also being copied by scribes.[46]

Print, like handwritten texts, was not intended to exist in isolation. It was intended to perform social functions, as manuscript publication and oral communication were also intended to do. Contemporaries recognised that print had a particular purpose within the range of possible ways of publication. The early seventeenth-century godly preacher Richard Olmstead prefaced one collection of his Irish sermons with the words 'as a picture expresseth not the life, so neither can writing demonstrate the lively energy of the voice which consists of an utterance and action, the two ornaments of speech'.[47] As the late seventeenth-century Dublin Presbyterian minister Robert Chambers expressed it, 'there is as much difference between hearing and reading, between a lively voice and breathless lines as much as is between cold meat and hot'.[48] Sermons, for example, were intended to be heard rather than printed and read. When a sermon moved from the medium of oral delivery to the printed word, significant changes were necessary to accommodate it to the new medium. Print allowed the sort of extended meditation on words that the performance medium of the sermon did not. As John Murcot claimed, when a sermon preached by him in Christ Church, Dublin, went into print in 1656, it would be useful to 'those whose frail memories may have lost the greater part of the sense of it and by a humble reading and meditation of it may do more good to those that have altogether been unacquainted with it'.[49] Such printed works did not rely on the presence of the minister to convey the authority of what was said; rather the meaning of the text was to be divined by a reader, possibly in consultation with others in a textual community.[50] One contemporary certainly adopted this strategy by annotating his copy of a Dublin printed sermon by the godly minister Faithful Teate with additional scriptural references. His annotations supported the argument and amended some of the printed references supplied in the text.[51]

While books and printed ephemera certainly carried ideas within the context of a wider communications network, they did not stop at that. Books were also creators of sociability. Books as gifts helped to bond particular groups together. In the 1560s the English jurist William Staunford sent a copy of his recently published book to his friend the Catholic palesman Nicholas Nugent, later chief justice of the common pleas.[52] In this case Protestant and Catholic found common space in the printed word of the law. In the late seventeenth century an English member of the Royal Society, Robert Plot, happily sent copies of his books to the Irish scientist and political philosopher William Molyneux.[53] Furthermore the borrowing and lending of books helped to cement social bonds. Both Luke Challoner, one of the first fellows of Trinity College, Dublin, and the early seventeenth-century archbishop of Armagh James Ussher opened their libraries to their friends. Some of these were clerical borrowers either in Dublin or in Trinity College itself but there were a number of lay friends who borrowed works on politics, history, geography and medicine, and a few borrowed devotional works. In some cases such contacts could produce what appear strange links. Ussher and David Rothe, the Catholic polemicist and future Catholic bishop of Ossory, for instance were on book and manuscript exchanging terms in the early 1620s. In turn Ussher borrowed from others.[54] In late seventeenth-century Dublin the Quaker Joseph Carleton, apparently with a much smaller collection, recorded in a notebook the books which he lent to others, crossing them out as they were returned.[55] Such communal sharing of books could create particular bonds between groups of people. In 1705, for instance, a group of Presbyterian ministers and students came together to form the Belfast Society at which they could read and discuss the books they read. A circular of 1720 described that about fifteen years ago divers ministers and students considering the many disadvantages which arise from our being hampered in our education from our low circumstances in the world which cannot afford us competent libraries ... we consulted of proper measures for procuring the best intelligence about books, enter into concerts for the buying of them, taking care that no two members purchase the same book (except where it is of constant use to all) by which means the whole reap the benefit of what every member possesseth. Everyone communicated to the whole what he has met with observable in the course of his private studies. After we had conferred upon some subjects one is appointed to reduce the substance of our reasonings into writing and upon the reading of it the conferences on that subject are resumed.[56]

Such sharing of books and ideas among groups of like-minded people was not unusual in late seventeenth-century Ireland. The Societies for the Reformation of Manners, established in Dublin in the 1690s, required that 'at their first meeting they [the members of the society] may discourse of what sermons they have heard, what good books they have seen and read or upon any other pious subject till a competent number come together'. Chapters of the New Testament, the church catechism 'or some other practical good book' were also to be read.[57] More informal groups also existed. In the 1680s a group of Quakers in Chapelizod obtained a copy of a printed work of the sixteenth-century German mystic Jacob Boheme. John Beckett, the first man who seems to have acquired it, lent it to three of his friends, including Thomas Smith, a linen weaver at Chapelizod. On the basis of reading the book and discussing its contents they arrived at rather unorthodox theological views for which they were censured by the Quakers.[58]

The sociability in which books played a part could be regularised in a number of venues which helped to change the way in which news moved and information was created in a culture of communication. Perhaps the most important of these was the coffee house. By the late seventeenth century coffee houses seem to have been a well-established feature of Irish urban life. The London bookseller John Dunton, visiting Ireland in 1698, recorded that there were coffee houses at Dublin, Limerick, Cork, Kilkenny, Clonmel, Wexford, Galway 'and other places'.[59] How large these operations were is not known but it seems likely that they operated on a smaller scale than their English counterparts. At such locations print was an important prompt for coffee-house sociability. Political and commercial news circulated together. Indeed in 1679 the Irish lord lieutenant, the duke of Ormond, unable to find copies of an address to the English parliament, which he was assured had been printed, asked that a search be made among the Dublin booksellers 'and coffee houses where such things possibly may be kept'.[60] Certainly in 1686 the Dublin coffee houses were said to be 'stuffed with news letters'.[61] Such communal reading made sense in the case of high-priced manuscript and imported printed newsletters since the cost could be spread widely. The coffee houses did not stop at being repositories of printed political information and they also took a role in reshaping and recirculating that intelligence through rumour and gossip.[62] In 1679, during the political uncertainty surrounding the popish plot, Sir William Petty in Dublin noted that he had written a tract on how to deal with a possible French invasion 'and yet I verily believe that the air which I have breathed on the coffee houses hath been very prolific and so I believe this paper will be'.[63] For this reason the government attempted to control coffee houses, although in Ireland this took the form of reissuing English proclamations for licensing rather than specific initiatives of the Dublin government.[64]

By the beginning of the eighteenth century the coffee houses were joined by another institution focused on print which generated public discussion of shared and contested ideas: the public library. The emergence of public libraries shifted the idea of a library from a private space where access to books was controlled by networks of friendship or patronage to a public space where civic, religious and commercial values converged and overlapped. Such a development helped to transform the print culture of eighteenth-century Ireland and shape the constituent parts of what might be termed 'public opinion'.

III

Books by their ability to spread ideas, in conjunction with manuscripts and the spoken word, could be either socially cohesive or disruptive. They also had another more tangible social attribute since the book as object also had the power to carry a wide range of messages.* The collecting of books for display in private libraries, for example, was seen as an indicator of social status. A large library, whether read or not, could act as a sign of learning, or pretention to learning. In 1680, for example, Narcissus Marsh, the newly appointed provost of Trinity College, Dublin, clearly linked learning with book ownership when he noted of the books of the vastly learned early seventeenth-century archbishop of Armagh, James Ussher, 'I would not have it divulged that Primate Ussher's library (both manuscripts and printed books) comes very far short of its owner's fame. It might have been thought a good library for another man but not for that learned primate.'[65] Some booksellers even used this perception to flatter potential purchasers. As the London bookseller John Dunton wrote of one of his Dublin customers, 'for the books he buys do by their number sufficiently declare his love to learning, and by their value and intrinsic worth the vastness of his judgement'.[66] Equally an individual's respect for books was part of what was regarded as acceptable conduct. Nicholas Bernard, the dean of Kilmore, contrasted the actions of the rebels in the 1640s in wanting to burn Archbishop Ussher's library and the more respectable treatment of

Viscount Marlington's library, which was sold by the Drogheda garrison.[67]

By the late seventeenth century a series of trappings had been developed for the display of books to underline learned or gentry status. In the early part of the century books were, in the main, kept in boxes or cabinets. In one case in the 1640s an insurgent in Wexford stole a trunk, claiming it would be useful for keeping his books, and Lady Lambert in Kilbeggan kept what was probably her only book, the Bible, in a cupboard in the main hall of the house.[68] By the latter half of the century bookshelves had become more important. A list of 1685 of goods in Dublin Castle included 'a bookcase' in one man's room and in Kilkenny the duke of Ormond certainly had bookshelves in his closet.[69] Richard Steele, the future dramatist, recalled growing up in Dublin where his guardian had a 'pretty large study of books' all arranged by size on bookshelves.[70] By the beginning of the eighteenth century glazed bookcases had begun to make their appearance in Ireland.[71] Bindings too had become an important element in book display. A poem attributed to Swift on the appearance of William Hamilton's *The life and character of James Bonnell, accomptant general of Ireland* (London, 1703) observed

> What's wanting to make the book worth minding,
> Is easily got, A pretty binding.[72]

Some people at least linked the style and quality of binding with the intrinsic value of the book. Dean Bernard, for instance, could comment in the early weeks of the rising of the 1640s of those who destroyed manuscripts 'howsoever valuable yet by their mean clothing likely to be least respected by such illiterate hands'.[73]

In the sixteenth century plain bindings or book covers, sometimes made of bone, served both to protect books and to make them usable.[74] Early seventeenth-century Irish bindings, on the basis of those which survive, are plain sheepskin bindings.[75] From the 1630s, at least, Irish authors had copies of their own works specially bound as presentation copies so that the appearance of the book would reflect its superior contents. Archbishop Ussher in the 1630s certainly had a number of copies of some of his works bound, possibly in Dublin, with his arms embossed on them for presentation purposes.[76] An even more lavish presentation volume was bound as a new year's gift to the Irish lord deputy, Thomas Wentworth, earl of Strafford, from students in Trinity College, Dublin, in 1640.[77] By the late seventeenth century such luxury bindings seem to have become more common. At least some of the work of the 'Devotional binder', who may have worked in Dublin for the bookseller William Norman, may have been done for the duke of Ormond's library and hence for display in bookcases rather than for storage in presses.[78] What impressed John Dunton when he visited Trinity College, Dublin, in 1698 was 'the many handsome folios and o[the]r books in Dutch binding gilt with the earl [of Bath's] arms impressed upon them, for he had sometimes been of this house'.[79] Certainly by the beginning of the eighteenth century a Dublin medical doctor, Edward Worth, was able to assemble an impressive library from auctions in England, Holland, Germany and Ireland which was at least partly for display purposes. Some of his books were purchased for their fine bindings rather than their contents.[80] Moreover Worth rebound many of his books to his own specifications. In some cases where the covers have not been tooled in gold the spines have been tooled. This suggests that Worth was trying to give a uniformly luxurious appearance to his library as part of the display function of the collection.[81]

A collection of books assembled at least partly for display did not disappear on its owner's death. After death, if the collection was sufficiently large, it could be used to perpetuate a person's memory. The Catholic lawyer John Grace of Brittas in his will of 1683 attempted to preserve his own memory by leaving a number of his books to his grandchild 'which I leave as a paraphanalis always to remain in the lineal family of the house'.[82] The fate of families could be uncertain and a more secure way of creating a memorial was bequeathing one's books to an institution. When Sir Jerome Alexander bequeathed his books to the library of Trinity College, Dublin, in the 1670s he specified that they should be known as the Alexander Library and required the college to take extra security measures 'to prevent loss and embezzlement of the said books etc., many of them being small and easily pocketed up'. For each book lost the library keeper was to be fined £5. The real loss was, of course, not financial but the loss of symbolic capital for the Alexander name.[83] Alexander was not the only donor to stipulate conditions for his bequest although he was probably the most exacting.[84] The memory of benefactors was important to the library, and in an early seventeenth-century listing of the furniture of the College the library had 'a table of benefactors' which was, presumably, to be displayed prominently.[85]

By the end of the seventeenth century this form of memorial had become particularly popular with bishops of the Church of Ireland. Sensing a growing interest in the world of print some began to establish a 'public library' to house their own books. In 1701 Narcissus Marsh, archbishop of Dublin, established Ireland's first public library which was, according to the parliamentary statute of 1707 establishing it, 'for the use of all persons who shall resort thereto'.[86] He presented his own books to this new foundation and augmented the collection by purchasing the books of Edward Stillingfleet, bishop of Worcester. That Marsh wished to preserve not just his books but also his own memory is clear from the fact that his arms were carved in the bookcases in the library. There were some earlier examples of such donations. George Wilde, bishop of Derry, willed his books to his family, St John's College, Oxford, and the Merchant Taylors' School in London.[87] This was not simply a Church of Ireland phenomenon since the 1693 will of the Catholic bishop of Ossory, James Phelan, stipulated that 'I leave all my books as a library for the diocese where the Ordinary for the time being and Col. Walter Butler and his heirs shall think best'. Political circumstances ensured that the library could not be established, and what happened to this collection is not known although one of Phelan's books, bearing his signature, is now in the Ossory diocesan library of the Church of Ireland. This suggests that some may have been dispersed locally.[88]

At a lower social level books likewise took on symbolic status. Books were held to have a particular religious significance, and stories of their power circulated. In the sixteenth and early seventeenth centuries older manuscripts, for instance, were often held to have special powers. In particular those which were thought to have been written by saints were venerated as wonder-working relics. In the late 1620s the translator of the Annals of Clonmacnoise claimed that he had seen the Book of Durrow, which was believed to have been one of St Columcille's books, used by a farmer as part of a ritual for curing sick cattle.[89] However books did not have to be that venerable or even to have sacred associations to be perceived as powerful objects. When Bishop Ram of Ferns died in 1635 he bequeathed his books to establish a cathedral library but by 1642 the books still remained in his son's house when it was attacked by rebels. It was reported that the insurgents would have destroyed the books had not a swarm of bees providentially intervened to protect them.[90] Particular religious books, of course, took on special powers. Protestants took oaths on the Bible and Catholics on mass books as symbols or gateways to what was holy for them. In the 1640s rebels swore on a missal.[91] They also appreciated the Protestant sense of the Bible as the word of God. A case in point is the action of a group of Kilkenny rebels in the 1640s who placed the leaf of a bible in the mouth of a dead minister and taunted him by demanding he preach a sermon.[92] The uses of the Bible were not always so orthodox. It might be displayed in the window of a house as a sign of the godly cast of mind of the inhabitants, but Ulster Presbyterians would also use it with keys as part of a divination ritual.[93] The vehement Dublin Protestant Robert Ware claimed that one culprit in the burning of Dublin castle in 1671 was a Catholic, but one who would proclaim his pretended Protestant piety for political reasons. He 'would walk before the lord lieutenant among the gentry to church with his Bible publicly under his arm to be seen' and 'at church he would seem very zealous turning to the texts of scripture as fast as they were quoted by the preacher'.[94] Among Protestants the iconic status of the Bible was reinforced in a number of ways. Swearing on the Bible was, for example, the normal way of taking an oath among Protestants. Similar display was clear from its use in churches. Church Bibles seem to have been larger than those in everyday use to judge from their cost. The parish of St Catherine in Dublin, for instance, not satisfied with what could be obtained locally, ordered their pulpit Bible especially bound from England.[95] The quasi-sacred status of Bibles was also reinforced by the way in which they were kept. The list of the library of the duke of Ormond in the 1680s has little to say about bindings except in the case of religious books, especially the Bible. A number of godly works are described as 'all richly bound in red Turkey leather'. The Books of Common Prayer and one Bible were similarly bound.[96]

That Bibles and Books of Common Prayer were so displayed and attention drawn to them by their bindings meant they were understood as special. In the rising of the 1640s they became the targets of Catholic insurgents wishing to destroy what they believed Protestants regarded as gateways to the sacred. This destruction took various forms. In some cases it was simply the ripping up of books. In late 1641, for instance, two Catholic merchants in Kilkenny 'in their houses tore Protestant Bibles and prayer books and other good English and Protestant books ... in pieces and used and employed them as waste paper to wrap soap, starch candles and other wares'.[97] Such reports of vandalism were rife. In Cavan Protestant books were reported burnt at the high cross in Belturbet, and in Armagh and Meath Bibles were burnt or simply thrown away. In Wexford, more spectacularly the Bible and Book of Common Prayer were both cut up and a piper played in the churchyard while the remains were trampled underfoot.[98] In other cases the destruction was more ritualised, emphasising not simply destruction but desecration also. In Queen's County during the rising of the 1640s one of the Catholic insurgents tore up Bibles 'with the most horrible indignities'.[99] What these might have been is suggested by events in Fermanagh where one rebel took a Bible and laid it 'the open side in a puddle of water, leapt and stamped upon it saying "A plague on it. This book hath bred all the quarrel"'.[100] In Armagh ritual defilement took the form of rebels who 'laid the sacred Bible on their privy parts in contempt of the same'. Another rebel 'opening the sacred Bible pissed on the same saying if I could do worse with it I would'.[101] Ritualised destruction was, of course, not the exclusive prerogative of the native Irish in the 1640s. At the beginning of the seventeenth century the Catholic revolt in the Munster towns had also been characterised by the destruction of Bibles and service books.[102] The lord deputy's secretary, Fynes Moryson, described how in Cashel a Protestant goldsmith had been tied to a tree and Catholics 'threatening to burn him and all his heretical books at which time he [the priest present] burnt some of our books which he so termed'.[103] Book destruction was not confined to those wishing to make a religious statement. In 1596 the Church of Ireland bishop of Cork discovered that in schools in his diocese the queen's arms had been torn out of the grammars despite the fact that 'they came new from the merchant's shops' which he attributed to a protest against the style of the queen as defender of the faith.[104] Such destruction was not limited to gestures of popular protest. The Irish government in the latter part of the seventeenth century began practising book burning as a ritual activity directed against books which were held to be dangerous. In 1661 the Irish parliament ordered that printed copies of the Oath of Association, or the Engagement, should be burned by the common hangman. Further works were burnt in 1663 and in 1689 it was said that Sir John Temple's 1646 history of the Irish rebellion was burnt by the Jacobite government.[105] In 1697 a seditious work of a different type, John Toland's *Christianity not mysterious*, was to be burnt by the hangman at College Green and in 1703 John Asgill's heretical work was to be burnt before the parliament and the Tholsel in Dublin. By 1711 the Presbyterian sermons of Joseph Boyse had been consigned to the hangman's flame before the Tholsel.[106]

The significance of such book destruction is not difficult to discern. To destroy a book was symbolically to destroy the ideas which it contained and to assert an alternative set of ideas. Those who besieged Drogheda in 1642, for instance, were said to have wanted to burn the library of James Ussher, Protestant archbishop of Armagh. Such an act was seen as a symbolic destruction of Ussher and his ideas, 'taking what revenge they could on it [the library] seeing he was too far out of their reach himself'.[107] Again to force an individual to destroy his or her own Bible was a way of forcing them to renounce their religious convictions and to adopt a new set of religious ideas based on other texts or different readings of the same ones. Thus it was no coincidence that rebels at Mountrath, in Queen's County, demanded of a woman that she should 'burn her Bible and go to mass'.[108] The conjunction of the two commands was not accidental.

IV

The printed word in early modern Ireland was a complex entity. Its main consumers may have been the upper social stratum of the literate population, those who had time and money to acquire books and possibly read them. Yet, in reality, books were integral to a much wider social world. No printed work existed in a vacuum. Each one interacted with oral and manuscript traditions to create ways in which people communicated with each other. Those interactions took place within social and cultural frameworks, such as coffee houses, which by the late seventeenth century helped to create a world which both depended on and dominated the world of print. The social situations in which print mattered were not confined to the library, reading circle or coffee house. The symbolic dimension of the printed word, especially in the world of religion, served to ensure that even those who were not technically literate appreciated the iconic status of books, hence making them targets in the various clashes of ideas which characterised early modern Ireland. In such ways did the book become an integral part of the social fabric.

NOTES

1 Lucien Febvre and Henri-Jean Martin, *The coming of the book: the impact of printing, 1450–1800* (London 1976), p. 11.

2 Ian Green, *Print and Protestantism in early modern England* (Oxford, 2000), p. 1.

3 The two main positions are set out by Elizabeth Eisentein and Adrian Johns in 'A.H.R. forum: how revolutionary was the print revolution' in *American Historical Review* cvii (2002), pp. 84–128. David McKitterick, *Print, manuscript and the search for order, 1450–1830* (Cambridge, 2003) is a particularly effective presentation of the latter view.

4 Richard Cox, *Hibernia Anglicana or the second part of the history of Ireland* (London, 1690), sig. e2.

5 T.W. Moody. 'Early modern Ireland' in T.W. Moody, F.X. Martin and F.J. Byrne (eds), *A new history of Ireland iii: early modern Ireland* (Oxford, 1976), p. lxiii.

6 R.F. Foster, *Modern Ireland, 1600–1972* (London, 1988), p. 163.

7 F.G. James, *Lords of the ascendancy* (Dublin, 1995), pp. 21, 100.

8 J.G. Simms, 'Land owned by Catholics in Ireland in 1688' in *Irish Historical Studies* vii (1950–51), pp. 180–90.

9 John Hanly (ed.), *The letters of Saint Oliver Plunkett* (Dublin, 1979), p. 74.

10 Raymond Gillespie, *Devoted people: religion and belief in early modern Ireland* (Manchester, 1997).

11 Raymond Gillespie, 'Faith, family and fortune: the structures of everyday life in early modern Cavan' in Raymond Gillespie (ed.), *Cavan: essays on the history of an Irish county* (Dublin, 1995), pp. 99–114.

12 Raymond Gillespie, 'A question of survival: the O'Farrells and Longford in the seventeenth century' in Raymond Gillespie and Gerard Moran (eds), *Longford: essays in county history* (Dublin, 1991), pp. 13–29.

13 *The life of Thomas Gent, printer of York; written by himself* (London, 1832) p. 32.

14 Presbyterian Historical Society, Belfast, PA 48, Notebook of John Kennedy, p. 56.

15 P[atrick] C[omerford], *The inquisition of a sermon* (Waterford, 1644), sigs a4–4v.

16 H.M.C., *Report on the Franciscan manuscripts* (London, 1906), p. 194.

17 T.C.D., MS 1354, ff. 1v, 241v.

18 George Rust, *A sermon preached at Newtown[ards] the 23 of October 1663 at the funeral of the Honourable Hugh, earl of Mount Alexander* (Dublin, 1664), sig. A1v.

19 Raymond Gillespie, 'The social thought of Richard Bellings' in Micheál Ó Siochrú (ed.), *Kingdoms in crisis: Ireland in the 1640s* (Dublin, 2001), p. 214.

20 Michael Perceval-Maxwell, 'The Anglesea–Ormond–Castlehaven dispute, 1680–1682: taking sides about Ireland in England' in Vincent Carey and Ute Lotz-Heumann (eds), *Taking sides: colonial and confessional mentalities in early modern Ireland* (Dublin, 2003), pp. 214–27.

21 Raymond Gillespie, 'Irish print and Protestant identity: William King's pamphlet wars, 1687–1697' in Vincent Carey and Ute Lotz-Heumann (eds), *Taking sides: colonial and confessional mentalities in early modern Ireland* (Dublin, 2003), pp. 231–4, 240–2, 247–9.

For another possible case of self-censorship see Thomas O'Connor, 'Custom, authority and tolerance in Irish political thought: David Rothe's *Analecta sacra et mira* (1616)' in *Irish Theological Quarterly* lxiv (2000), p. 136.

22 *No pamphlets but a detestation against all such pamphlets as are printed concerning the Irish rebellion* (London, 1642), sig. A2.

23 H.M.C., *Report on the manuscripts of the marquess of Ormonde* (new series, 8 vols, London, 1902–20), v, p. 543.

24 T.C.D., MS 809, ff. 180, 182, 184, 186, 190, 192, 196.

25 T.C.D., MS 821, f. 39.

26 H.M.C., *Report on the manuscripts of the marquess of Ormonde* (old series, 3 vols, London, 1895–1909), ii, p. 283.

27 For example the manuscript collection of sermons from late seventeenth-century Youghal in N.L.I., MS 4201, claim to have been taken down from the preacher, or probably rewritten from notes made at the sermon.

28 Henry Jones, *A sermon on antichrist preached at Christ Church Dublin* (Dublin, 1676), sig.. B3v. Richard Olmstead's *A treatise on the union betwixt Christ and the church* (Dublin, 1627) seems to have had a similar origin according to the dedication (sig. A3).

29 Barnaby Rich, *A true and kind excuse written in defence of that book entitled* A new description of Ireland (London, 1612), pp. 6, 8.

30 Alan Bruford, *Gaelic folk-tales and medieval romances* (Dublin, 1969), pp. 55–64; George Denis Zimmermann, *The Irish storyteller* (Dublin, 2001), pp. 44–78.

31 Paul Walsh, *Irish men of learning* (Dublin, 1947), p. 29.

32 Hanly (ed.), *The letters of Saint Oliver Plunkett*, p. 332.

33 For example, Hanly (ed.), *Letters of Saint Oliver Plunkett*, p. 220; Andrew Sall, *A sermon preached in Christ Church in Dublin* (Dublin, 1674), p. 57.

34 Thomas Gogarty (ed.), *The council book of the corporation of Drogheda* (Drogheda, 1915), pp. 129, 130.

35 This case is fully examined in Maighréad Ní Mhurchadha, 'Contending neighbours: society in Fingal, 1603–60' unpublished Ph.D. thesis N.U.I. Maynooth, 2002, pp. 83–93. For another case of beating to remember events see Raymond Gillespie, *The proctor's accounts of Peter Lewis, 1564–1565* (Dublin, 1996), p. 75.

36 Geoffrey Keating, *Foras feasa ar Éirinn*, eds David Comyn and P.S. Dinneen (4 vols, London, 1902–14), ii, pp. 325, 348; Bernadette Cunningham, *The world of Geoffrey Keating* (Dublin, 2000), pp. 116–19.

37 Denis Murphy (ed.), *The annals of Clonmacnoise* (Dublin, 1896), pp. 7–8.

38 Lambert McKenna (ed.), *Iomarbhágh na bhfileadh* (2 vols, London, 1918), i, pp. 18–19, 52–3, 54–7, 78–9, 92–3, 136–7; ii, pp. 180–1, 184–5, 188–9, 206–9, 220–1.

39 McKenna (ed.), *Iomarbhágh na bhfileadh*, i, pp. 136–7; Keating, *Foras feasa ar Éirinn*, i, pp. 78–81; John O'Donovan (ed.), *The annals of the kingdom of Ireland by the Four Masters* (7 vols, Dublin, 1851), i, pp. lxiv–lxv. For a long list of works, both Irish and classical, consulted by one poet in the 1650s see Cecile O'Rahilly (ed.), *Five seventeenth-century political poems* (Dublin, 1952), pp. 42–3.

40 McKenna (ed.), *Iomarbhágh na bhfileadh*, i, p. 31; Cunningham, *The world of Geoffrey Keating*, pp. 136, 189; Keating, *Foras feasa ar Éirinn*, ii, pp. 348, 325.

41 Cunningham, *The world of Geoffrey Keating*, pp. 173–81.

42 Patrick Thomas, *The collected works of Katherine Philips* (3 vols, Stump Cross, 1992), ii, pp. 59–61.

43 Gearóid Mac Niocaill (ed.), *Crown surveys of lands, 1540–1* (Dublin, 1992), pp. 312–14, 355–6.

44 Bodl., Rawlinson MS B480, ff. 69b–78.

45 T.C.D., MS 1375; B.L., Egerton MS 136.

46 Royal Irish Academy, MS 23 L 19, ff. 49–104, T.C.D., MS 1383, pp. 110, 121; B.L., Sloane MS 3567, ff. 36ff.; Egerton 196, ff. 36–69v.

47 Richard Olmstead, *Sion's tears leading to joy* (Dublin, 1630), sig. A6v.

48 Union Theological College, Belfast, Robert Chambers MS 'Explanation of the shorter catechism', sig. A2.

49 John Murcot, *Saving faith and pride of life inconsistent* (London, 1656), sig. A3v.

50 Raymond Gillespie, 'The reformed preacher: Irish Protestant preaching, 1660–1700' in Alan J. Fletcher and Raymond Gillespie (eds), *Irish preaching, 700–1700* (Dublin, 2001), pp. 140–2.

51 Faithful Teate, *A discourse grounded on Prov. 12.5, 'The thoughts of the righteous are right'* (Dublin, 1666). This copy is now in Dr Williams's Library, London, 2094. E33.

52 The copy of William Staunford, *An exposition of the king's prerogative collected out of the great abridgement of Justice Fitzherbert* (London, 1567) with the inscription is now in Tony Sweeney's Arranmore collection.

53 Capel Molyneux, *An account of the family and descendants of Thomas Molyneux* (Evesham, 1820), p. 76.

54 Elizabethanne Boran, 'The libraries of Luke Challoner and James Ussher, 1595–1608' in Helga Robinson-Hammerstein (ed.), *European universities in the age of Reformation and Counter Reformation* (Dublin, 1998), pp. 109–15; William O'Sullivan (ed.), 'Correspondence of David Rothe and James Ussher, 1619–23' in *Collectanea Hibernica* nos 36–7 (1994–95), pp. 13, 47–9.

55 N.L.I., MS 4715.

56 *A narrative of the proceedings of the seven general synods of the northern presbyterians in Ireland by the ministers of the presbytery of Antrim* (n.p., 1717), p. 18.

57 Benjamin Scroggs, *A sermon preached before the religious societies in the city of Dublin on the 29th of September 1695* (Dublin, 1695), pp. 39, 46, 47.

58 Society of Friends Historical Library, Dublin, MS MM II F1, ff.. 165–7; MS MM II A1, ff.. 139, 140, 151, 155, 162.

59 John Dunton, *The Dublin scuffle*, ed. Andrew Carpenter (Dublin, 2000), p. 19.

60 H.M.C., *Ormonde MSS*, n.s., v, p. 210.

61 B.L., Add MS 21494, f. 2.

62 For example *A short view of the methods made use of in Ireland for the subversion and*

destruction of the Protestant religion and interests in that kingdom (London, 1689), pp. 14, 27.

63 Marquis of Lansdowne (ed.), *Petty–Southwell correspondence* (London, 1928), p. 73.

64 The spreading of rumours in coffee houses was prohibited by proclamation in 1672 and 1685 which were reissues of English proclamations, R.R. Steele (ed.), *Tudor and Stuart proclamations* (2 vols, Oxford, 1910), ii, Ireland nos 824, 952. On the context see Brian Cowan, 'The rise of the coffee house reconsidered' in *Historical Journal* xlvii (2004), pp. 21–46.

65 Bodl., Smith MS 45, f. 19.

66 Dunton, *The Dublin scuffle*, p. 248.

67 Nicholas Bernard, *The whole proceedings of the seige of Drogheda in Ireland* (London, 1642), pp. 66, 81.

68 T.C.D., MS 818, f. 15; MS 817, f. 38.

69 N.L.I., MS 2554, no. 2, f. 35, no. 6, f. 35.

70 *The Guardian: volume the first* (London, 1767), p. 257.

71 For an early example see T.C. Barnard, 'Libraries and glazed bookcases in eighteenth-century Ireland' in *Eighteenth–Nineteenth Century Irish Fiction Newsletter* no. 14 (Feb. 1999), [p. 4].

72 Harold Williams (ed.), *The poems of Jonathan Swift* (2nd edn, 3 vols, Oxford, 1958), iii, pp. 1144–5.

73 Bernard, *Whole proceedings*, p. 7.

74 For example P.F. Wallace and Raghnall Ó Floinn (eds), *Treasures of the National Museum of Ireland: Irish antiquities* (Dublin, 2002), p. 281.

75 Anthony Cains, 'The Long Room survey of sixteenth and seventeenth-century books' in Vincent Kinane and Anne Walsh (eds), *Essays on the history of Trinity College library, Dublin* (Dublin, 2000), p. 58.

76 Maurice Craig, *Irish bookbindings, 1600–1800* (London, 1954), p. 1.

77 Joseph McDonnell, *Five hundred years of the art of the book in Ireland* (Dublin and London, 1997), p. 122.

78 McDonnell, *Five hundred years of the art of the book*, pp. 127–30.

79 John Dunton, *Teague land or a merry ramble to the wild Irish (1698)*, ed. Andrew Carpenter (Dublin, 2003), p. 130.

80 Vincent Kinane, 'Some red morocco bindings by Christopher Chapman in the Worth library, Dublin' in *Long Room* no. 42 (1997), p. 22.

81 Muriel McCarthy, 'An eighteenth-century Dublin bibliophile' in *Irish Arts Review* iii, no. 4 (Winter 1986), pp. 31–2.

82 J.D. White, 'Extracts from original wills' in *Journal of the Royal Society of Antiquaries of Ireland* v (1858–59), p. 319.

83 Charles Rogers, 'Notes in the history of Sir Jerome Alexander' in *Transactions of the Royal Historical Society* n.s. ii (1873), pp. 99–100.

84 For this idea see Elizabethanne Boran, 'The function of the library in the early

seventeenth century' in Kinane and Walsh (eds), *Essays on the history of Trinity College library, Dublin*, pp. 41–5.

85 J.P. Mahaffy (ed.), *The particular book of Trinity College, Dublin* (London, 1904), p. 202.

86 6 Anne, c. 19.

87 N.A., Prerogative will book, 1644–84, f. 80.

88 William Carrigan, 'Catholic episcopal wills' in *Archivium Hibernicum* iv (1918), pp. 87, 89. Phelan's copy of *Alithonologia: a defence of the Roman Catholic church in Ireland as the true church of the country* ([London] 1664), is now in the Ossory diocesan library.

89 Murphy (ed.), *Annals of Clonmacnoise*, p. 96.

90 [Steven Stevens], *Exceeding happy news from Ireland* (London 1642), sig. A3.

91 T.C.D., MS 831, f. 99v.

92 T.C.D., MS 812, ff. 203, 220, 247v.

93 G.T. Stokes (ed.), *The memoirs of Mistress Anne Fowke, née Geale* (Dublin, 1892), p. 21; Presbyterian Historical Society, Belfast, Carnmoney Session Book, 1 August 1703.

94 [Robert Ware], *The second part of foxes and firebrands* (Dublin, 1683), p. 112.

95 R.C.B., MS P117/5/1, p. 189.

96 H.M.C., *Ormonde MSS*, n.s. vii, pp. 526–7.

97 T.C.D., MS 812, f. 213v.

98 T.C.D., MS 832, ff. 69, 91; MS 833, ff. 99, 279; MS 836, ff. 49, 58v; MS 816, f. 138; MS 830, f. 144; MS 818, ff. 8v, 12v, 22, 25; MS 824, f. 149; MS 834, ff. 57, 70v; MS 835, ff. 36v, 109; MS 815, ff. 23v, 24v, 32, 41, 42.

99 T.C.D., MS 815, f. 25.

100 T.C.D., MS 835, f. 38.

101 T.C.D., MS 836, ff. 63v, 64.

102 *Cal. S. P. Ire., 1603–6*, p. 34; Edmund Hogan (ed.), *Ibernia Ignatiana* (Dublin, 1880), p. 118.

103 *An itinerary written by Fynes Moryson, gent.* (London, 1617), p. 295.

104 *Cal. S. P. Ire., 1596–7*, p. 17.

105 B.L., Add MS 4784, f. 249; Add MS 21494, f. 108. In fact Temple's work does not seem to have been burnt although there was a plan to do so.

106 *Journals of the House of Commons of the kingdom of Ireland* (19 vols, Dublin, 1796–1800), i, p. 401; ii, pp. 190, 317; *Journals of the House of Lords [of Ireland]* (8 vols, Dublin, 1779–1800), i, p. 249; ii, pp. 70, 414, 415.

107 Bernard, *Whole proceedings*, p. 81.

108 T.C.D., MS 815, f. 60.

Chapter 2

The prelude to print:
the rise of writing

Across early modern Europe the development of the technology of print created the possibility of significant social transformations. The extent to which those possibilities would be realised, and to what ends, was determined by a wide range of factors. How local communities responded to print was one of the most important variables. That response was to a large degree determined by the pre-existing ability of those communities to deal with the written word, in manuscript form, as a way of shaping and preserving social memory. Clearly those who were familiar with the world of writing and the keeping of records dealt with print in a rather different, and more assured, way from those who had previously used the written word much more sparingly. In Ireland the strategies available to deal with written texts – what may be described as a textual culture – varied greatly over the island. For those in the early sixteenth-century Dublin-administered pale familiar with English legal practice, and more practised in centralised record keeping, a textual culture and a set of social boundaries associated with the use of the written word were already familiar. In Gaelic Ireland the social rules for writing were significantly different. To understand the impact that print would have in these two worlds the history of the development of a textual culture is central.

I

In the course of the sixteenth century English and Anglo-Irish commentators on, and analysts of, the Irish world came into increasing contact with those parts of Ireland outside the pale. What they discovered there was a world which operated on social and political principles that were very different from those they were accustomed to.[1] In order to produce a range of strategies for the reformation of that world, so that its power relationships could be managed, they tried to identify the basic social constructs which made it function. A number of these structures, such as the systems of inheritance known as gavelkind and tanistry, were quickly recognised as central elements requiring reform. Beyond these many commentators thought they recognised a more basic problem. Ireland, they felt, was a world ruled by custom rather than law. The lord deputy's secretary at the beginning of the seventeenth century, Fynes Moryson, repeatedly referred to Irish social traits as 'customs', and his contemporary Barnaby Rich noted that 'custom is a metal amongst them that standeth whichsoever way it be bent'.[2] A few commentators went further and defined what they meant by the term 'custom'. Edmund Spenser came closest when he declared that at the end of the sixteenth century 'it is the manner of barbarous nations to be very superstitious and diligent observers of old customs and antiquities which they receive by continual tradition from their parents, by recording of their bards and chronicles, in their songs, and by daily use and example of their elders'.[3] Others also came close when they described the workings of Irish brehon law. The Anglo-Irish analyst Rowland White, in the 1570s, noted that the Irish 'maintained their old customs which were the laws of the brehons'.[4] Edmund Spenser described such laws as 'a certain rule of right unwritten but delivered by tradition from one to another'.[5] As Fynes Moryson put it, brehon law judges 'determined their causes by an unwritten law, only retained by tradition which in some things had a smack of right and equity and in some other was contrary to all divine and humane laws'.[6] Even when the brehons had acquired some of the principles of English common law it was, according to the Irish solicitor general Sir John Davies, 'rather by tradition than by reading'.[7]

The essence of this perceived world of custom was that it was understood as an oral construct with little or no writing. As Spenser expressed it, the Irish were 'always without letters, but only bare traditions of times and remembrances of bards, which used to forge and falsify everything as they list to please or displease any man'.[8] All this had repercussions. Contemporaries well knew the difference between the character of the written word and ideas held in oral tradition as part of the social memory. As one late sixteenth-century partition of land by a Gaelic Irish lawyer, Flann Mac Egan, in Tipperary written in Irish observed, 'writing is better than memory ... that is, writing lives, and memory departs'.[9] Later, in the seventeenth century, the Dublin Presbyterian minister Robert Chambers put the matter equally succinctly: 'writing is of singular use to keep things on record which else would be forgotten'.[10] The oral, and therefore unstable, nature of custom was, it was assumed by commentators, at least part of the difficulty with the Irish polity. The mutable nature of oral tradition, for instance, led to succession disputes and other internal factional warfare. At the less practical, but equally important, level of learning the oral world of Gaelic Ireland left a good deal to be desired. The sixteenth-century Dubliner Richard Stanihurst noted in his tract on Ireland's past that in the use of language Irish people 'blab whatever comes to mind first. Instead of weighing their words with the grammarian's precision and paying attention to syllabic qualities, they use the inconstant standard of breathing in articulating their sentences'.[11] In almost every area of life the oral tradition, which the commentators on Gaelic Ireland thought was so pervasive, proved to be defective in organising society.

As in their descriptions of many aspects of Gaelic Irish life in the sixteenth century, the commentators had found what was, at best, a half truth. They certainly identified the fact that social memory in Gaelic Ireland functioned rather differently from the way it did in the pale or in England. In the latter regions central record-keeping and record-generating bodies, such as the courts, acted as a way of remembering property and power structures. In contrast Ireland outside the pale was a fragmented polity. At the beginning of the sixteenth century one commentator observed that Ireland was composed of 'more than sixty countries', each one presided over by its own lord and each lord 'obeyeth no other temporal person ... and hath imperial jurisdiction within his room'.[12] At the beginning of the seventeenth century, just as that fragmented world was about to disappear with the extension of royal authority across the island, Sir John Davies still described a similar situation. On the basis of discussions with brehon lawyers he noted that there were over sixty 'countries or territories possessed by the Irish', each of which had a chief lord or captain who made peace and war and 'the whole profits of the country were at his disposition when he listest'.[13] In this localised world with its regionalised customs writing was of limited use. Its main function was for those who operated on a regional or national level and hence needed a way of communicating over long distances. Social memory in matters such as landownership and genealogy was regulated by oral tradition rather than written documents. Writing was, however, part of the world of those who operated on a wider stage; the world of the learned classes who dealt with religion, the law, medicine and literature. Manuscripts from Gaelic Ireland in the sixteenth century are, for example, heavily dominated by medical texts. Some 40 per cent of surviving manuscripts from this period are medical works drawing on the classical world of medical learning and supplementing it with charms, prayers and recipes for various cures. Such precise knowledge had permanent value and hence writing was an important way of preserving this. Such manuscripts tended to have long lives. One medical manuscript written in the 1460s, for instance, was used by members of medical families until the early eighteenth century when it passed into the hands of antiquarian collectors.[14]

While writing was clearly important in this world of the learned classes, the way in which it was used differed somewhat from the way English commentators were familiar with. Written documents were located firmly within an oral culture and were used to promote that tradition. In the area of law, for instance, books were used as a way of teaching legal principles which were then enunciated orally, giving the impression that those principles derived entirely from oral tradition. The English Jesuit Edmund Campion, for example, noted of students of law and medicine, 'I have seen them where they keep school, ten in some one chamber grovelling upon couches of straw their books at their noses themselves lying flat, prostrate and so chant out their lessons by piecemeal'.[15] Even in the case of bardic poetry, which was the quintessential performance art of sixteenth-century Ireland, it appears that poets may have composed some of their work in writing prior to recitation and, indeed, may have presented the manuscript to their patron.[16] That such written works, particularly literary works, were used for reading aloud also seems clear. In the Annals of Ulster, for instance, the obit for Seon Ó Croidhein and his wife in 1528 asked, 'And every one who shall read or listen to this year, let him bestow benison on the souls of that couple aforesaid we mentioned above'.[17] It may well be that annalistic entries for a year were read publicly or were quarried for public reading.[18] Writing was certainly a well established technology in Gaelic Ireland in the sixteenth century but it was clearly surrounded by a set of social conventions which dictated how and when it should be used.

In the course of the sixteenth century the social conventions which surrounded the use of writing began to shift as an ever-increasing range of situations generated written texts, almost always as a result of local develop-ments. At least two sets of pressures were involved in this process. The first was the emergence of documents reflecting largely local concerns within Gaelic Ireland in the sixteenth century, and the second impetus resulted from a national trend by which the authority and institutions of the Dublin administration penetrated into the regions outside the pale.

The local pressures which resulted in areas of life formerly remembered in oral tradition being committed to paper in the form of 'charters' are largely the result of lords wishing to consolidate their hold on their lordships by regulating their relationships with their sub-lords and using writing as one strategy of achieving this. This was usually dictated by local circumstances and in that sense such developments were local rather than national ones. The earliest surviving example of such a document dates from November 1532 and deals with the overlordship of the earl of Kildare over the Mac Ranald lordship. In return for a shilling from every quarter of land controlled by Mac Ranald the earl promised to defend the family and its property.[19] It is clear that Mac Ranald was unused to this sort of written arrangement since he had no seal with which to seal the document and the seal of the chantry college at Maynooth had to be affixed instead. It seems highly likely that the initiative for such a development had come from the earl of Kildare. It is also unlikely that the Mac Ranald charter was the only such document. At this time Kildare was also regulating his dealings with other native Irish lords who held land from him. In 1508, for instance, he entered into a written lease for the lands of Omeath with the O'Hanlon family and made other written agreements with the O'Farrell family over land. In a number of these cases brehon lawyers were actively involved in such agreements and their signatures appear among the witnesses to their making.[20] In 1518 the earl compiled a 'rental' setting out in some detail the duties payable by a number of Irishmen to Kildare and it is at least possible that agreements about lordship similar to that with Mac Ranald underlay this list.[21] In other Gaelicised lordships, such as parts of the Ormond lordship where the habit of preserving written records of transactions was better developed, similar agreements regulating relationships between different types of lordships also begin to appear in the late fifteenth and early sixteenth centuries. In some of these cases native lords already owned seals which they attached to the documents, suggesting that they authenticated documents on a regular basis.[22]

There is also some evidence that about the same time written charters dealing with lordship began to be used in other parts of Gaelic Ireland. The Ulster annalist noted after an outbreak of hostilities between O'Neill and O'Donnell in 1514: 'they went to meet each other on the bridge of Ard-stratha and gossipred was made by them with each other. And new charters, along with confirmation of the old charters, were granted by Ua Neill to Ua Domnaill for Cenel-Moen and for Inis-Eogain and for Fir-Manach.'[23] No indication of what these 'charters' were or the form in which they were made has survived but it seems clear that the written document was intended to stabilise relations between two powerful lords. It did so by setting down in writing their respective rights, rights that previously had been determined by tradition or force of arms. A variant on this sort of lordship agreement was that of 1539 between O'Donnell and Tadhg O'Connor over Sligo castle. O'Connor promised to be a loyal follower of O'Donnell and to surrender the keys of Sligo to him when required. He also promised to send the cocket of the port of Sligo to O'Donnell.[24] A more sophisticated form of the same sort of agreement was concluded in August 1566 between Conor Mac Geoghegan and Bresal Fox in King's County. In this it was agreed that Mac Geoghegan would be overlord to Fox and a tribute of pigs was to be rendered to Mac Geogheghan as 'the sign of lordship'. Provision was also made for mortgages, the payment of cess levied on the territory by the crown. In return Mac Geogheghan promised to defend Fox and his followers and resolve their legal disputes.[25] Such ideas also seem to lie behind the late fifteenth-century Irish religious tradition of the 'charter of Christ' in which the charter of peace between God and humankind was written as a document on Christ's breast.[26] In the latter part of the sixteenth century, references to such 'charters' become more common. Such documents are clearly what the poet Tadhg Dall Ó hUiginn had in mind in a late sixteenth-century poem to Cormac O'Hara of Sligo as 'The old charters of the tributes of the plain of Leyney have fallen out of remembrance, so that it is a bright, clear charter this is renewed for his heirs'.[27] Such charters were almost certainly part of the textual culture from which emerged the sixteenth-century prose tracts on the rights of individual lords. Thus in the 1570s the rights of MacWilliam as they were set down in the north Connacht prose tract *Seanchus Búrcach* were 'according to the testimony of the stewards and of the charters'.[28]

None of these written agreements seems to have related specifically to the ownership of land. Rather they were recorded simply as memoranda of agreements already made in a traditional, oral form. In themselves they had no legal effect. Thus the 1566 agreement between Mac Geoghegan and Fox noted that the agreement was made on Wednesday and the document recording the agreement was written two days later, on Friday. It is also clear that the agreement between Kildare and Mac Ranald was made and sworn on 'the oath of the church' before it was written down by a traditionally trained brehon lawyer, Maoilin Óg O'Mulconry, at the dictation of one of the parties.[29] However the models on which these agreements are based are clearly those associated with English common law. The Kildare agreement with Mac Ranald, for example, describes itself as '*curadh agus denitiure*', covenant and indenture. '*Denitiure*' was in the early sixteenth century a recent linguistic borrowing from English which had appeared for the first time in a late fifteenth-century religious manuscript.[30] In the sixteenth century it became the normal description of a legal agreement but the timing of the borrowing, and its source, points to growing awareness of how the written word increasingly came to affect the power relations at a local level in Ireland.

One example of how the concerns of lords to consolidate their local authority resulted in their recourse to writing to confirm existing rights, and in some cases to establish new ones, is provided by the *Seanchus Búrcach* of the 1570s. The date of the text can be established with some accuracy since it seems to contain a reference to the making of the first composition of Connacht, which occurred in 1577. The aim of this agreement between local lords and the Dublin administration was to restructure power relationships in the province by regulating relationships between lords and their followers.[31] In this context of shifting power relationships it seems that the Mayo Burkes turned to the written word as a way of confirming their own political position. They seem to have used the written indentures of composition in a way that they were never intended and in doing so strengthened their own position vis-a-vis their followers.[32] The *Seanchus Búrcach* contained a Latin genealogical history of the family, a traditional collection of bardic poems and a long statement of the rights and duties of the family as lords of north-west Ireland. All this was imbedded firmly in a religious context, which is also apparent in many of the sixteenth-century charters, since the volume includes a series of images not only of long-dead Burkes of the line of the patron of the manuscript, giving life to the genealogical tract, but also images of the Passion of Christ. The same religious context of the claim of lordship is repeated in the text on the duties leviable by Burke, since the document claimed: 'it is not to this writing which we have just read on the other side of this leaf that we yield or give credence but to almighty God, and to truth as we have seen it written'.[33] That this book was not for private consumption but was aimed at several public audiences is suggested by the fact that it was written in both Irish and Latin. That this represented two different audiences also seems clear from the comment which separates the family history from the statement of dues payable to Burke that 'this is the portion of the country people, and of the readers of the Gaelic tongue of the book and of the lordship of Mac William. And the chronicle of MacWilliam in Latin is written before us down here.'[34] This desire in the 1570s to write a work which would appeal to the varying groups in the lordship, the country people and the 'literate' or Latin speakers, seems to be a way of marshalling traditional ways of demonstrating authority. Again the collection of bardic poetry reflected both oral and written traditions. The religious and genealogical imagery of the volume again blended the visual and the written. Central to the whole endeavour was the written description of traditional rights and duties, then perceived to be under threat. Writing down such a survey, in the same way as the composition indentures were written down, was a new and important element in the armoury of asserting local power relationships, and denying other claimants, in a turbulent political world.

The second set of forces which helped to move the world of Gaelic Ireland into a culture more affected by texts resulted from administrative penetration into that world by the Dublin government. Perhaps the greatest effect this movement had was to shift the basis of landownership from a world domin-ated by family and genealogical custom to a world in which the written document became central. From the 1540s the process of surrender and regrant had made the written contract an important means of regulating relationships between central and local authority using grants of land. Within Gaelic Ireland at regional level also records began to be kept of local land transactions. Most of these have now disappeared but in a land dispute of 1605 the annals referred to the production of much older charters relating to an exchange of property between O'Neill and O'Donnell, probably dating from the 1540s.[35] This was a reality of life clear to all but it was not without its limitations. One native Irish poet, writing in praise of Maguire towards the end of the sixteenth century, attempted to clinch his argument by claiming: 'documents agree with me, let me hear a certain story [*sgél*] from the charter, a charter in which the account of every land is found'.[36] The notion that a charter contained a story rather a set of legal provisions points to the growth of the written word but it also shows how that world was penetrated with the traditions of oral cultures. However, that oral world was increasingly restricted in the late sixteenth and early seventeenth centuries as the Dublin administration expanded its influence in the localities. One aspect of the administration, the law courts, especially the court of chancery, attracted a growing volume of business from the native Irish. Certainly by the 1640s the world of legal and administrative documents, particularly those related to land, and a knowledge of the workings of the law had penetrated deeply into Gaelic Ireland. According to one deponent during the rising, the Irish in Leitrim not only established justices of the peace but also sent out written warrants in imitation of English models. Meanwhile another rebel in Wicklow reflected the importance of the court of chancery when he observed, 'we have no chancery to try the title [of land]'.[37] The consequence of this was it became necessary to ensure that legal matters, especially those relating to land, were in writing and in proper form. As one Irish deed from County Clare in 1611 expressed it, the lessor promised to 'put this writing into the form of law of the English king as the law advisers of the above Sean [the lessor] may advise' and there were a number of attempts to imitate English legal form in Irish deeds.[38]

The growing dominance of legal forms is perhaps most clearly seen in the dating of documents in Irish. Dates were important for a number of reasons. Not only did they put documents into a temporal context but they could also be used to authenticate a document. In the early part of the sixteenth century the normal way of dating legal documents written in Irish was simply by the 'year of Christ' sometimes with a more specific date related to a saint's feast day or other religious festival. By the early seventeenth century a day, month and year were normal although older forms persisted. Moreover by the 1580s many documents written in Irish were dated by regnal year, suggesting a concern with legal form.[39] In 1584 one deed drafted by a parish priest in Mayo was so concerned that his form of dating should be correct that he covered all options declaring that it was written 'the fourth day before the feast of the Nativity, the most serene princess Elizabeth ruling and John Perrot being deputy in Ireland, Richard Bingham ruling the provinces of Thomond and Connacht, Richard Fitz-Oliver de Burgo being created MacWilliam'.[40] By the early seventeenth century at least some of these problems had been solved by the mass production of legal deeds by scribes which required only the filling in of blank spaces, as in the deeds used in the releasing of the earl of Antrim's estate in the 1630s. Such scribal products in time gave way to printed forms of leases.[41]

In legal actions the production of deeds and their form became increasingly important, and accusations circulated on how documents had been stolen, fraudulently obtained and even embezzled. As the Cork landowner Henry Boyle observed during the Jacobite regime of 1668, Irishmen were claiming land which settlers held 'for it is so usual a practice now to produce old smokey parchments which they swear to be ancient entails that nobody can be sure of their purchase any longer than the party lives that sold it'.[42] In one Roscommon case in chancery in the late sixteenth century, Anthony Brabazon, a New English settler, was alleged to have taken advantage of one native Irish landowner, who was 'single and illiterate and well stricken in years', to get deeds for lands despite the fact that the landowner's two sons believed them to be in safe hands.[43] Lost or embezzled deeds were a serious matter, and deeds damaged beyond repair likewise created difficulties.[44] These matters were not irreparable. One County Roscommon landowner asked to have some of his deeds enrolled in Chancery so that they would be safe.[45] In another Galway case of 1621 when a bargain and sale had been made 'by word only and without writing' a commission was established to take the evidence of witnesses to the transaction and the resulting papers enrolled in Chancery.[46] More traditionally a dispute in 1593 was resolved by a brehon lawyer who gave a written judgement 'and accordingly subscribed the said order under their hands' which allowed the plaintiff to ask this to be enrolled in Chancery as evidence of a local agreement on the matter.[47]

By the early seventeenth century, when the legal process of the Dublin administration had extended across the whole island, the dangers of not understanding what written documents contained were clear. In the 1680s, for instance, one woman claimed that one of her relations

> brought a piece of paper and desired me to sign it to which paper I being an illiterate woman and not knowing what it was did sign it never thinking it was in the manner of a release from me to him of the said debt for there was no reason I should give him a release ... but [I] thought the paper to be some account passed between him and his shepherd.[48]

At the simplest, failure to navigate one's way through a growing number of written agreements might involve the loss of money. One soldier in the 1570s, for instance, claimed that he had lost a debt of £700 by the 'falsehood of his clerk, who deceived him [he] not knowing how to read or write'.[49] As paper documents spread so did the possibility of dubious practices. Government, through parliament in the 1630s, attempted to tighten the rules on fraud to make the possibility of subverting the written word more difficult. The importance of this new world of paper was clearest in the area of land titles in which the danger of not understanding how documents conveyed those titles to land and how they worked were very considerable. In 1634, for example, one Faghney Reynolds claimed that thirteen years earlier during the plantation of Leitrim he had held two catrons of land but he

> being ignorant and altogether unskilful what course to take for himself did put the said two catrons of land into the hands of Charles Reynolds esq to have the same

passed out in his patent and for passing of the same the petitioner did give to the said Mr Reynolds two fat beeves.

Reynolds, perhaps predictably, passed the lands in his own name.[50] This was not an isolated example of sharp practice in which one individual, who understood the workings of the world of documents, took advantage of one who did not. The example of Reynolds's actions had other parallels.[51] There were other ways to lose land through not knowing how the textual world worked. Charles O'Molloy complained that during the plantation of King's County in the 1620s his father 'being but an illiterate man' did not know how to make his rights known to the plantation commissioners and consequently the family lost their land.[52] The Irish court of Chancery heard similar stories such as that of Teige Farrell in the Longford plantation in the 1620s who, as in the case of Reynolds, employed an adjoining landowner as his agent to pass a grant of lands who duly passed it in his own name. Some alleged that the government manipulated this situation of uncertainty about the world of documents to its own ends. The Catholic bishop of Ossory, David Rothe, for instance, claimed that those who held land by descent rather than deeds had that land confiscated and even if one did have deeds 'on the same being produced [and] perused if there could be found but one ambiguous word out of which might be framed any cavil or if any thing should be wanting of the ordinary form of law' the property was confiscated. The flimsiest evidence, according to Rothe, made a Chancery case against existing proprietors.[53] That such techniques were actually deployed in some circumstances is suggested by a number of cases. In the 1560s, for instance, the power balance in south Leinster was disrupted by the claims of Peter Carew to the barony of Idrone in Carlow based on a number of older and much defaced documents.[54] Again the importance of paper title to land was demonstrated in the case of the debt-ridden landlord of the southern part of the Ards peninsula in Ulster, Patrick Savage. In the 1620s his brother-in-law, Sir James Montgomery, attempted to reorganise the Portaferry estate lands but he met resistance from native Irish and Old English freeholders. Having despatched Savage to the Isle of Man, where he could not be pressured by his followers, Montgomery, according to a history of the Savage family from the 1690s, 'put the most stubborn and refractory to the law to make them examples for there were flaws in their deeds and their titles were defective, sealing leases of ejectment against them whereby they were overcome and subdued'.[55] The best protection against such action was the ability to understand what documents did and how they did it.

II

As a result of all these developments the native Irish elite, like their Anglo-Irish counterparts, during the late sixteenth and early seventeenth centuries, were increasingly drawn into a textual culture. To demonstrate their mastery of the world of documents they showed an interest in reading and writing and began to acquire the accessories of that world such as seals and spectacles.[56] In 1558 Maelmórdha O'Reilly, lord of Breifne, had to borrow the seal of the Franciscan friary of Cavan to authenticate a deed, suggesting that the use of seals by the family was uncommon, yet his grandson, Sir John, owned his own seal which, since it allowed him to authorise large numbers of documents, suggests definite familiarity with the world of texts.[57] Law was not the only variable in this shift. Since this growing awareness of the importance of texts in the sixteenth century was a social phenomenon rather than the result of a geographical diffusion process, it is difficult to trace its development precisely. For this reason the earliest sixteenth-century legal documents occur, almost simultaneously, in both the south-east of Ireland, where, given the presence of common law, it might be expected, and in Sligo, where awareness of the written word is rather unexpected. The spread of textuality seems to have been largely the product of local circumstances. As individual lords became aware of the importance of the written word they began to explore the possibilities which it presented for their own lordship. This resulted in a rather patchwork pattern of development of the use of written documents in the sixteenth century which is very loosely related to the spread of the influence of the Dublin administration outside the pale. In the early seventeenth century the spread of common law practices through the assizes and quarter sessions brought ideas of textuality to almost all parts of Ireland. The spread of central-ised government with its printed proclamations and statutes also enhanced the status of writing. Moreover, growing commercialism of the economy, together with a shortage of coin, required the keeping of written records of transactions. At the same time colonisation introduced new practices of estate management based on the written lease. These developments took place piecemeal but by 1600 written documents in the form of leases, court pleadings and proclamations, for example, were all very much more familiar to the inhabitants of Ireland than they had been a century earlier.

Such changes inevitably had an impact on language use. By the end of the sixteenth century the language of legal deeds was English, although Latin might still be used to keep a formal record of legal proceedings. English and Anglo-Irish commentators agreed that Irish was not a language well adapted to writing. They believed that the script which was normally used, for instance, was not well suited to writing quickly in the way that cursive hands were. Surviving letters in the script of professional Irish scribes were individually made, resulting in a slowing down of the writing process. By the 1640s one French traveller to Ireland claimed of Irish that it was 'a tongue which you must learn by practice because they do not write it. They learn Latin in English characters with which character they also write their own language.'[58] Whether this is true or not is unclear. On the one hand extant manuscripts in Irish do not contain any examples but since these were written by professional scribes this need not be conclusive. Certainly when the Old English priest Theobald Stapleton published his catechism in 1639 the Irish text was set in roman type which, he claimed, made it easier to read for the unlettered sort.[59] Such considerations clearly helped English letter forms, if not fluency in the language, to become more common in early modern Ireland. Given that English language and letters became the main way in which legal, and later economic, transactions operated, some basic knowledge of the language, or an interpreter, was necessary for those who moved at this social level.[60] Just as there were cases of those not conversant with the workings of documents losing land, there were also cases of land in the Leitrim plantation passing into the wrong hands because the grantees did not speak English and had to trust others to pass their grants.[61] Such practical arguments compelled at least some to develop a bilingual approach to their world although the knowledge of the acquired language could be rudimentary.[62] In turn the ability to manage documents in English reinforced the textual world.

One indication of the spread of a textual culture is the apparent growth of the practice of letter writing in the sixteenth and seventeenth centuries. Letters do not require the author or recipient to be either able to write or read since scribes or readers were available. In late medieval Ireland letters were rare and most messages were conveyed orally with messengers remembering the text.[63] By the late sixteenth century letters became a more common feature of the world of Gaelic Ireland. The increased political penetration into that world by the Dublin administration gave rise to the exchange of letters between the Irish lord deputy and some of the greater Gaelic lords, usually in the medium of Latin although a number of letters in Irish also survive.[64] In the main these dealt with diplomatic affairs. By the end of the sixteenth century there is evidence of letters being used as a mechanism of communication between Irish lords on more general topics. In 1589 Conaire Fitzpatrick, for example, wrote in Irish to the earl of Thomond about the behaviour of soldiers and specifically requested a reply in writing.[65] In this case Fitzpatrick had certainly been exposed to a textual world and English writing practices for some time. Although in one report of 1576 it was claimed that he had 'no writings to show' for his property, since it was held by Irish custom, at the same time he was issuing deeds for his lands to his tenants.[66] Again during the Nine Years' War O'Neill seems to have used letters written in Irish as a way of communicating with other lords although only a few intercepted letters now survive.[67] Within forty years, during the rising of the 1640s, letters were used frequently by the native Irish insurgents as a way of communicating with settlers. In the 1642 seige of Carlow castle, for instance, letters were exchanged between besiegers and those within the castle as a way of establishing terms.[68] Elsewhere, at the seige of Geashill castle and Wicklow castle letters were also used for communicating. Again the O'Byrnes of Wicklow also issued safe-conduct documents which were 'signed and sealed'.[69]

The process of drawing Ireland into a wider textual work was, of course, much accelerated by the process of colonisation from the late sixteenth century and especially after 1603. Colonists from England were more familiar with the world of the written lease and similar written legal documents, and their arrival did much to accelerate the process of disseminating texts. When Sir Peter Carew established his early settlement in Carlow one of his first actions was to applot 'portions of land by writing'.[70] Leases, although a rarity in Scotland in the late sixteenth century, became one of the touchstones of settler society in areas such as Ulster. As part of the plantation scheme in the province it was stipulated that property was to be divided between fee farmers, leaseholders and tenants at will. The imposition of such a hierarchy was an attempt to plan the social structure and determine the social relationships of the new settlement.[71] However, leases conveyed rights, and leaseholders sought to ensure that those rights were observed. In 1622 the commissioners surveying the state of Ireland were bombarded by complaints from tenants in Ulster concerning the failure of undertakers to deliver the written documents to their tenants. They also complained of the failure of undertakers to remove the native Irish from their lands. As one settler put it, they 'have so little encouragement as they wish themselves again in their own country'.[72] Whatever the reality of landlord–tenant relations, the symbolic and economic importance of the written document was clear. Perhaps even more important than the spread of legal documents was the dramatic commercialisation and monetisation of the Irish economy which accompanied this process of colonisation.[73] Such a shift necessitated a considerable expansion in record keeping since coin was in short supply in this economy and records of debts and credits had not only legal but also economic importance. Certainly in the 1640s settler deponents frequently listed among their losses bills, bonds and books of accounts holding records of paper transactions.[74] Again in the 1690s disturbances led to many landowners sending their papers as well as their valuables to places of safety. As one observer of the panic which ran through Ulster in 1688 put it, 'several [gentlemen] of the country sent in their best household furniture and papers to Enniskillen thinking them more secure there than with themselves'.[75] Similar concerns for safety of deeds and writings prompted Sir William Petty to suggest, on a number of occasions from the 1660s, the establishment of a land registry to keep copies of deeds so 'that to buy and sell lands in Ireland will be a business of no craft, but that ignorant and absent persons may safely do the same'.[76] That the Dublin administration listened to such concerns is suggested by the fact that its own record-keeping procedures were tightened significantly in the course of the seventeenth century, culminating in the establishment of the Paper Office in 1702 and a registry of deeds in 1708.[77]

III

Thus in the course of the late sixteenth and seventeenth centuries both Gaelic Ireland and Anglo-Irish Ireland were drawn increasingly into a dominant textual culture. This equipped them with an ability to recognise forms of texts and to respond to the demands of the different types of documents that became part of their lives. It did not necessarily provide them with the ability to decode the words of those documents in order to generate new texts for themselves. That was a more complex skill of literacy. A case in point is that of a County Clare deed of 1585 by which Shaen O'Dea conveyed the manor of Tullagh to Nora Ny Brien. The list of witnesses on the deed is endorsed 'when this deed was read & interpreted to thabove Shaen O Dea' and 'when he sealed & delivered the same'.[78] That O'Dea seems to have been used to dealing with documents is suggested by his possession of a seal but he clearly could not read the deed nor, since it was in English, understand it. O'Dea was a man who had mastered the culture of the text but not the skill of literacy. A rather similar case occurred in 1594 in Tipperary when according to witnesses 'the contents of this deed were duly expressed in Irish before the within named Thomas Butler'. Butler, like O'Dea, sealed his deed with an armorial seal which suggests a familiarity with documents.[79] This rather limited understanding of how texts worked was appreciated by at least some contemporaries for their own ends. At the beginning of the seventeenth century Fynes Moryson described the 'crafty uses' some lords made of orders made by magistrates refusing petitions sent to them 'who coming home would show this hand [signature] to their tenants and adversary without reading the words to which it was set and, so pretending the magistrates' consent to their request, many times obtained from ignorant people their own unjust ends'.[80] Something of this process of using parts of a document to make a particular point operated in the early 1640s when, as part of a propaganda campaign by those in rebellion, Sir Phelim O'Neill forged a king's letter claiming that he had royal support for his uprising. In the depositions taken after the rising the document itself is rarely referred to but the seal attaching to it is frequently mentioned, the insurgents claiming that they had the 'king's broad seal' for their actions.[81] One woman from Tyrone, Gertrude Carlisle, who was certainly unable to sign her name on her deposition, was impressed at being shown 'a seal which they [the rebels] said was the king's seal to a commission [that] warranted them to do the same'. The Catholic bishop of Derry in 1643 reportedly admitted that the document had been forged not to encourage the gentry but the 'common sort of people', adding that the power of the written document 'induced and led them into those forward actions and cruelties'.[82]

As a textual culture spread in early modern Ireland there was a need to engage with it more fully by acquiring the more complex skills of literacy. Measuring the extent and development of the skill of literacy is a difficult task. The association of oral culture with native Irish society in the minds of many contemporaries led to wild generalisations about the ability to read in Gaelic Ireland. For instance, the bishop of Kilmore in the 1630s, William Bedell, claimed that not one in a thousand of the native Irish population in Cavan could read.[83] One obvious problem in measuring the truth of such statements is a scarcity of sources. There are, for instance, no large-scale bodies of evidence from Gaelic Ireland in the late sixteenth and early seventeenth centuries which would allow the charting of the spread of a literate culture. There is certainly some impressionistic evidence that the spread of a textual culture in the sixteenth century encouraged at least some of the elite outside the learned class to acquire the skills of reading, writing, or both. As early as the 1540 the Annals of Loch Cé described a son of O'Neill as 'a man full of knowledge and learning in regard to reading' although at this stage it may be its unusual nature that made the annalist record the fact.[84] By the later sixteenth century there are more references to lordly reading. One late sixteenth century bardic poem, for instance, depicted Cú Chonnacht Maguire reading books with stories of Ireland's past before a battle and using a reed to mark his place. He was also praised for the speed of his reading.[85] Again the ability to, at least, read must be ascribed to the lordly patron of Tadhg Dall Ó hUiginn in the late sixteenth century since his patron read to the blind poet from a book.[86] In one collection of deeds from Roscommon in the 1590s about a third of those who can be identified as native Irish, on the basis of their names, could sign their deeds, the others making marks; while almost all the other lessees, who were settlers, could sign their names.[87] From the upper social levels in one petition of the 1629, signed by a significant number of native Irish from Cavan, signature literacy is rather higher than might be expected; only three out of forty-seven Cavan natives could not sign their names.[88] Such impressionistic evidence certainly suggests a growing literacy among the Gaelic Irish over this period. By the 1630s it is possible to measure something of its progress on one Ulster estate. Using a large quantity of leases from the earl of Antrim's estate in the 1630s, and distinguishing ethnic groupings on the basis of surnames, 40 per cent of those identifiable as Irish had the ability to sign their leases against three-quarters of the settlers. Such figures are, of course subject to considerable qualification. They represent the elite on an estate, and below this level estimates are much lower. Certainly two-thirds of those Irish who described themselves as 'gentleman' could sign their leases while over a fifth of yeomen could do so.[89] Such estimates suggest a growth in literacy among the native Irish. By the late seventeenth century the evidence of leases would suggest that this sort of technical literacy had expanded considerably. Of the 203 persons who signed leases on the Herbert estate at Castleisland in County Kerry between 1653 and 1687, over 73 per cent signed their names as opposed to making a mark.[90] In Ulster on the Hill estate in County Down over 85 per cent could sign their names.[91] Among those who can be identified as native Irish on the basis of surnames on the Herbert estate two-thirds could sign their names, a proportion which rose to 83 per cent in the case of the settlers.

The reasons for this expansion in the skill of writing, as measured by the ability to sign one's name, are clearly complex but at least part of this was related to the growing accessibility of print but also the practical need to keep records and learn about new developments in an increasingly complex economic environment. Reading, for example, was seen by many as a practical skill. James Wolveridge, a medical graduate of Trinity College, Dublin, but practising in Cork in the 1660s, wrote of the skill of midwifery that 'the best midwife is she that is ingenious, that knoweth letters, and having a good memory, is studious, neat and cleanly over the whole body'.[92] By the end of the century Samuel Foley was convinced that reading was the answer to poverty, declaring that 'those that are so poor that they can scarce do that [learn a trade] may have them taught to read, the neglect of which is the great cause of that fatal ignorance which does so lamentably reign among the meaner sort of people'.[93] Certainly in the case of the Adair estate around Ballymena in County Antrim the ability to sign one's name on a lease was related to occupation. Of those describing themselves as farmers or yeomen and having land outside the town only one-third could sign their names on their leases while of the thirty-three leases to tradesmen – cutlers, shoemakers, butchers, glovers, masons and tanners – inside the town only two were unable to sign their names.[94] In Dublin, the commercial hub of the country, signature rates were probably even higher. In the parish of St Werburgh's in the 1650s only three out of fifty-eight persons on a list for the collection of money to support a minister could not sign their names.[95] A rather broader measure is provided by the surviving bail books of the corporation, recording sureties on behalf of those involved in debt cases before the city's Tholsel Court. These records depict a growing ability to sign one's name from about two-thirds in the middle of the seventeenth century to about 80 per cent at the end of the century, again reflecting a growing trend of writing ability among the middling sort.[96]

It seems clear that there was a significant increase in the technical skill of writing in the course of the seventeenth century. This was driven by a wide range of pressures.[97] Practical concerns of government, which saw education as a way not only of governing but also of improving Ireland, saw the foundation of schools as an important issue to be tackled. A sixteenth-century legislative framework provided for parish and diocesan schools, although much of this remained ineffective. More practically, 'royal' schools were established in Ulster as part of the plantation scheme and at Carysfort in County Wicklow. Inevitably, linked to this was the interest of the established church in education as a way of promoting religious conformity and the interest of Catholics and dissenters in using the same techniques in promoting their own confessional loyalties. However it was not until the latter part of the seventeenth century that the full impact of cells of the literate on moral reform was appreciated by the Church of Ireland clergy which provided an impetus to the growth of parish schooling. By the latter half of the seventeenth century others, landowners and merchants, became increasingly concerned for the sort of practical education in literacy and trade skills which the rapidly expanding Irish economy demanded. At local level landlords, and urban corporations such as Derry, founded schools to teach practical skills as well as more conventional literacy. Thus over the course of the seventeenth century, as well as a growing demand for literacy skills for economic and other reasons, there was also a surge in the supply of those skills. Measuring how extensive that growth in provision was is an impossible task since outside the net of parish, diocesan and landlord schools there was a network of informal, highly localised schools which often fragmented into smaller schools and as often failed to survive long. Many were informal arrangements, shifting repeatedly, as demand for education or the toleration of state or local churches allowed. Archbishop King, for instance, commented in the 1690s that there were 'many little fellows' who set up in parts of a parish for three or four months before moving on.[98] King himself in the 1650s, when younger, had attended such schools, usually for a few months before they 'dissolved' so that he was 'at leisure and forgot what I had learnt'.[99] Equally impossible is measurement of the quality of the teaching provided in these schools. One schoolmaster in County Down, for instance, was said in 1679 to be 'merely a weaver who hath left his looms and professes the mathematics'.[100] For all these reservations the general pattern of an expansion in both the demand for and supply of literacy skills over the seventeenth century in Ireland seems clear, though difficult to quantify.

Problems with sources for measuring access to texts through literacy are compounded by problems of definition and measurement. The traditional technique of measuring literacy by counting signatures is fraught with difficulty. The ability to sign one's name may well conceal a range of abilities from that of a frequent and accomplished writer to one who had learnt no more than to trace the letters forming the name. Moreover it is a crude measure of the ability to interact with a textual world. Descriptions of early learning experiences in an Irish context are not common, but such as do exist, mainly on the experience of learning to read the Bible, do suggest that reading came before writing. Thomas Gent, who grew up in Dublin, described in his autobiography how his mother taught him to read the Bible at home.[101] Learning to read at home seems to have been a relatively common experience, and one Waterford man in the 1660s described how he had learnt to read before he went to school.[102] In more detail William King, the future arch-bishop of Dublin, described how after a long period at small schools 'I learnt to repeat the alphabet by rote, but could not distinguish a letter'. Subsequently, the young King, by knowing the letters, managed to pronounce words so that when a book was placed in his hands he could read it but 'I did not understand the words, nor was I capable of understanding what I read'. Eventually taking the Bible from a sleeping woman 'and by enumerating the letters, according to my habit, I pronounced the words in its beginning and immediately perceived it to contain some sense'. Enthused by his success 'I procured books and made unexpected progress at reading', reading all he could find at home. It was only after this that he attempted the skill of writing when 'I formed wretched and exceedingly rude letters, and being often flogged on account of them, I trembled at pens and ink'.[103]

If King's experience was typical then writing was a complex skill which was usually taught after reading, the basis of dealing with texts, and many who had learnt to read did not progress to learning to write. Thus in the 1640s a Clare brewer claimed that 'all his writings were taken away by the rebels': despite the fact he was unable to sign his name he was presumably able to read his 'writings'.[104] Again in Waterford Elizabeth Hoope, though again being unable to sign her name, claimed that rebels had torn leaves 'out of this deponent's Bible or Testament' and another man in Queen's County while unable to sign his name owned books which he valued at £10.[105]

Even inflating estimates of signature literacy to provide indications of the sort of numbers who might be able to read does not provide any real indication of the impact the written word might have on early modern Irish society. Much reading was not done individually but rather as a social activity. Within Gaelic Ireland public reading is suggested by a note in a late sixteenth-century O'Reilly poembook which referred to those who 'will read this book or hear it read' and there is evidence that stories were read in Irish to groups of listeners.[106] Again one poet writing praise poetry to the Maguires in the late sixteenth century referred to a tale which, he claimed, was not difficult to read but he proposed to recite it.[107] Among settlers also people might read in twos or threes. The Dublin butcher Hugh Leeson, for instance, recorded how he had been converted by having the Bible read to him by his wife; and in the late seventeenth century the Presbyterian minister Robert Craghead observed 'as for those who cannot read which God giveth a heart for it they take the help of their neighbours who can read'.[108] Again the preface to a prayerbook compiled for the use of the Enniskillen force in 1696 observed, 'it may be objected that many of the army are illiterate and that they shall profit nothing by this method of instruction. I shall answer that in such a case the soldier may find a comrade that will read for him.'[109] Public readings of scripture in church and the reading of proclamations all helped to close the gap between the world of those who had achieved mastery of reading and those who had not.

Once heard, a text could be recirculated by committing it to memory. Within Gaelic Ireland the learned class were well used to considerable feats of memory, and Edmund Campion claimed to have seen medical and legal scholars learning 'by rote'.[110] One Maguire poet in the late sixteenth century claimed that the lord of Fermanagh had learnt the art of kingship since 'he has it from books and he memorised it when it was recited'.[111] Within settler Ireland there were those capable of similar feats. The blind aunts of the young James Ussher, later archbishop of Armagh, were said to have had 'such tenacious memories that whatever they heard read out of the scriptures, or what was preached to them, they always retained and became such proficients that they were able to repeat much of the Bible by heart'.[112] Lesser feats were also possible. The Dublin Presbyterian William Cairnes, for instance, on his deathbed could repeat large parts of the scripture as well as singing psalms, while his co-religionist Anne Reading of Rathfarnham could also recite long passages of scripture.[113] Indeed the chaplain to the earl of Cork, Steven Jerome, in dedicating his 1624 work to the sovereign of Tallow in County Cork, claimed that Ireland was 'a little bookish country' and 'my chief library indeed being that which is living and walking, carried about with me ... by that portion of memory'.[114] From a Catholic perspective at Waterford in 1627 the vicar general tried to combat illiteracy among his clergy by insisting that they learn by heart the short form of the principal chapters of the catechism to teach their parishioners.[115] Such memorisation was particularly effective when the material was cast in verse form. The earl of Orrery noted in the 1680s there were those who could hardly recite a verse of scripture but could repeat entire metrical psalms and other rhymes.[116] Indeed the response of some settlers in Galway in the 1640s under attack by the rebels was to sing psalms which they had memorised.[117] One priest in Laois in the 1640s recited to a settler 'seditious verses' about the Bishop's Wars in Scotland which he had probably memorised from a printed sheet.[118] For this reason a good deal of the seditious material which circulated in seventeenth-century Ireland was cast in verse form since it was clearly memorable and recitable. Remembering a written document for recitation is clearly less effective than being able to navigate one's way around the document itself. It was difficult to isolate specific passages or to analyse the detail of the text but it did provide a mechanism by which the written and oral worlds could overlap.

IV

During the early modern period the social boundaries which surrounded the act of writing shifted. Changing social relationships, particularly those controlled by the legal framework, shifted the boundaries which determined what should be written down and what should be remembered. As a result the written document was a much more common part of Irish life in 1700 than it had been in 1500. One instance is the charters, grants and deeds of the corporation of Kilkenny. Over 280 survive of which twenty predate 1400. There are twenty-nine fifteenth-century deeds, eighty-two from the sixteenth century and 157 dating from the seventeenth century.[119] That pattern was repeated across the country. Writing came to be seen as one of the signs of civility, with one pamphleteer from the 1640s claiming that the rebels had not merely destroyed books but 'they also designed to annul and destroy all the laws, customs, civility ... and all monuments, records, charters, writings any way relating thereto ... all things ... tending to civility'.[120] Individuals grew increasingly confident of their ability to manage what may be described as a 'textual' society even though they may not have mastered the full technicalities of writing or, in some cases, even of fluent reading.

Such a change was revolutionary although not all welcomed it. In 1641 Sir Richard Blake, the Galway lawyer, complained that too much legal work was being done through writing, and in particular 'paper petitions'. Such documents, he claimed, were recent innovations which could be drawn by 'an illiterate clerk ... whose knowledge soars no higher than his mother tongue'. The oratorical skills of the lawyer, he argued, were under threat from such 'paper blasts' which were 'robbers of our goods and supressors of our intellectual parts'.[121] The argument was an old one, dating back into the medieval period, and, in reality, Blake had little to worry about. The seventeenth-century experience was that written (or printed) texts were part of a much wider visual and oral communications network, although in some areas, such as land-ownership, they were decidedly privileged texts. A case in point is the way in which the corporation of Drogheda chose to conduct its business in the late seventeenth century. In 1656 they agreed that before the end of each assembly the clerk was to read out what they had decided and if that was acceptable to all concerned then the formal record of the proceedings would be written down. It was also agreed that the roll of freemen would be read aloud at each assembly. In 1688 they further agreed that 'whatever acts have passed or do pass in this assembly for the future be transcribed fairly every assembly and openly read and laid up in the chest with the charters'.[122] Documents and reading, especially following the arrival of printing and the triumph of the common law after 1603, became central to the way in which the early modern Irish world worked. While this was not yet a culture dominated by print one precondition for the triumph of print, the ability to understand and utilise the written word in everyday life, was slowly becoming established.

NOTES

1   The best description of this remains D.B. Quinn, *The Elizabethans and the Irish* (Ithaca, 1966).

2   Graham Kew (ed.), 'The Irish sections of Fynes Moryson's unpublished *Itinerary*' in *Analecta Hibernica* no. 37 (1998), pp. 35–6; Barnaby Rich, *A new description of Ireland* (London, 1610), p. 27.

3   Edmund Spenser, *A view of the present state of Ireland*, ed. W.L. Renwick (Oxford, 1970), p. 60.

4   Nicholas Canny (ed.), 'Rowland White's "The dysorders of the Irishery"' in *Studia Hibernica* no. 19 (1979), p. 154. White also referred to 'the customary law of the brehons' in another tract, Nicholas Canny (ed.), 'Rowland White's "Discors touching Ireland, *c.* 1569"' in *Irish Historical Studies* xx (1976–77), p. 454.

5   Spenser, *View of the present state*, p. 5.

6   Kew (ed.), 'The Irish sections of Fynes Moryson', p. 59

7   Hiram Morgan (ed.), '"Lawes of Irelande": a tract by Sir John Davies' in *Irish Jurist* n.s. xxviii–xxx (1993–95), p. 313.

8   Spenser, *View of the present state*, p. 39.

9   *29th Report of the deputy keeper of the public records of Ireland* (Dublin, 1897), pp. 40–1.

10   Union Theological College, Belfast, Robert Chambers MS 'Explanation of the shorter catechism', sig. A2.

11   Printed in Colm Lennon, *Richard Stanihurst: the Dubliner, 1547–1618* (Dublin, 1981), p. 149.

12   Printed in Constantia Maxwell (ed.), *Irish history from contemporary sources, 1509–1610* (London, 1923), p. 79.

13   Morgan (ed.),'"Lawes of Irelande"', pp. 310–11.

14   N.L.I., MS G11.

15   Edmund Campion, *Two bokes of the histories of Ireland*, ed. A.F. Vossen (Assen, 1963), p. [24]. A similar story is repeated in Stanihurst's history of Ireland, Liam Miller and Eileen Power (eds), *Holinshed's Irish chronicle* (Dublin, 1979), p. 114.

16   Pádraig Ó Macháin, 'The early modern Irish prosodic tracts and the editing of bardic verse' in H.L.C. Tristram (ed.), *Metrik und Medienwechsel/Metricks and Media* (Tübingen, 1991), pp. 273–87.

17   W.M. Hennessy and B. MacCarthy (eds), *Annála Uladh, Annals of Ulster* (4 vols, Dublin, 1887–1901), iii, pp. 574–5.

18 For further details see Bernadette Cunningham and Raymond Gillespie, *Stories from Gaelic Ireland* (Dublin, 2003), pp. 104–6.

19 Charles W. Russell, 'On an agreement in Irish between Gerald, ninth earl of Kildare and the Mac Ranald' in *Proceedings of the Royal Irish Academy*, x (1866–9), pp. 480–96.

20 P.R.O.N.I., D3078/1/23/1; D3078/1/26/1–17; D3078/1/15/13; Gearóid Mac Niocaill (ed.), *Crown surveys of lands, 1540–1* (Dublin, 1992), p. 272.

21 Mac Niocaill (ed.), *Crown surveys*, pp. 235–6.

22 For example Edmund Curtis, *Calendar of Ormond deeds* (6 vols, Dublin, 1932–43), iv, pp. 11–12, 218–19, 224–5, 296–7.

23 Hennessy and MacCarthy (eds), *Annála Uladh*, iii, pp. 514–15. A similar entry appears in the Annals of Connacht, A.M. Freeman (ed.), *Annála Connacht* (Dublin, 1944), pp. 626–7.

24 Maura Carney (ed.), 'Agreement between Ó Domhnaill and Tadhg Ó Conchobair concerning Sligo Castle (23 June 1539)' in *Irish Historical Studies*, iii (1942–43), pp. 288–91.

25 John O'Donovan (ed.), 'Covenant between Mageoghegan and the Fox' in *The miscellany of the Irish Archaeological Society, i* (Dublin, 1846), pp. 190–7. For discussion of the correct dating of the document see Paul Walsh, *Irish chiefs and leaders* (Dublin, 1960), pp. 255–6.

26 Andrew Breeze, 'The charter of Christ' in *Celtica* xix (1987), pp. 116–20.

27 Eleanor Knott (ed.), *The bardic poems of Tadhg Dall Ó hUiginn* (2 vols, London, 1922–26), i, p. 240, ii, p. 158.

28 Tomás Ó Raghallaigh (ed.), 'Seanchus Búrcach' in *Journal of the Galway Archaeological and Historical Society* xii (1926–27), p. 111.

29 For O'Mulconry see John O'Donovan (ed.), *Annals of the kingdom of Ireland by the Four Masters* (7 vols, Dublin, 1851), sub anno 1519.

30 Royal Irish Academy, *Dictionary of the Irish language based mainly on Old and Middle Irish materials* (Dublin, 1983), sub 'denitiur'.

31 Art Cosgrove (ed.), *New history of Ireland, ii: medieval Ireland, 1169–1534* (Oxford, 1987), pp. 814–15; Raymond Gillespie, 'Negotiating order in seventeenth-century Ireland' in M.J. Braddick and John Walter (eds), *Negotiating power in early modern society* (Cambridge, 2001), pp. 190–1.

32 Cunningham and Gillespie, *Stories from Gaelic Ireland*, pp. 192–4.

33 Ó Raghallaigh (ed.), 'Seanchus Búrcach', pp. 106–7.

34 Ó Raghallaigh (ed.), 'Seanchus Búrcach', pp. 118–19.

35 O'Donovan (ed.), *Annals of the kingdom of Ireland*, sub anno 1605.

36 David Greene (ed.), *Duanaire Mhéig Uidhir* (Dublin, 1972), pp. 136–7.

37 T.C.D., MS 831, f. 6v; MS 811, f. 69v; Gillespie, 'Negotiating order', pp. 199–202.

38 For examples see J.H. Todd, 'On some ancient Irish deeds' in *Proceedings of the Royal Irish Academy* vii (1858), p. 17; James Hardiman (ed.), 'Ancient Irish deeds and writings' in *Transactions of the Royal Irish Academy* xv (1826), p. 95; Gearóid Mac Niocaill (ed.), 'Seven Irish documents from the Inchiquin archives' in *Analecta Hibernica* no. 26 (1970), p. 65.

39 Hardiman, 'Ancient Irish deeds', p. 75, Mac Niocaill, 'Seven Irish documents', p. 53.

40 Tomás Ó Raghallaigh (ed.), 'Seanchus Búrcach' in *Journal of the Galway Archaeological and Historical Society* xiv (1928–9), p. 161.

41 For the earl of Antrim deeds see P.R.O.N.I., D265; D2977.

42 Edward MacLysaght (ed.), *Calendar of the Orrery papers* (Dublin, 1941), pp. 355–6.

43 N.A., Salved Chancery pleadings F6, for other examples of deeds being forcibly seized see N.A., Y5, K22, H20, H119, I228, I234, J186, J206, J210.

44 For examples see N.A. Salved Chancery pleadings, AA125, AA72, BB149, AA90, K11.

45 N.A., Salved Chancery pleadings, C65.

46 N.A. Salved Chancery pleadings, K59.

47 N.A., Salved Chancery pleadings, R38.

48 N.A., Dublin Prerogative will book, 1644–84, f. 367.

49 P.R.O., SP63/62/9.

50 B.L., Harley MS 4297, f. 140.

51 For example B.L., Harley MS 4297, f. 141v; N.A., Salved Chancery pleadings, B371.

52 B.L., Harley MS 4297, f. 157v.

53 N.L.I., MS 643, ff. 62v–3.

54 John Hooker, *The life and times of Sir Peter Carew*, ed. John Maclean (London, 1857), pp. 71–2.

55 G.F. Savage-Armstrong, *A genealogical history of the Savage family in Ulster* (London, 1906), p. 124.

56 Katharine Simms, 'Literacy and the Irish bards' in Huw Pryce (ed.), *Literacy in medieval Celtic societies* (Cambridge, 1998), pp. 251–3.

57 Gearóid Mac Niocaill (ed.), 'Cairt o Mhaolmhordha Ó Raighilligh, 1558' in *Breifne* i no. 2 (1959), pp. 134–6; E.C.R. Armstrong, *Irish seal matrices and seals* (Dublin, 1913), pp. 19–20.

58 T. Crofton Croker (ed.), *The tour of M. de la Boullaye Le Gouez in Ireland, 1644* (London, 1837), p. 37.

59 J.F. O'Doherty (ed.), *The 'Catechismus' of Theobald Stapleton* (Dublin, 1945), 'Address to the reader', para. 33.

60 For example the comments of Richard Hadsor in B.L., Cotton MS Titus B X, ff. 180–80v. For interpreters see Patricia Palmer, *Language and conquest in early modern Ireland* (Cambridge, 2001), pp. 188–96.

61 B.L., Harley MS 4297, f. 156, for instance.

62 For example the, perhaps fictional, exchange between the Irishman and the merchant in the 1630s in N.J.A. Williams (ed), *Pairlement Chloinne Tomáis* (Dublin, 1981), pp. 40, 97–8.

63 Simms, 'Literacy and the Irish bards', p. 251.

64 John O'Donovan (ed.), 'Original letters in the Irish and Latin languages by Shane O'Neill' in *Ulster Journal of Archaeology* 1st ser., v (1857), pp. 259–73; John O'Donovan

(ed.), 'The Irish correspondence of James Fitz Maurice [earl] of Desmond' in *Journal of the Royal Society of Antiquaries of Ireland* ii (1859), pp. 354–69.

65 J. Fraser, P. Grosjean and J.G. O'Keeffe (eds), *Irish texts: fasciculus iv* (London, 1934), pp. 27–9.

66 Charles McNeill, 'Lord Chancellor Gerrard's notes of his report on Ireland' in *Analecta Hibernica* no. 2 (1931), p. 166; for the deeds see N.L.I., MS 16471.

67 For example P.R.O., SP 63/195/244c.

68 T.C.D., MS 812, ff. 74v–5.

69 T.C.D., MS 814, ff. 71–2, 168v–9; Ms 811, f. 155; MS 835, f. 2v; MS 815, ff. 99v–100, 100v–1

70 Hooker, *The life of Sir Peter Carew*, p. 85.

71 T.W. Moody (ed.), 'The revised articles of the Ulster plantation, 1610' in *Bulletin of the Institute of Historical Research* xii (1935), p. 181.

72 B.L., Add MS 4756, ff. 104v, 118–18v.

73 Raymond Gillespie, *The transformation of the Irish economy* (Dundalk, 1991), pp. 24–7, 31–2, 55.

74 For examples T.C.D., MS 836, f. 44v; MS 829, f. 207; Ms 821, f. 153, 177; Ms 839, f. 27; Ms 812, f. 57; MS 814, f. 44; MS 831, f. 12v; MS 811, ff. 55v, 101, 130; MS 810, ff. 75v, 162; MS 822, f. 20; MS 823, f. 216; MS 824, f. 66

75 William McCamick, *A further impartial account of the actions of the Inniskillen men*, ed. W.T. Latimer (Belfast, 1896), pp. 1–2. For the same process in Munster see Maclysaght (ed.), *Orrey papers*, pp. 326, 332, 338.

76 Marquis of Lansdowne (ed.), *The Petty papers* (2 vols, London, 1927), i, pp. 77–9.

77 For a survey of these trends see Herbert Wood, 'The public records of Ireland before and after 1922' in *Transactions of the Royal Historical Society*, 4th ser., xiii (1930), pp. 20–3; Peter Roebuck 'The Irish registry of deeds: a comparative study' in *Irish Historical Studies* xviii (1972–73), pp. 61–73.

78 John Ainsworth (ed.), *The Inchiquin manuscripts* (Dublin, 1961), p. 282, for other examples, pp. 284, 285, 287, 288, 297; N.A., Salved Chancery pleadings, U154, BB107.

79 John Ainsworth (ed.), 'Doneraile papers' in *Analecta Hibernica* no. 20 (1958), p. 58.

80 Kew (ed.), 'The Irish sections of Fynes Moryson', p. 62.

81 Raymond Gillespie, 'Destabilising Ulster, 1641–2' in Brian Mac Cuarta (ed.), *Ulster 1641: aspect of the rising* (Belfast, 1993), p. 114.

82 T.C.D., MS 839, ff. 32, 45v.

83 E.S. Shuckburgh (ed.), *Two biographies of William Bedell* (Cambridge, 1902), pp. 125–6.

84 W.M. Hennessy (ed.), *The Annals of Loch Cé* (2 vols, London, 1871), ii, pp. 344–5.

85 Greene (ed.), *Dunaire Mhéig Uidhir*, pp. 92–3, 94–5, 200–1.

86 Knott (ed.), *Bardic poems of Tadhg Dall Ó hUiginn*, i, p. 170, ii, p. 113.

87 John Ainsworth (ed.), 'Dillon papers' in *Analecta Hibernica* no. 20 1958), pp. 29–32.

88 PRO, SP63/249/19 iii; Raymond Gillespie, 'Church, state and education in early modern Ireland' in Maurice O'Connell (ed.), *O'Connell: education, church and state* (Dublin, 1992), pp. 40–59.

89 Raymond Gillespie, *Colonial Ulster: the settlement of east Ulster, 1600–41* (Cork, 1985), p. 230.

90 N.L.W., Aberystwyth, Powis Caste deeds, passim.

91 P.R.O.N.I., D671/LE 1, 3, 4, 8.

92 James Wolveridge, *Speculum matricis or the expert midwives handmaid* (London, 1671), p. 27.

93 Samuel Foley, *An exhortation to the inhabitants of Down and Connor concerning the religious education of their children* (Dublin, 1695), p. 27.

94 P.R.O.N.I., D929/F1/1, 3, 4.

95 R.C.B., P326/27/3/35.

96 T.C. Barnard, 'Learning, the learned and literacy in Ireland, 1660–1760' in T.C. Barnard, Dáibhí Ó Cróinín and Katharine Simms (eds), *'A miracle of learning': studies in manuscripts and Irish learning* (Aldershot, 1998), pp. 220–1.

97 For much of what follows see Gillespie, 'Church, state and education', pp. 40–59.

98 Armagh Public Library, Dopping correspondence, no. 256.

99 C.S. King (ed.), *A great archbishop of Dublin* (London, 1908), pp. 3–4.

100 H.M.C., *Report on the manuscripts of the marquess of Ormonde* (new series, 8 vols, London, 1902–20), v, p. 125.

101 *The life of Mr Thomas Gent, printer of York, by himself* (London, 1832), p. 23.

102 *A brief account of Mr Valentine Greatrix ... written by himself* (London, 1666), p. 15.

103 King (ed.), *A great archbishop*, pp. 3–4.

104 T.C.D., MS 829, f. 160.

105 T.C.D., MS 820, f. 50v; MS 815, f. 169.

106 James Carney (ed.), *Poems on the O'Reillys* (Dublin, 1950), p. xiv; Alan Bruford, *Gaelic folktales and medieval romances* (Dublin, 1969), pp. 55–68.

107 Greene (ed.), *Duanaire Mhéig Uidhir*, pp. 230–1.

108 John Rogers, *Ohel or Beth Shemesh* (London, 1653), p. 412(10); Robert Craghead, *An answer to a late book entitled a discourse concerning the inventions of men in the worship of God* (Edinburgh, 1694), p. 86; Edward Wetenhall, *A practical and plain discourse of the form of godliness visible in the present age* (Dublin, 1683), p. 158.

109 *The soldier's best exercise* (Dublin, 1696), preface.

110 Campion, *Two bokes of the histories of Ireland*, ed. Vossen, p. [24].

111 Greene (ed.), *Duanaire Mhéig Uidhir*, pp. 24–5.

112 Richard Parr, *The life of the most reverend father in God James Ussher* (London, 1686), p. 2.

113 *The works of the Rev. and learned Joseph Boyse* (2 vols, London, 1728), i, p. 440; J[oseph] B[oyse], *Sermons preached on several subjects* (2 vols, Dublin, 1708), ii, pp. 583–4.

114 Steven Jerome, *Ireland's jubilee and joyes io paen* (Dublin, 1624), sig. A3.

115 Michael Olden, 'Counter Reformation problems: Munster' in *Irish Ecclesiastical Record* 5th ser., civ (July–Dec. 1965), p. 45.

116 Roger Boyle, earl of Orrery, *Poems of the festivals of the church* (Cork, 1681), sig. B1v.

117 T.C.D., MS 830, f. 173v.

118 T.C.D., MS 815, ff. 105–5v.

119 John Bradley (ed.), *Treasures of Kilkenny: charters and civic records of Kilkenny city* (Kilkenny, 2003), p. 96.

120 T[homas] W[aring], *A brief narration of the plotting, beginning and carrying on that execrable rebellion and butchery in Ireland* (London, 1658), pp. 18–19.

121 *Richard Blake his speech in the house of commons at the grand committee for the bills against paper petitions* (London, 1641).

122 Thomas Gogarty (ed.), *Council book of the corporation of Drogheda* (Drogheda, 1915), pp. 33, 77, 262.

Part II

The development of print

Chapter 3

The coming of print, 1550–1650

In 1551 the first book printed in Ireland using movable type was produced on a printing press in Dublin. By European standards this was a late development. Most countries on the fringes of Europe had adopted printing as a technique half a century earlier. On the eastern edges of Europe, Bohemia had a press since the 1460s and on the northern edge of the continent Stockholm had a press by the end of the fifteenth century. In Scotland, Edinburgh had its first press by 1500.[1] Ireland in European terms has only two parallels. In Norway – a dependency of Denmark – a printing press was not established until 1643, with Copenhagen having a monopoly on printing for Norway up to that point.[2] In the British Isles only Wales failed to establish an early sixteenth-century press, relying on London for its printing needs.[3] In other ways too Ireland was different from the European norm. In Scotland the printed word arrived as a result of local initiatives linking mercantile wealth and private patronage with the result that printing was controlled by the towns rather than the state.[4] In England too commercial incentives formed the impetus for the development of printing but here the state came to play a more active role in the organisation of the trade than in Scotland.[5] In Dublin printing was initiated and promoted by government. The first printer, Humphrey Powell, had come from London, where he had issued some ten books between 1548 and 1550. In 1550 he was given £20 by order of the privy council in London to establish himself in Ireland, and on the title page of his first Irish book he described himself as 'king's printer', an office probably created by the government to regulate the trade.[6] His initial production was the first Edwardian Book of Common Prayer, issued presumably in line with the government's desire to promote reformed religion. These circumstances of the establishment of a printing press in Dublin were to have a profound influence on the shape of the book trade in its first century.

I

The history of the Irish printing press in the late sixteenth and early seventeenth centuries is, in the main, a story of inactivity. Before 1600 the output of the Irish press was insignificant. On the basis of surviving evidence it appears that the bulk of printing was for government. Before the 1550s printing for Irish purposes had been done in London but with the establishment of Powell as a printer in Dublin it became possible, in theory at least, to execute larger-scale projects in Ireland. In practice little materialised. A case in point is the publication of the Irish statutes, of which, although planned since the 1540s, the volume, when finally published in the 1570s, had to be produced in London.[7] When Powell died is unknown although his last work published in Dublin was issued in 1567. The effect of his demise was to bring the development of the Irish press to a premature halt. When in 1571 the next significant printed work appeared in Dublin it was under the imprint of John Kearney, the treasurer of St Patrick's Cathedral, who was not a professional printer. This book was a translation of the catechism into Irish, printed in an Irish type used for the first time. It should probably be viewed as a once-off religious work, the printing of which was organised by Kearney to promote the spread of religious reformation rather than as a commercial exercise in developing printing as a means of communication. As Kearney himself expressed it, he had undertaken the work 'as I saw no one else would do so'.[8] Kearney produced nothing else for the press and the office of queen's printer which Humphrey Powell had held does not seems to have been filled in Ireland until 1588. In that year William Kearney, a relative of John who had trained as a printer in England, was appointed queen's printer in Ireland. William Kearney's output was no more impressive than that of his predecessor Powell. From 1588 there were some discussions between the privy council and Kearney concerning the printing of an Irish Bible. However, while work began it was not completed when Kearney died, probably in 1598 or 1599, leaving little to show for his ten years in office.[9] The sheets of the Bible, and the type and ornaments of his workshop passed to his apprentice John Franckton, who by 1600 was printing government proclamations and who in 1604 was formally appointed king's printer in Dublin, an office which he held for the next fourteen years, producing eleven works, apart from proclamations and two reprints, over that time and importing books from Chester.[10]

By any standards this was not a distinguished record for the Dublin printers in the late sixteenth century. One might excuse this on the grounds that the market for books was thin in late sixteenth-century Ireland. It was significant that Dublin, its chief town, did not have a university which might act as a stimulant to the print trade. Outside the pale area the marketing system for books was non-existent, most trade being carried on by itinerant merchants in an area where English, the language of print, was little spoken. The establishment of Trinity College in 1592 and the reinvigoration of cathedral life in Dublin during the 1590s might have been expected to generate work for the Dublin press but this did not materialise. There were two main problems with the sixteenth-century Irish press. The first was that it was undercapitalised. Printing was a business which tied up significant amounts of capital over long periods of time. Paper, for instance, was expensive and since it was not produced in Ireland all the paper used had to be imported. Thus in the 1580s one contemporary noted that 'paper in Dublin is very dear, scant and bad'.[11] Once printed, books had to be stored and then transported for sale. Failure to sell a print run tied up capital for long periods of time and discouraged further investment. The sixteenth- and early seventeenth-century press relied on government grants for its capitalisation. Powell had been given £20 to establish his business in Dublin, over £80 had been provided to make punches, matrices and fonts for the Irish type used by John Kearney and money had been allocated to William Kearney for the printing of the Irish New Testament. However government was prepared to pay only for the practical necessities of prayerbooks, Bibles and proclamations rather than subsidising a press for book production on an ongoing basis. The second problem experienced by the Dublin press before 1610 was lack of copy. Publication in Dublin did not carry the sort of cultural status to the author that publication in London did. There were few in Ireland with sufficient cash to spare to patronise literary endeavour and, apart from a brief period in the 1570s, there was little that resembled a royal court attached to the vice-regal officials in Dublin castle. Thus those with literary pretensions in Ireland, such as Barnaby Rich, Lodowick Bryskett or Edmund Spenser, looked to London for publishing outlets rather than relying on the rather disorganised press in Dublin. The literary output of Gaelic Ireland remained in either oral or manuscript form with little commercial potential. Some argued this was due to a lack of fonts of Irish type but such an argument reflects only the conservatism of the Dublin printers. In the 1630s, for instance, one Irish-language catechism printed in Brussels was set in Roman type 'so that it can be more easily understood'.[12] In reality it was more likely that printers saw the Irish-language market as not profitable enough to justify their attention. For this reason a considerable part of the Irish world was, at least initially, closed to the world of print. Within the pale and surrounding areas there seems to have been a good deal of bilingualism in the late sixteenth and early seventeenth centuries.[13] However, outside the pale the provinces of Connacht and Ulster had a large proportion of monoglot Irish speakers at the beginning of the seventeenth century. By the 1640s bilingualism seems to have made some headway in those regions. Such people were, as the previous chapter suggests, not as well used to handing the written word as they would later become.

By 1619 the shortcomings of the Irish press were all too obvious. The king's printer John Franckton was elderly, and died in the following year. The English privy council was well aware of the problems when it commented in 1618 that Franckton was not fit for the office 'both in respect of his weak estate and his insufficiency otherwise'. There had already been some discussion with the London Stationers' Company about taking responsibility for the Irish press by sending over an agent 'to settle a factory of booksellers and bookbinders there at Dublin'. They do not seem to have envisaged that, at least initially, there would be a printer at Dublin. The problem was that two reversionary interests had been granted for the position of king's printer but neither of these individuals was deemed suitable for the post. The reversionary interests were stayed and the Stationers were granted the office of king's printer in Ireland with the sole right to print and sell books in the country. To advance this they formed the Irish Stock to raise funds on behalf of and to manage the Irish business.[14] This allowed a substantial capital injection into the Irish press although this came as much by accident as by design. The original plan may have been not to print in Ireland but simply to sell London-printed books there. In 1620, for example, the Irish Stock purchased £900 worth of books from the Stationers for sale in Ireland. A list of about this date suggests that they intended to corner the lucrative market in schoolbooks, Bibles and liturgical works.[15] If this was the original design it does not seem to have been effective. The Stationers discovered they needed to maintain a press for government work, and that press was technically capable of producing substantial works. Certainly by June 1618 within months of acquiring the patent as king's printer Archbishop James Ussher reported that the Stationers were beginning to print a new edition of the Irish statutes prepared by Richard Bolton, although this did not appear until late 1620 or early 1621.[16] Over the next five years they produced a number of the archbishop's own scholarly works at rates which could be slow. In one case it took a year for the Stationers to produce a three-hundred-page volume by Ussher.[17]

There is little doubt that the introduction of the Stationers' Company as king's printers in Ireland had a significant impact on the output of the press. By the late 1630s the output of the Dublin press increased to almost ten items a year, or five times what it had been under Franckton.[18] However, this was still low by the standards of other parts of the British Isles. The Edinburgh press, for instance, which operated in a country with a population about the same size as that of Ireland and with similar problems for publishers in respect of the language of its inhabitants, produced an average of twenty-eight items a year over the late 1630s against Dublin's average of ten titles. Moreover, what sustained the Dublin press was not the entrepreneurial skill of the Stationers but rather the need of government for printing services. From 1620 to 1640 well over half of the output of the Dublin press was for administrative purposes.[19] Indeed when in the 1650s the Welsh puritan John Jones attempted to have a godly work printed in Welsh in Dublin he found the progress of the printing much delayed by the amount of government work which the Dublin press had to do.[20] The Stationers were clearly unhappy with their Irish venture and in 1639 they sold their monopoly for printing and sale of stationery to their factor, William Bladen, for £2,600 although he only ever paid £947. For the next twenty-one years Bladen acted as printer first to the king and then to the commonwealth until his death in 1663.[21]

The Stationers' expectations from the Irish trade are unclear. Many of the sixteenth-century problems with the press, including the problems with the supply of paper, remained.[22] It does seem clear that they grossly overestimated the speed at which the Irish market for print would expand in a growing economy in the early seventeenth century as English and Scottish settlement expanded across the country. It is clear that they gained a basic market for Bibles and schoolbooks, most of which they imported from England.[23] The Stationers operated in Dublin through a number of factors each of whom tried to exploit the market to which he had been given access, often reprinting English bestsellers in Ireland. This led to a rather erratic pattern of output from the Dublin press. Thus Arthur Johnson, the factor from 1624–1631, reprinted a number of bestselling English works, including a twelfth impression of Sir Thomas Overbury's *His wife now a widow*, in 1626, but all to no avail since he failed to make a profit from the Irish operation.[24] However, what the Stationers may have thought they were acquiring was spare printing capacity with lower wage rates than in London. Certainly within months of acquiring the patent as king's printer the Stationers were reprinting Sir Philip Sidney's *Arcadia* for sale not in Dublin but in London. In 1624 they printed another book in Dublin for the English market.[25] This pattern clearly continued and in 1633 the Stationers' agent in Dublin is recorded exporting between 8 and 10 cwt of unbound, presumably Dublin-produced, books to Chester.[26] By the 1640s Dublin-produced books may have relatively common in London and its hinterland. Inventories of twenty-six libraries from London seized by parliament in 1643 include four recorded copies of James Ussher's *Britannicarum ecclesiarum antiquitates*, published only in Dublin in 1639. Other lists of London libraries from the sample had sets of the Irish statutes and Richard Bolton's manual for justices of the peace, again available only in Irish printings.[27]

In terms of works for the Irish market the Stationers established a press on a more commercial basis than before 1620 and produced more than their predecessors had done. Yet the Irish market for print was still limited. Distribution mechanisms were poorly developed, and the commercialisation, which would open up a marketing structure along which books would flow, had a good deal of progress to make. The outbreak of war in Ireland in the

1640s gave a considerable fillip to the printing press. In England the collapse of censorship in the early 1640s saw an explosion of print there. Much of this was political propaganda or pamphlets expressing the sort of heterodox religious views which had previously spread only through word of mouth or manuscript tract. In Dublin there was also an expansion in the activity of the press but in a different way. Government control of the one printing press that existed in Dublin was maintained in a way that control of the complex world of print in London, with its many presses, could not be. As a result the output of the Dublin presses expanded significantly because of government need rather than political or religious debate. Secondly, and more importantly, print in Ireland became an important weapon in the propaganda war which was fought alongside the military campaigns of the 1640s. From this perspective the issues which preoccupied authors and printers in London had little to say to the small Irish market. Divisions between Catholics and Protestants were of more concern than dissenting theological views, which did not make their way into Ireland until the early 1650s.

However print as a propaganda tool in the war was important both to the government and to the body set up to manage the war on behalf of the insurgents, the Kilkenny Confederation. Where the Confederation set up its earliest press is not known. In April 1642, for instance, there are references to 'laws' being printed by the Confederates and it is just possible that a press of some sort existed in their capital, Kilkenny.[28] On the evidence of the printed works themselves, the earliest surviving items, mostly proclamations, date from 1643 and are from Waterford. There, a Thomas Bourke who described himself as 'printer to the Confederate Catholics of Ireland' on his imprints, established a press. Nothing is known about Bourke save that on the evidence of his productions he seems to have been a trained printer. It is not clear either why the press should have been established in Waterford since the Confederate capital was in Kilkenny. This must have represented considerable inconvenience for the printing of government documentation such as proclamations. The most likely explanation is that Bourke was trained as a printer somewhere in Europe and had imported his press into the port of Waterford where, not wanting a further journey to Kilkenny, he set himself up in business. While his initial business was derived from the Confederation he clearly wanted to diversify, and in a preface from 'the printer' to 'the reader' in a sermon published in 1644 Bourke claimed that 'I will shortly publish other learned works which hitherto through the iniquity of former times lay lurking in darkness'.[29] A number of other significant Catholic works were published, although after 1645 Bourke's name disappeared from the imprints and almost nothing was produced in Waterford after 1646. By 1646 a second press had been established in Kilkenny, probably under Jesuit control, but was seized by the supreme council of the Confederation. One 1648 imprint of this press carries Thomas Bourke's name although the type and ornaments are different from that of the Waterford press. The Kilkenny press continued to issue material until the town fell to the Cromwellian forces in the early 1650s. Printing was established at one further centre in the 1640s. A press was set up in Cork in 1648 by Peter Pienne, of whom nothing is known except that, to judge from imprints, he ran the Waterford press in its closing years. The Cork press used some of the type and ornaments from the Waterford press. It produced, probably on the initiative of the earl of Inchiquin, mainly royalist propaganda. In the early 1650s the Cork press was seized by parliamentary forces who used it to print their own material. By 1651 the types and ornaments in use at Cork again appear in Waterford-printed items, now under the control of the Cromwellian regime, suggesting that the press had returned there. However this move did not last long and in 1653 the press was re-established at Cork under Pienne. By 1657 this press was being run by William Smith, who had been a printer at the Kilkenny press in its latter years. Where Smith had been in the interim is not known but by 1657 he was using an assortment of type not previously known in Kilkenny or Waterford and which may have been acquired in England.[30] Such provincial printing was of relatively short-term significance in terms of increasing the volume of print in Ireland, with Dublin and the government press remaining the main location for printing in Ireland. Although Cork continued to print books throughout the late seventeenth century they were few and of limited significance. They did, however, point out the importance of print in stating and defending one's position.

II

The restricted nature of the output of the Dublin presses throughout the sixteenth and early seventeenth centuries does not mean that Ireland was isolated from the wider world of print and the culture of books. One of the main characteristics of the world of books in sixteenth-century Ireland was that demand was fed not by the Dublin press but by imports, a fact which served to shape the nature of the Irish book trade in the early modern period. The dominance of imports, for instance, gave the trade a colonial feel and meant that it was reliant on the English-speaking market for its success. Even by the time of the first printing in Dublin, eastern Ireland had already been exposed to the world of print through trade. By 1503–4 the parish church of St Werburgh in Dublin had acquired a printed missal, presumably from England, although it also continued to pay for manuscript copies of liturgical works.[31] Other clergy also presumably acquired books in this way. Certainly in 1537 a priest in Waterford was robbed of 'much linen cloth and a book' and earlier in 1526 Archbishop Cromer of Armagh required each curate to acquire named books under a penalty of 40s.[32] The trade developed rapidly and by 1545 the Dublin stationer James Dartas was already importing a wide range of printed works for retail in Dublin.[33] Indeed by the 1540s London printers may even have been producing books specifically for the Irish market.[34] Individuals and groups also imported printed works from both England and continental Europe for their own use, and both the earl of Kildare in the 1520s and the Franciscans in Youghal by the early sixteenth century had substantial libraries, presumably imported by themselves to meet their own needs.[35]

Throughout the sixteenth century some families in eastern Ireland had access to the world of books. One Anglo-Irish magnate, Christopher Nugent, claimed that his hobbies were 'books and building'. The Stanihurst family library in Dublin seems to have been significant and it was used by the Jesuit Edmund Campion in compiling his history of Ireland in 1570.[36] Many of the same works cited by Campion, and indeed by Richard Stanihurst in his history of Ireland, reappear in a manuscript compilation of the late sixteenth century, the Book of Howth.[37] From this we might infer something of their reading interests but this is clearly a very selective approach. Since some important classes of work, such as religious works, rarely appear as references in historical works they are underrepresented in this sort of survey. In the writings of Stanihurst and Campion, in the middle of the sixteenth century, history and law are clearly predominant with standard English chronicles, including those of Fabyan and Hall and the *Polychronicon*, as well as the work of Hector Boece and John Major on Scotland, being listed as sources. Similar titles are found also in the earl of Kildare's library. Hooker's annals and the chronicles of Grafton and Holinshed were also being read in Kilkenny in the late sixteenth century.[38] In such ways did the Anglo-Irish of eastern and southern Ireland participate in the English and European intellectual life of the sixteenth century, and this connection lay at the core of their self-understanding. The works of Barnaby Rich written in Dublin in the late sixteenth century provide a New English perspective on what was available there, although it is possible that Rich may have been using notes of books he had read elsewhere. The books cited by Rich suggest that contemporary English works were certainly available in the city, including George Pettie's *Petite palace of Pettie his pleasure* and William Painter's *Palace of pleasure*. If Lodowick Bryskett's *Discourse of civil life* (1606) is based around a discussion in Dublin in the late sixteenth century, then a range of classical works must also have been available there. More mundanely, churches, such as St Werburgh's, invested in printed books (presumably liturgical ones) and had those repeatedly rebound throughout the late sixteenth century.[39]

All this was supported by booksellers comprising the queen's printer but also a few independents, such as William Leath who was active in 1566.[40] In addition, individual readers were able to find books that they wanted through their personal network of contacts outside Ireland. In 1548 'little French books' were being sent from London to the Irish lord deputy.[41] In the 1550s Lord Deputy Sidney also expended five shillings on a French book in Dublin.[42] In the 1570s Lord Deputy Fitzwilliam also bought 'little' prayerbooks and a whole service book. He must have had a larger collection of imports since he also paid 10*d* 'for a register of my lord's books'.[43] Certainly by the beginning of the seventeenth century print culture was well established within the area of the pale and supported by the external contacts of the New English in London and elsewhere.

To what extent the culture of print spread outside the area of Dublin and its hinterland in the late sixteenth century is less clear. Language differences and a restricted market structure certainly retarded the trade. However, existing networks of trade and church ensured that the wider population in these areas was not untouched by the world of print. In the 1590s merchants from Limerick and Galway, as well as the Munster towns, were importing books for distribution into a wider hinterland. In many cases these were cheap, popular books such as chapbooks and almanacs which were sold. In other cases schoolbooks formed the spine of the trade, presumably for the larger towns.[44] Again in 1572 William Piers, the governor of Carrickfergus, noted that 'a barque from England has arrived here with news in print that Sir Thomas Smith hath a gift of part of Ulster and the Ards' and the local native Irish lord, Brian mac Phelim O'Neill, knew about the 'certain books in print' spreading that message. That print had some impact in this case is suggested by a note by Lord Burghley, the queen's principal secretary of state, on Piers's letter that the 'matter in print' was causing problems among the Irish in Ulster.[45] Religious works, particularly Catholic ones, may have found a different route. In 1584 it was reported from Connacht that missals and primers were being confiscated from the common people, for which action the provost martial claimed, 'I am threatened with the greatest curses they have'.[46] In other cases there are reports of oaths being taken on printed primers or missals.[47] Smuggling Catholic books into Ireland in the late sixteenth century was not uncommon.[48] These may have been distributed by clergy or sold by merchants but were certainly common enough to be noticed. By the late sixteenth century few in Ireland could have escaped the presence of print but it would be wrong to overstate this. Contemporaries who had wider acquaintance with the world of books were able to place their Irish experience in context. Ireland, observed Barnaby Rich in 1578, was a country 'where there is no great choice of books to be had' and fifty years later Steven Jerome, the chaplain to the earl of Cork, declared Ireland to be a 'little bookish country'.[49] These were men who were professionally involved with books so their requirements were exacting but nevertheless in comparison to England Ireland remained underdeveloped in the world of print.

In many respects the early seventeenth century intensified the contacts between those who lived in Ireland and the wider world of print. Migration strengthened trade links between Scotland, England and Ireland. Books were one of the many items that flowed along those trade routes. The Bristol port books, for instance, record a near fivefold increase in the number of books imported into southern Ireland between the 1590s and 1612.[50] The book trade in the early part of the century was small and unspecialised. Its nature is clearer from one ship, the *Joseph*, which sailed from Bristol to Youghal in March 1612. Eleven Limerick merchants had cargoes on board and while all had books none specialised in them. The cargo consigned to Miles Arthur of Limerick, for example, included two dozen hornbooks intended to teach reading, two dozen copies of Francis Seagar's *The school of virtue*, six copies of the chapbook the *Seven wise masters*, four 'little books called histories' and six copies of *The right pleasant and variable tragical history of Fortunatus*. However these books were a small part of the cargo consigned to Arthur, which also contained wire, necklaces, starch, soap, pipes, knives, hatbands, lace, nutmeg, wooden combs, playing cards, silk points, cinnamon, papers, stockings, girdles, hats, candlesticks and cambric bands.[51] Arthur's activities were not unusual for the beginning of the seventeenth century since all those who shipped books to Ireland did so as part of wider trading activities. Richard Rothe of Kilkenny in 1593 brought not only two dozen hornbooks to the town but also needles, hats, raw silk and webs of silk, hops, coarse glass, paper, pins, kerseys, trenchers and fustian. In 1590 John Creagh of Waterford, the owner of one of seven cargoes in the *Jesus* of Waterford (two of which had books) imported from Bristol seven primers as well as pocket knives, gloves, locks, thimbles, combs, glass buttons, silk points, paper, nails, hops and hats.[52] These general merchants traded widely and books were only part of their cargoes. Of almost 120 merchants recorded in the Bristol port books who shipped books from Bristol to Ireland between 1590 and 1612 most did so on only one occasion and then disappeared from the trade. Only eleven of the merchants who carried books are recorded as doing so on two occasions and only one, Walter Ryan of Kilkenny, imported books on three occasions, in 1591, 1592 and 1601. However this trade was more characteristic of the sixteenth than the seventeenth century. The monopoly given to the king's printer to sell books, together with the spread of royal authority in Ireland after 1603 to enforce that monopoly, should have meant that such activity by private merchants was severely curtailed. Certainly in the port books for Bristol books bound for Ireland disappear from the list of cargoes after 1612. However books were certainly available in provincial Ireland after 1603, as testified by the presence of a bookbinder at Youghal in 1638.[53] Since there are relatively few sets of corporation records before 1641 it is impossible to tell how widespread such book arts were in provincial Ireland. After the outbreak of hostilities in 1641 it does seem that books were imported into provincial Ireland. According to one sermon preached in Waterford in 1643 the preacher had come across an older sermon to which he intended to reply 'among other pamphlets brought hither out of London'.[54] Again in 1648 and 1649 when the Cork press produced editions of English-published royalist works they must have obtained their copy texts from an English source, and trade is the most likely means.

In contrast to the provincial trade the Dublin trade was rather more organised. The king's printer was based there and could operate as a book-seller and could license others to do so. Certainly in the 1630s the Stationers' factor William Bladen was active in importing books to Ireland through Chester. In 1632, for instance, he probably imported over 20 cwt of books, some bound and some unbound, to meet his bookselling requirements in Dublin.[55] However the king's printer was not the only person prepared to sell books in Dublin. In 1614, for instance, the London stationer John Gwillam imported 10 cwt of books into Dublin and in 1634 John Stepney and Michael Spark, both London stationers, imported 2 cwt each.[56] These were once-off shipments and may be regarded as speculative, with a few London dealers testing the market with the consent of the Stationers. That they did not continue with the shipments suggests that they found the Irish business unprofitable or uncongenial. By 1640, however a few Dublin-based merchants were showing some interest in the book trade. William Crawford, a general merchant, imported a dozen grammars from Chester in 1641 and another Dublin merchant, Bartholomew Droppe, shipped 40 lb of books from Chester to Dublin in the same year. One other merchant shipped 15 cwt of books in 1639 and 1640.[57] All this points to the development of a bookselling trade in Dublin despite the rather retarded state of the print industry. One important sign of this was the establishment of the first significant bookshops in the city. In 1637 John Crooke, a London-trained printer, established a bookselling partnership in Dublin with his brother Edmond, Thomas Allot and Richard Sergier. John probably settled in Dublin only in 1639. All their stock was printed in London and imported. In 1639 John Crooke shipped almost 80 cwt of books, both bound and unbound, to Dublin from Chester and almost 15 cwt the following year, a much higher quantity than the king's printer William Bladen.[58] The position of their shop close to the centre of political power and patronage, probably in Castle Street near the gate of Dublin castle, may be significant for the development of the print trade. It may also be important that they sold the plays of the English playwright James Shirley, attracted to Dublin by the emergence of a vice-regal court under the patronage of Lord Deputy Wentworth, earl of Strafford.[59] The emergence of a fashionable centre in the city, of which book buying was a part, certainly provided considerable incentive to the development of the print trades.[60] Certainly by 1641 Crooke and Segier could claim that they, for the previous five years, had run a stationer's shop 'well furnished with marte and English books', which implies they drew their stock from a wide range of sources, which they then sold 'at such rates as formerly this kingdom was not supplied withal'.[61] In terms of bookselling this was the way of the future. That it took so long to develop in Dublin does demonstrate how difficult it was for the print trade to exploit the commercial opportunities of the city and Ireland at large.

Merchants operating under licence from the king's printer who imported and distributed books printed elsewhere were undoubtedly the mainstay of the Irish book trade in the early seventeenth century. It is clear, however, that some of those who lived in early modern Ireland had other ways of obtaining books. Many of those who moved to Ireland as part of formal plantation schemes or more informal colonisation arrangements brought with them their possessions which sometimes included books. In 1615, for instance, Edward Sanders sailed from Chester to Dublin bringing with him his apparel and books and in 1620 Edward Hatton brought two trunks from Chester including apparel and books. Other migrants had books with their linens or bedding as they moved to Ireland.[62] Indeed a few English printers may have tried to exploit this market. When one work on surveying appeared in London in 1610 its title page announced that it was of use not only in England but 'no less remarkable for all undertakers in the plantation of Ireland or Virginia', hoping to encourage those leaving for Ulster to buy the book.[63] If migrants subsequently wanted books available in England or Scotland links were often maintained with relations at home and they might be in position to obtain such works from bookshops in Scotland or England to supply their wants. Certainly in 1623 the testament of Richard Lawson, an Edinburgh bookseller, revealed that he was owed £43 16s Scots by Robert Semple, a minister in Ireland.[64] For those in search of books from wider horizons there were a number of sources which could be tapped. The Irish antiquary James Ware in the autumn of 1632 made a note of the books he wished to send for '*ex catalogus Francafurtensi*'.[65] This may be a catalogue of 'marte' from the Frankfurt book fair or it may be a London reprint of the catalogue. At any rate Ware had access to a wider supply of books than that provided by the Dublin bookshops. For those who knew merchants trading to continental Europe it is likely that private commissions could be obtained. The earl of Clanricard, for instance, used merchants to buy books for him in Lisbon.[66] It also seems highly likely that a volume of the lives of the saints together with a Latin and English office, bequeathed by Thomas Rice, merchant of Dingle, to his family in 1633 had its origin in a personal purchase abroad.[67] What appears to be a rather dramatic example of this sort of activity is provided by the extensive library of the Limerick doctor Thomas Arthur, which contained works with imprints from across continental Europe. Some of this may have been ordered specially by Arthur but the majority had probably been acquired during the time Arthur had lived in Paris.[68] Some in the pale may have had more systematic access to the wider European world of print. The accounts of the Plantin press in Antwerp, for instance, contain a number of individuals with Old English names, such as Luke Plunket, who are described as 'Irelandois', as book purchasers. Most of these transactions were carried out with a Thomas Strong as intermediary, who was probably an Irish merchant acting as agent for Old English book purchasers on a regular basis.[69]

Outside the commercial world of trade, books moved along other routes. Friendship networks allowed borrowing and lending of books, even over considerable distances. The Dublin antiquary James Ware, for instance, frequently borrowed both books and manuscripts from the London scholar Sir Robert Cotton as did James Ussher, archbishop of Armagh, the Irish lord deputy Oliver St John and the Ulster planter Basil Brooke.[70] More commonly large libraries in Dublin, such as that of Ussher, were the resort of a number of borrowers and the cathedral library at Christ Church in Dublin also seems to have been used as a lending library.[71] Outside Dublin the extensive range of English and Latin titles cited by Geoffrey Keating in his history of Ireland, written in 1634, hints at the diversity of publications to which he had ready access, many of them probably borrowed from others.[72] A further way of circulating books in this less than fully commercial world was giving books as presents, a practice which often crossed confessional and social boundaries. Some of the works of James Ussher, archbishop of Armagh, made their way into the library of the Catholic Thomas Arthur, presumably by way of gifts since Ussher and Arthur were on manuscript-borrowing terms.[73]

By 1640, therefore, there are a number of important indications of the extent to which the inhabitants of Ireland increased their access to the printed word. In some ways this was still restricted to English language users, though that market was growing. Despite problems with the economics of the Dublin printing press by 1640 the city could support professional booksellers. As well as serving the city, such booksellers also fulfilled direct orders for those living in the countryside. Travellers between rural Ireland and the capital would also carry books for friends and relations. In the 1630s the young Donogh Clancy from Clare used his brother, Thomas, a student in Trinity College, Dublin, to buy copies of books for him including Cicero, Ovid and Aesop's *Fables* so that he could be 'as handsome a scholar as any of my age'.[74] Those in provincial Ireland were not as well supplied with print, but imports into the regional ports suggest that at least basic works, such as schoolbooks and readers, were available there.

III

The result of the rising demand for books in Ireland, suggested by the growing literacy examined in the previous chapter and the mechanisms of supply sketched above, meant that in the late sixteenth and early seventeenth centuries collections of books began to be formed. Scholars certainly acquired substantial libraries early. Luke Challoner, one of the first fellows of Trinity College, Dublin, had a library of 853 titles in 1596, rising to 885 titles by 1608. James Ussher, the first professor of ecclesiastical controversies, and later bishop of Meath and archbishop of Armagh, had an even larger collection. Both men were sophisticated book buyers, bought regularly on journeys to England and applied their expertise to buying books for the newly established library of Trinity College.[75] Ussher continued to buy books in England in small quantities and import them for his own use well into the 1630s.[76] The college also purchased continentally published books directly from the Company of Stationers in London.[77] Outside this scholarly world by the 1640s there were a number of libraries of varying sizes in Ireland. Some could be substantial. At one end of the scale a 1639 inventory of the goods of the Oxford-educated fifth earl of Thomond included a list of two hundred books 'of all sorts' valued only at £10.[78] At Castleisland in County Kerry, an area settled as part of the Munster plantation, the landlord's house, according to one list, had a hundred 'great and little books' including a Book of Common Prayer and a Geneva Bible.[79] A few years later an inventory of the goods of the duchess of Buckingham in Dunluce castle included a much more modest collection of forty folios, twelve quartos and five octavos.[80] At the lower end of gentry libraries Lady Lettice Digby of Geashill in County Offaly could muster only twelve books in the inventory of her estate in 1628 and in Dublin ten years later Lady Anne Hamilton had fourteen books and Eleanor Luttrell twenty-three 'old books'.[81] At the lowest end of the scale those of more modest means might have only one or two books, often a Bible or prayerbook.[82] Such book collections were not the sole prerogative of settlers. James Hussey, the Catholic parish priest of Smarmore in County Louth, for instance, seems to have built up a substantial library by 1635, part of which he acquired from the Franciscan convent in Armagh.[83] Increasing bilingualism and the desire to demonstrate status meant that by the 1640s at least some native Irish gentry had begun to build book collections. As one insurgent claimed in 1641 when stealing a trunk in County Wexford, 'it would be a fine trunk to keep his the McMahon's books in'.[84]

The scale of the libraries assembled in early seventeenth-century Ireland depended a great deal on social pretensions and wealth. Perhaps the largest of these, that of Lord Conway at Portmore in County Antrim, accounted for eight thousand titles in the 1630s.[85] A library of this size clearly required special arrangements, and the chaplain to the family and local schoolmaster, Philip

Tandy, took on the role of librarian, unpacking books from chests, placing them on shelves and attempting to make a catalogue of the collection.[86] Conway was an inveterate book buyer and much of this library was clearly imported as the requirement of a gentleman's house although a few locally published titles occur. Some titles, it appears, were shipped to Ireland by mistake and had to be returned to England.[87] The library reflects all branches of learning from divinity through philosophy and science to literature, history, music and 'useful arts'. More restrained was the library of the Limerick Catholic doctor Thomas Arthur with 293 titles, mainly of a medical nature. Arthur's contemporary the Protestant Christopher Sexton had a library in Limerick of 131 titles.[88] Christopher's library was the product of both his father's book buying and his own and had been accumulated over a number of years. Rather over a third of the books concerned religion, the remainder being works of history, law and practical treatises.

A wider view of book ownership is possible from the lists of losses provided by those who were caught up in the rising of 1641.[89] These depositions are not a random sample of the population. There are few depositions from the very rich or poor and some groups, such as the clergy, are clearly over-represented. A further problem is that books were not systematically recorded as losses and in some cases may be buried in a general rubric such as 'household stuff' or 'other goods'. Of those who did report losses of books in their list of losses over half were described as clergy. Slightly over a quarter of those who lost books were either self-styled gentlemen or those whose scale of losses would qualify them for that title. In some cases these book losses may be related not simply to gentry status but to the sort of roles the gentry were to carry out. Gentry were variously described as justices of the peace, an estate agent, the registrar of the vice-admiral of Connacht and surveyor of the king's mines in Tipperary. All these functions required the regular consultation of printed books as practical manuals. At the lower social ranges of those who lost books 6 per cent were classified as yeomen and the remainder comprised a miscellaneous group of the wives of murdered book owners, a weaver, an innkeeper, a clothier and a doctor. Clergy undoubtedly had significant libraries. Using the valuations of book losses by clergy it appears that their books accounted for between 3 and 16 per cent of their total losses, with most above 5 per cent, while in the case of gentlemen most book losses were under 5 per cent of total losses and in many cases less than 1 per cent.[90]

This broad pattern of a large group of book owners drawn from those professionally involved with books, such as clergy and probably (although not represented in the depositions) lawyers, seems to be confirmed from other evidence. The 1641 deposition of the Dublin booksellers Crooke and Sergier, for instance, claimed that they supplied books to 'ministers and other customers of all professions throughout the kingdom'.[91] It is equally clear that books did penetrate further down the social scale, and some of those who migrated to Ireland as craftsmen and tenants owned books. William Billingsley, a joiner, who came to Ireland from Liverpool in 1621, brought with him not only clothes, bedding and joiner's tools but books also.[92] Social status was, however, only one determinant of book ownership. Since books do not seem to have trickled down from 'elite' to 'popular', a more important variable in explaining book ownership may be the simple matter of availability. The evidence, unfortunately, is not sufficiently good to allow an examination of the geography of this pattern of book ownership but it would seem reasonable to suggest that the greatest concentration of book ownership was in the eastern part of the country and perhaps nearest to ports, but this is an area requiring further exploration.

IV

The spread of print in early seventeenth-century Ireland is a complex story. On the one hand the development of Irish printing was slow. Problems with capitalisation and the supply of copy were only gradually reduced, although not eliminated, in the course of the early seventeenth century. Yet, despite this the world of print does seem to have penetrated deeply into Irish society by 1640. In part this can be seen as the result of a growing commercialisation of the country with the emergence of markets and fairs, for example, which allowed printed items to move around with more freedom than before. In particular overseas trade with London through Chester allowed large quantities of print to be brought to Ireland with relative ease, accompanying migrants or following more general trade routes. This situation had considerable repercussions. It gave the book trade a distinctively colonial feel. It was, for instance, dominated by English-language books since these were cheaper to import than risking local editions of Irish-language texts for a native Irish population which, as the previous chapter suggests, was only coming to grips with the social world of writing and reading. Only slowly, as the use of English spread, did the print trade penetrate into the world of the native Irish. It also meant that those who read in Ireland were exposed, in the main, to the ideas of England although smuggled and Catholic works provided alternatives for those who had networks to acquire them. For those who read godly tracts it was the language of English Puritanism which they absorbed, notwithstanding the Church of Ireland's claims to be independent of its English counterpart. For those interested in government and law it was the language of the English common law which they absorbed. If Ireland was to develop solutions to the problems which settlers were presented with, those solutions were articulated in the terminology of English print. That situation would have far-reaching ramifications in almost every area of Irish life in the future.

NOTES

1 For the spread of print see Lucien Febvre and Henri-Jean Martin, *The coming of the book: the impact of printing, 1450–1800* (London, 1976), pp. 180–205.

2 Anne Riising, 'The book and the Reformation in Denmark and Norway' in Jean-François Gilmont (ed.), *The Reformation and the book* (Aldershot, 1990) p. 434.

3 P.H. Jones and Eiluned Rees (eds), *A nation and its books: a history of the book in Wales* (Aberystwyth, 1998), pp. 55–65.

4 A.J. Mann, *The Scottish book trade, 1500–1720* (East Linton, 2000), pp. 7–8.

5 Lotte Hellinga and J.B. Trapp (eds), *The Cambridge history of the book in Britain: iii 1400–1557* (Cambridge, 1999), pp. 65–8.

6 Mary Pollard, *A dictionary of members of the Dublin book trade 1550–1800* (London, 2000), pp. 465–6.

7 For this area see D.B. Quinn, 'Government printing and the publication of the Irish statutes in the sixteenth century' in *Proceedings of the Royal Irish Academy* xlix sect. C (1941), pp. 48–63.

8 Pollard, *Dictionary*, pp. 330–1; Brian Ó Cuív (ed.), *Aibidil Gaoidheilge agus caiticiosma* (Dublin, 1994), p. 13.

9 Pollard, *Dictionary*, pp. 330–1; D.B. Quinn, 'John Denton requests William Kearney to print books for use in Down c. 1588: a sidelight on printing in Ireland' in *Irish Booklore* iii (1976–77), p. 89.

10 Pollard, *Dictionary*, pp. 225–7; P.R.O., E179/1329/9, f. 11 for example.

11 *Cal. S. P. Ire., 1588–92*, p. 373. For an attempt to make paper in Ireland see Mary Pollard, 'Paper making in Ireland in 1590' in *Irish Booklore* iii (1976–77), pp. 83–6.

12 J.F. O'Doherty (ed.), *The 'Catechismus' of Theobald Stapleton* (Dublin, 1945), 'Address to the reader', para. 33.

13 Vincent Carey, '"Neither good English nor good Irish": bi-lingualism and identity formation in sixteenth-century Ireland' in Hiram Morgan (ed.), *Political ideology in Ireland, 1541–1641* (Dublin, 1999), pp. 45–61.

14 *Acts of the privy Council, 1617–18* (London, 1922), pp. 65–6. R. Stewart, 'The king's printer' in *The Library* 3rd ser., xvii (1926–27), p. 322. For the history of the Irish Stock see H.R. Plomer, 'Some notes on the Latin and Irish stocks of the Company of Stationers' in *The Library* 2nd ser., viii (1907), pp. 295–7; Cyprian Blagden, *The Stationers' Company: a history, 1403–1959* (London, 1960), pp. 108–9.

15 Raymond Gillespie, 'Irish printing in the early seventeenth century' in *Irish Economic and Social History* xv (1988), pp. 81–8.

16 C.R. Elrington and J.H. Todd (eds), *The whole works of the most reverend James Ussher* (17 vols, Dublin, 1847–64), xv, p. 135.

17 Elrington and Todd (eds), *The whole works*, xv, pp. 135, 482, 540–1

18 Appendix, table 1.

19 Appendix, table 2.

20 N.L.W., MS 11440D, p. 137.

21 Pollard, *Dictionary*, pp. 37–9.

22 A paper maker did come to Ireland with the army: *Cal. S. P. Ire.*, 1608–10, p. 5.

23 Gillespie, 'Irish printing in the early seventeenth century', pp. 81–8.

24 W.A. Jackson (ed.), *Records of the court of the Stationers' Company, 1602 to 1640* (London, 1957), pp. 202, 208.

25 Jackson (ed.), *Records of the court of the Stationers' Company*, pp. 116, 141, 170.

26 P.R.O., E190/1334/14, f. 4.

27 P.R.O., SP20/7. For the context of these lists see Ian Roy, 'The libraries of Edward, second viscount Conway and others: an inventory and valuation of 1643' in *Bulletin of the Institute of Historical Research* xli (1968), pp. 35–46.

28 H.M.C., *Report on the Franciscan manuscripts* (London, 1906), p. 134.

29 P[atrick] C[omerford], *The inquisition of a sermon* (Waterford, 1644), sig. A4v.

30 For the history of all these presses see W.K. Sessions, *The first printers in Waterford, Cork and Kilkenny pre-1700* (York, 1990) on which the above relies.

31 J.L. Robinson, 'Churchwarden's accounts 1484–166, St Werburgh's church, Dublin' in *Journal of the Royal Society of Antiquaries of Ireland* xliv (1914), pp. 138–9.

32 H.F. Hore and James Graves (eds), *The social state of the southern and eastern counties of Ireland in the sixteenth century* (Dublin, 1870), p. 55; L.P. Murray (ed.), 'Archbishop Cromer's register' in *Journal of the County Louth Archaeological Society* viii (1933–36), p. 342.

33 L.M. Oliver, 'A bookseller's account book' in *Harvard Library Bulletin* xiv (1965), pp. 149–52.

34 D.B. Quinn, 'Edward Walsh's *The office and duety in fightyng for our country* (1545)' in *Irish Booklore* iii (1976–77), pp. 28–31. Copies of this work were being imported into Dublin by James Dartas: Oliver, 'A bookseller's account book', p. 151.

35 Gearóid Mac Niocaill (ed.), *Crown surveys of lands, 1540–1* (Dublin, 1992), pp. 312–14, 355–7; Catherine Moore, 'The library catalogues of the eighth and ninth earls of Kildare' Trinity College, Dublin, M.Phil., 1998; Colmán Ó Clabaigh, *The Franciscans in Ireland, 1400–1534* (Dublin, 2002), pp. 160–80.

36 P.R.O., SP63/160/9; Colm Lennon, *Richard Stanihurst: the Dubliner, 1547–1618* (Dublin, 1981), p. 28.

37 *Calendar of the Carew manuscripts preserved in the archepiscopal library at Lambeth: Book of Howth* (London, 1873).

38 J.T. Gilbert (ed.), *Facsimiles of the national manuscripts of Ireland* (4 vols, Dublin, 1874–84), iv, no. xlvii.

39 R.C.B., P326/27/1/15, 17, 19, 20.

40 Pollard, *Dictionary*, pp. 225–7, 330–1, 357. For binding see Raymond Gillespie (ed.), *The proctor's accounts of Peter Lewis* (Dublin, 1996), p. 68.

41 *Cal. S. P. Ire.*, 1509–73, p. 95.

42 H.M.C., *Report on the manuscripts of Lord L'Isle and Dudley* (6 vols, London, 1925–66), i, p. 381.

43 Northampton County Record Office, Fitzwilliam of Milton MSS, Irish no. 55.

44 Raymond Gillespie,'The book trade in southern Ireland, 1590–1640' in Gerard Long (ed.), *Books beyond the pale: aspects of the provincial book trade in Ireland before 1850* (Dublin, 1996), pp. 1–17.

45 P.R.O., SP63/35/2, 45.

46 P.R.O., SP63/108/13.

47 *Cal. S. P. Ire., 1601–3*, p. 446; *Cal. S. P. Ire., 1600*, p. 152, 294.

48 For example, *Cal. S. P. Ire., 1574–85*, p. 286; *Cal. S. P. Ire., 1608–10*, p. 192.

49 Barnaby Rich, *Alarm to England* (London, 1578); Steven Jerome, *Ireland's jubilee or Ireland's joys io paen* (Dublin, 1624), sig. A3.

50 Gillespie, 'The book trade in southern Ireland', p. 12.

51 P.R.O., E190/1133/12, ff. 8–11, 15.

52 P.R.O., E190/1270/9, f. 7; E190/1130/19, f. 4.

53 Richard Caulfield (ed.), *The council book of the corporation of Youghal* (Guilford, 1878), p. 211.

54 C[omerford], *The inquisition of a sermon*, sig. b1.

55 P.R.O., E190/1334/14, ff. 15v, 18, 20v, 25v, 34v, 43.

56 R.J. Hunter, 'John Gwillam and the Dublin book trade in 1614' in *Long Room* no. 36 (1991), p. 17; P.R.O., E190/1334/14, f. 16, 19v; Pollard, *Dictionary*, p. 548.

57 P.R.O., E190/1336/12, ff. 28v, 29; E190/1336/8, f. 10; E190/1336/18, f. 13.

58 P.R.O., E190/1336/3, ff. 7, 9, 12; E190/1336/12, ff. 13a, 15.

59 A. Stevenson, 'Shirley's publishers: the partnership of Cooke and Crooke' in *The Library* 4th ser., xxv (1945), pp. 140–61.

60 For the emergence of this courtly society see Raymond Gillespie, 'Dublin, 1600–1700: a city and its hinterlands' in Peter Clark and Bernard Lepetit (eds), *Capital cities and their hinterlands in early modern Europe* (Aldershot, 1996), pp. 85–7.

61 T.C.D., MS 809, f. 266.

62 P.R.O., E190/1330/14, f. 19; E190/1332/1, f. 25; E190/1336/3, ff. 5v, 7, 11; E190/1336/12, ff. 12, 23v, 26v; E190/1332/1, f. 27v; E190/1334/14, ff. 18, 19v, 22, 26v, 31; E190/1335/12, ff. 22, 28v; E190/1334/25, f. 32.

63 William Folkingham, *Feudigraphia: the synopsis or epitome of surveying methodised* (London, 1610), title page.

64 David Laing (ed.), *The Bannatyne miscellany, iii* (Edinburgh, 1855), p. 201.

65 B.L., Add. MS 4821, f. 236v.

66 *Cal. S. P. Ire., 1601–3*, p. 484.

67 N.A., RC5/20, f. 89.

68 B.L., Add MS 31885.

69 Plantin-Moretus Museum, Antwerp, MS AR319, Grootboek 1655–71, p.1; MS AR131 p. 21, 251; MS AR127, pp. 8, 9, 99, 263.

70 B.L., Cotton MS Julius C III, ff. 323–9, 380, 381, 388, 386.

71 Elizabethanne Boran, 'The libraries of Luke Challoner and James Ussher, 1595–1608' in Helga Robinson-Hammerstein (ed.), *European universities in the age of Reformation and Counter Reformation* (Dublin, 1998), pp. 109–15; Raymond Gillespie (ed.), 'Borrowing books from Christ Church cathedral, Dublin, 1607' in *Long Room* no. 43 (1998), pp. 15–19.

72 Anne Cronin, 'Printed sources of Keating's *Foras feasa*' in *Éigse* iv (1943–44), pp. 235–79.

73 B.L., Add MS 31885, f. 12. Arthur's transcript of a volume of saints' lives lent to him by Ussher in now in the Russell Library, Maynooth.

74 T.C.D., MUN/P/23/252.

75 Elizabethanne Boran, 'Luke Challoner's library' in *Long Room* no. 37 (1992), pp. 17–26; Boran, 'The libraries of Luke Challoner and James Ussher, 1595–1608', pp. 75–115; Mary Pollard, *Dublin's trade in books, 1500–1800* (Oxford, 1989), pp. 36–7.

76 P.R.O., E190/1336/3, f. 14; E190/1330/11, f. 37; E190/1334/14, f. 20.

77 R.J. Roberts, 'The Latin stock (1616–1627) and its library contacts' in Robin Myres, Michael Harris and Giles Mandelbrote (eds), *Libraries and the book trade* (New Castle, Delaware, 2000), p. 17.

78 Brian Ó Dalaigh, 'An inventory of the contents of Bunratty castle and the will of Henry, fifth earl of Thomond' in *North Munster Antiquarian Journal* xxxvi (1995), p. 157.

79 N.L.I., MS 7861, f. 167v.

80 Hector MacDonnell (ed.), 'A seventeenth-century inventory from Dunluce castle, Co. Antrim' in *Journal of the Royal Society of Antiquaries of Ireland* cxxiii (1992), pp. 118, 119.

81 B.L., Add. Charter 13340, m.4d; Dublin City Archives, MS C1/J/2/4, p. 228; B.L., Add. MS 11687, f. 125v.

82 For example, Dublin City Archives, MS C1/J/2/4, pp. 200, 216, 228.

83 L.P. Murray (ed.), 'The will of James Hussey of Smarmore, Co. Louth "priest", 1635' in *Journal of the County Louth Archaeological Society* viii (1933–36), pp. 303, 315.

84 T.C.D., MS 818, f. 15.

85 Public Library, Armagh, Library catalogue of the second Viscount Conway.

86 *Cal. S. P. Ire., 1633–47*, pp. 81, 118–19.

87 *Cal. S. P. Ire., 1633–47*, p. 129.

88 B.L., Add MS 31,885, ff. 8–13; Add MS 19,865, ff. 74–8.

89 T.C.D., MS 809–39.

90 Much later in the 1690s clergy were urged to spend 10 per cent of their annual income on books: Robert Matteson, 'Archbishop King and the conception of his library' in *The Library* 6th ser., xiii (1991), p. 239.

91 T.C.D., MS 810, f. 4.

92 P.R.O., E190/1332/11, f. 20.

Chapter 4

The triumph of print, 1650–1700

In the years before 1660 print established itself, albeit in a rather precarious position, within Irish society. Undercapitalisation of the press, a thin market for its products and a world that was only just coming to terms with the ideas of literacy, texuality and reading were all contributory factors to the slow spread of a print culture in early seventeenth-century Ireland. After 1660, however, the power of print grew dramatically so that by 1680 one Irish letter writer could enquire 'what are the most considerable things of news in this age of printing'.[1] There are a number of important indicators of this trend. The print trades within Dublin expanded considerably. In 1670 printers and stationers organised themselves, with others, into the guild of St Luke. The power of the king's printer in determining what would be published waned and by the 1690s the king's printer no longer controlled what was produced by the Dublin presses. The guild increasingly assumed the role of deciding what would be published in the city and vouching for its authenticity.[2] The number of printers at work in Dublin increased in the 1680s and again in the 1690s. The number of booksellers in the city quadrupled in the late seventeenth century.[3] This commercial expansion was reflected in a significant growth in the volume of material from the Dublin presses in the latter half of the seventeenth century. Some were scathing about the Dublin press. One visitor to the city in 1699, James Verdon of Market Dereham in Norfolk, complained 'they have, moreover, a printing house which, I must own, is no great glory for them because they seldom print anything but news and tickets for funerals'.[4] Some of the growth in output certainly comprised reprints of works already available in London but by the end of the century new indigenous works were being produced also. In the 1690s, for instance, the Dublin presses were being utilised by religious controversialists in a way that had not been done earlier in the century. William King, dean of St Patrick's cathedral and later bishop of Derry, used print to attack Catholics in the 1680s, and also

75

Presbyterians in the 1690s, and his work provoked spirited replies from both parties.[5]

There was also a significant rise in provincial printing in the late seventeenth century. The Kilkenny confederation had established presses in Kilkenny and Waterford in the 1640s but by the early 1650s the Kilkenny press had been closed and the Waterford press, under Cromwellian control, had moved to Cork. The Cork press continued to produce works throughout the late seventeenth century. By the 1690s printing had been established in Belfast.[6] There were probably also smaller endeavours elsewhere, producing ephemeral items for local use, which have left no trace in extant imprints. Combined with this was a steady increase in the volumes of print being imported into Ireland. If the customs figures for imports of books in the late seventeenth century are to be believed, the weight of books imported into Ireland, mainly from England, probably doubled in the 1690s alone.[7] Certainly by the late 1690s Ireland was England's single largest customer for books, with 175 cwt being exported there. Next was Holland with 131 cwt and then Scotland with 119 cwt followed by Virginia with 108 cwt.[8] In addition books arrived in Ireland from Scotland although the evidence of the Scottish port books suggests that this was a localised northern trade with imports of Bibles and catechisms into Ulster being the mainstay of the trade.[9] There was also some direct trade with Ireland in continentally produced books. In the late 1680s, for instance, two Dublin Catholic booksellers, James Malone and Christopher Jans, were importing missals and breviaries from the Antwerp firm of Plantin-Moretus into Dublin but this seems to have been an exceptional case made possible by the Jacobite triumph in the city.[10] Holland, and to a lesser extent France, were more normal sources for books to be dispersed in the Irish trade but in comparison to the English trade this was insignificant. In 1699–1700, for instance, Holland and France accounted for about 10 per cent of total Irish book imports according to customs valuations.[11]

I

One of the first indications of the growing importance of the role of print in Irish society in the late seventeenth century was the rapid expansion of the print trades. While the world of print was, in theory, still dominated by the king's printer, that control was much less evident than it had been before the 1640s. In 1660 the crown appointed John Crooke as king's printer in Dublin although William Bladen, who had held the post before and during the Interregnum, was still working in the city also. For the next decade William Bladen, and after 1663 his heir the Rev. Thomas Bladen, challenged the monopoly of the king's printer.[12] Bladen's press produced at least six books before 1670 and it was not until 1673 that it was finally shut down and confiscated. After 1680 Bladen's challenge was followed by another from Joseph Ray, a London stationer who had established himself in Dublin, bringing with him his own fonts of type from London. In contrast to the challenge of Bladen, which was motivated by property rights, Ray's attack on the monopoly was inspired by the potential profit to be made in Dublin as a consequence of the increased demand for print. Ray, for instance, was appointed printer to Dublin corporation and the Dublin Philosophical Society, thus demonstrating the range of business that could be picked up in Ireland by those with a sense of entrepreneurship. Moreover, Ray printed books for Quakers and Presbyterians, and was suspected of producing a Catholic work in 1685. The range of his business demonstrates that profit rather than conformity with licensing restrictions was his main motivation. Most significantly Ray's 1681 challenge to the monopoly of the king's printer was backed by the newly formed guild of St Luke, which included the print trades among its members.[13] Ray's challenge was ultimately unsuccessful although he continued to print throughout the 1680s, possibly under licence from Crooke. However, in 1693 Andrew Crooke received a new patent as king's printer with unchanged terms. But the power of the king's printer had effectively been broken and from the 1680s the terms of the patent were honoured more in the breach than the observance. By 1700 there were seven printers in Dublin offering their services to the booksellers and others as compared with two in 1660.[14]

The consequence of this expansion of the trade was that the output of the Dublin press grew significantly. The total number of items produced in the 1660s was ten times that printed in the 1610s. By the 1690s the Dublin presses were producing almost twice as many items as a year as they had been thirty years earlier. Of course such a comparison by items is rather misleading since by the 1690s the presses were used for a much wider range of ephemeral items, such as tickets for funerals, which tend to inflate the estimates of production.[15] Clearly some of this expansion is accounted for by government activity but a growing part of the activity of the press was explained in other ways. The number of locally conceived and produced books, for instance, grew steadily. In part this was the result of the entrepreneurial activity of individual booksellers who thought they saw gaps in the market which could be filled.[16] In the early 1660s the bookseller Samuel Dancer, for example, sold the usual staples of statutes, sermons and proclamations but also started his own newsheet and published five hundred copies of Katherine Philips's play *Pompey* which had recently been performed in Dublin.[17] Dancer also produced a poetic miscellany, entitled *Poems by several persons*, in 1663 which included works by local writers such as Philips and Peter Pett alongside pirated work from better known and more fashionable poets, such as the English royalist Abraham Cowley. In such ways could the entrepreneurial skill of an individual bookseller, working with a Dublin printer, increase the range of works available in the city. The second significant element in the growth of late seventeenth-century Dublin output was the rise of the reprint trade. By the late 1650s unauthorised reprints of English works began appearing from the Dublin presses and in the late seventeenth century up to a third of the output of the press may have originated in this source. In particular during the popish plots of the late 1670s and early 1680s the demand for news from England prompted the reprinting in Dublin of a number of tracts on the plots originally issued in London.

There were important limitations on what the Dublin print trades produced. As in the early part of the century there were technical limitations. As with the early seventeenth century, for instance, paper for printing had to be imported. The Franciscan Peter Walsh, producing his work on the Remonstrance in the early 1670s complained that 'the Dublin printing house was not well furnished with them [paper, ink and type] but very ill at least with paper and letter when I printed there'.[18] These technical problems were compounded by a lack of copy and shortage of capital which limited output. London publishing still overshadowed Dublin in terms of status, tempting some authors to take their work there. There were, however, some encouraging signs that the market for print in Ireland was growing. Those who commented on the languages of late seventeenth-century Ireland all agreed that more people than before could speak English and that this language was percolating down the social hierarchy.[19] Such a development clearly enlarged the market for books in Ireland. A second development, intended to ameliorate the problem of undercapital-isation, was the emergence of subscription publishing, in part in imitation of developments in London. In 1683, for instance, the Dublin bookseller William Norman advertised a history of Dublin by Robert Ware. It was intended that this should be a large folio volume of a hundred sheets with forty copper plates. To raise capital to support this work potential purchasers were invited to subscribe 23s. For those who did not subscribe, the purchase price would be 30s.[20] It seems the project drew insufficient attention since the volume was never published. Again in 1701 John Whalley proposed to publish his edition of Ptolemy's *Quadriparta* by subscription but lack of support forced him to scale down his original proposal and produce the work in a smaller format.[21] The problem of capital remained unresolved until the early eighteenth century when the growth in the export trade of Irish books, mainly in pirated reprints of English works, allowed printers to recover their investment more quickly.

By the end of the seventeenth century the rise of provincial printing came to supplement the production of the Dublin presses. Cork had been producing books from the 1640s but over the late seventeenth century that output was fitful, of small scale and of poor quality. In the 1690s a press was established at Belfast by the Scottish Presbyterian Patrick Neill. Neill was invited to the town probably in 1694 by the sovereign, William Crawford, although it is possible that the impetus for this development came from the Presbyterian church in the town since Neill's early works were all Presbyterian. What may have crystallised the realisation among Presbyterians that a printer was needed in the town was the failure of that group to be able to produce a printed rebuttal to the pamphlets of William King, bishop of Derry, against their church.[22] While the Belfast press contributed little before 1700, its importance in articulating the Presbyterian political and theological position during the eighteenth century was to be considerable.

II

The growing output of the Dublin and provincial presses was only one sign of a growing demand for print in Ireland. Perhaps more importantly for the book trade in the longer term was the dramatic improvement in the distribution mechanisms. By the late seventeenth century there were a number of ways in which printed items could be acquired and distributed within Ireland. Institutions such as the state and the various churches had developed mechanisms for distributing their own sponsored works among their followers.[23] Godly groups outside Ireland might also seek to support their brethren in the country by sending them books to comfort and support them. Welsh Baptists in the 1650s, for example, sent books to their Irish co-religionists to support them.[24] Individuals within Ireland could use their friends in London to buy books for them. In the 1650s Toby Bonnell corresponded from Dublin with a London bookseller in Pope's Alley. He requested particular books by Richard Baxter as well as other works. In the 1680s his relative James Bonnell mused over the cheapest way of getting books from England: 'whether to employ some solicitor at auctions (as I suppose there are such) or to employ an honest bookseller (if such to be had)'.[25] Oliver Plunkett, the Catholic archbishop of Armagh, used his friends in London to buy books for him and Robert Southwell in Cork used a London agent, Philip Maddox, to find a copy of Thomas à Kempis's work for him in the 1680s.[26] Again in the 1680s when the young Thomas Molyneux of Dublin went to university at Leiden he kept his brother William supplied with scholarly gossip and books from across Europe.[27] Others with more regular demands might establish an account with a London bookseller to help satisfy their requirements. Archbishop Marsh of Dublin, for instance, had an account with the London bookseller Brabazon Aylmer of Cornhill and by 1700 another account with Thomas Leigh of St Paul's churchyard. Marsh sometimes relied on friends to send him books from Oxford and buy books at library sales for him.[28] His contemporary William King, bishop of Derry, also had an account with Robert Clavell of London and he too was supplied with books by friends and he in turn bought books for them.[29] Entries in the Chester port books suggest that other clergy were likewise buying books in England which were then shipped to Dublin.[30] Similarly laymen of a scholarly cast of mind such as William Molyneux, wishing to keep abreast of specialist works published in England, imported them directly.[31] Other individuals, such as the historian Robert Ware and the earl of Orrery, appear as debtors in London booksellers' accounts, suggesting they too were purchasing direct in London.[32] Developments in the English book trade, particularly subscription publishing, facilitated such direct access. From the 1670s, in an endeavour to spread the cost of large volumes, English publishers sought subscriptions from purchasers for works which they proposed to produce. A number of these included Irishmen who wished to acquire copies of these prestige works. Richard Blomme's *Britannia or a geographical description of the kingdom of England, Scotland and Ireland* (London, 1673) included a list of 812 subscribers, of whom fifteen had Irish connections. Some of these, such as the duke of Ormond, the earl of Arran, the earl of Burlington and Sir Robert Southwell, were regular visitors to London and hence well placed to acquire books. Others were less public individuals from provincial Ireland for whom subscription publishing provided a means to acquire London published works. The number of Irish subscribers to works varied a good deal according to the popularity of the volume. *The great historical, geographical and poetical dictionary being a curious miscellany of sacred and profane history* (London, 1694) attracted only eight Irish subscribers but these were scattered from Sligo to Edenderry and Cork. The 1695 edition of *The poetical works of John Milton* on the other hand found seventeen Irish subscribers from around the country. One copy of this, owned by Lord Donegall in Belfast, who had acquired it in London, was lent to both John Mc Bride, the Presbyterian minister in the town, and the local Church of Ireland incumbent.[33] In such ways did books acquired outside Ireland make their way into circulation within the country.

More important than these ad hoc ways in which books might arrive in Ireland were the formal channels of trade. In the late seventeenth century the Irish economy became much more commercialised than previously. The export of unprocessed goods was replaced by manufactures such as butter, barrelled beef and linen cloth. This required a complex internal marketing network of markets and fairs and along this network books travelled also. One emerging figure in this process was the bookseller. In early seventeenth-century Ireland such men had been rare in Ireland but after 1660 the bookseller became the main point of contact between the producer and the consumer of print although it is clear that the older pattern of general merchants dealing in cheap books continued. In 1694, for instance, Isachar Wilcocks, a Dublin Quaker grocer, had among the stock of his shop five dozen hornbooks, valued at a shilling a dozen, and over six hundred primers.[34] There were clearly a number of general merchants who engaged sporadically in the Dublin book trade, and the Chester port books for the late seventeenth century show a number of individuals who were general merchants and imported books on one or two occasions.[35] Such men were of very limited significance for the development of the trade. In Dublin what might be recognised as professional booksellers had begun to become established by 1660. Bookselling took many forms. Most importantly, there was a cadre of professional booksellers who dealt almost exclusively in books and stationery and who can be identified both in imprints and in trade records. The number of such men rose in the late seventeenth century from three in the 1660s to thirteen in the 1680s, pointing to the expansion of book retailing over the period. Finally by the 1690s there was the rise of the book auction in Dublin as booksellers, some like John Dunton from London, imported large quantities of books into Dublin which were to be sold quickly to gratify immediate desires, mainly of collectors.[36]

The Dublin booksellers had two main sources for their stock. The first was obviously the products of the Dublin printers themselves. Even more important, as in the early seventeenth century, were the imports from the London trade. Dublin and London booksellers moved in similar cultural worlds and at least some links had developed between them. Some sort of link is suggested by the fact that in 1646 political pamphlets printed in Ireland under Ormond's direction were being shipped into London.[37] Again in the 1650s George Thomason in London was able to purchase a copy of a Dublin printed book by Edward Worth from a London bookseller.[38] By the late seventeenth century some London booksellers were developing links with their Dublin counterparts. The London bookseller Benjamin Tooke, for example, acted as king's printer in Ireland, with his sister Mary, from 1669 to 1693. Although he took little part in the Irish business, remaining in London to run his stationer's business there, he did provide a link between the two branches of the trade and may have provided Dublin booksellers with stock.[39] There were also links between other individuals in the Dublin and London trades. In the 1680s, for instance, William Norman in Dublin was said to be linked with Edward Darrell who had a shop in Paternoster Row in London.[40] From the 1670s books originating in Ireland were being printed in Dublin by arrangement between London and Dublin booksellers to be retailed in both places. The imprint of Edward Wolley's *Ho typos* which appeared in 1670 read 'Printed at Dublin and are to be sold in London by Christopher Wilkinson at the Black Boy against St Dunstan's church in Fleet Street'. Ten such imprints can be identified from the 1680s. A wide variety of Dublin characters appear in these imprints including Joseph Ray, Joseph Howes and Eliphal Dobson, all significant players in the Dublin trade. In London the most important contact was Awnsham Churchill, who had a shop at the Black Swan in

Paternoster Row and was a significant player in the London trade.[41] Personal contacts were important in developing this trade. By May 1687 Peter Manby's *The considerations which obliged ... to embrace the Catholic religion*, first published in Dublin in 1687, was available in both Dublin and London.[42] The route by which it arrived there highlights the linkages between the Dublin and London presses. Both the London editions of Manby's work were published by a well-known Catholic bookseller in London, Nathaniel Thompson. Thompson had served his apprenticeship in Dublin and must have retained strong contacts there. Copies of Manby's later work, the *Reformed catechism*, on sale in London had been printed by Joseph Ray in Dublin and shipped to London.[43] The trade evidently worked in both directions since a sermon by the archbishop of Tuam, John Vesey, *A sermon preached at Windsor the second Sunday after Easter 1684*, was printed by Robert Clavel in London 'and are to be sold by Samuel Helsham, bookseller in Dublin' according to the imprint. At a provincial level Richard Minshul, a bookseller of Chester, clearly had Dublin agents to sell his wares since he imported a few cargoes of books into the city in the 1690s although he continued to live and trade in Chester.[44]

Aside from such personal contacts the key element in bringing English books to Dublin was the normal mechanisms of trade. In the 1660s, for example, about two-thirds of all Irish book imports came from London.[45] By the 1690s the English trade accounted for almost 90 per cent of the value of bound books imported into Ireland. Dublin dominated this trade, with almost three-quarters of all imports going there.[46] There are two ways of trying to measure this trade and its impact on Dublin. The first is to attempt to find the evidence for the activities of the Irish booksellers among the records of their London counterparts. Certainly in the inventories of late seventeenth-century London booksellers there are mentions of debts due to them from the Irish trade. In the 1674 inventory of the debts of the London stationer Thomas Seward the Dublin booksellers William Winter, Joseph Howes and John North appear, owing £27, £91 and £40 respectively, presumably for books purchased from Seward for sale in Dublin.[47] Again in the case of the inventory of Thomas Leigh, taken in 1704, the names of six Dublin booksellers appear as debtors: William Norman, Luke Dowling, Patrick Campbell, John Forster, John Ray and Eliphal Dobson. Their debts are small-scale, ranging from £2 for Joseph Ray to £30 for Luke Dowling, suggesting that these booksellers did limited business with Leigh.[48] More substantial in its coverage is the 1681 inventory of George Sawbridge, probably one of the largest and most successful booksellers in London at the time. Sawbridge, at the time of his death, had £3,716 owing to him from people in Ireland out of total debts owing to him of over £15,000. Not all of these debts seem to be the results of trade in books but about two-thirds of the total Irish debts are to seven Dublin booksellers. Undoubtedly the most important of these was Samuel Helsham, who owed

Sawbridge £1,020. Helsham is followed in importance by Joseph Howes and John North, who owed £541 and £479 respectively. The remaining four Dublin booksellers, Eliphal Dobson, William Mendy, Joseph Ray and Dr William Bladen, owed much smaller sums of money from £50 (in the case of Ray) to £153 (in the case of Mendy).[49] Such an inventory conveys a picture of a few Dublin booksellers dominating much of the trade with, at least, one of the largest stationers in London.

The evidence of inventories, while important, presents considerable problems of interpretation. The snapshot they paint of the Irish debts owing to the London bookseller at the point of his death may be unrepresentative of the nature of the trade he engaged in over the course of his life. Moreover some Dublin booksellers may have been better at paying their debts than others, so, again, the snapshot in an inventory may give a distorted picture of the shape and scale of the Irish trade. An alternative way of examining the activities of the Dublin booksellers is to look at the custom records. Most of Dublin's trade in books from London and elsewhere passed through Chester, and by using the port books for Chester port it is possible to reconstruct something of the involvement of the Dublin booksellers in that trade.[50] Such an attempt at reconstruction is not without its problems. Port books are often incomplete and damaged but nevertheless they probably represent the main outlines of the trade in the 1680s. Perhaps the most striking feature of the pattern of imports into Dublin is the dominance of a few booksellers in the trade. On the basis of the port book evidence in 1680, for example, the top four booksellers, Eliphal Dobson, James Malone, William Mendy and Samuel Helsham, accounted for almost two-thirds of the trade. Three of these appear also in the list of Sawbridge's Irish debtors discussed above, and Helsham topped it. The individuals and proportions recorded in the port books varied slightly over time but the general pattern of a trade in a few hands seems to apply throughout the period. In the port books for the 1690s this pattern is repeated with fewer booksellers overall but two or three being predominant.[51]

In part this seems to be the result of some degree of specialisation. In contrast to those who dealt in imports, the Crooke family, as king's printers, imported little over the 1680s presumably because most of what they sold they produced from their own press. On the other hand, Patrick Campbell imported considerable quantities of books yet his name does not appear as a bookseller in any Dublin printed work in the 1680s, although he does feature in the 1670s and 1690s. Again William Mendy produced nothing but imported a good deal. By contrast Joseph Ray, a printer himself, imported little but is named in a large number of imprints. Other printers in the same category are William Winter, William Weston and William Norman, who imported little. The correlation is not perfect. There are a number of booksellers who both imported a good deal and who also feature as booksellers on the imprints of

Dublin published works. The most significant of these are Samuel Helsham, Eliphal Dobson, John North and Joseph Howes. This evidence suggests that there was a hierarchy of booksellers in Dublin. The largest dealers handled a wide range of books, both domestic and imported, and had markets extending well beyond the city.[52] A few, probably four or five, monopolised most of the import trade which, given the importance of this trade, made them significant players. Some of these men may also have acted as wholesalers supplying imported works to smaller booksellers. Samuel Helsham, for instance, seems to have sold on to other booksellers copies of works which he imported.[53] Finally there were those who dealt in locally produced works or retailed imported works possible acquired from wholesalers.

It is possible to get a sense of what these varying types of booksellers might have offered to the inhabitants of late seventeenth-century Dublin. Some consumers were scathing about what the Dublin bookshops might supply. The book collector and archbishop of Dublin, Narcissus Marsh, complained in 1689 that he could not obtain the books he wanted in Ireland since 'our booksellers being rather to be called sellers of pamphlets than booksellers'. By 1706 he claimed the situation had not improved, noting: 'nor are our book-sellers' shops furnished any thing tolerably with other books than new trifles and pamphlets and not well with them also'.[54] Marsh was a demanding book buyer who assembled a large and rather specialised library and his views cannot be taken as representative of the needs of the more modest purchaser. It is clear however that the thinness and unpredictability of the Irish market meant that forecasting demand, and hence deciding on stock levels, was difficult. Printers for instance produced widely varying lengths of run based on unpredictable demand. In the early part of the century the run of a scholarly work, such as a volume by Archbishop Ussher, might be of the order of a thousand to fifteen hundred copies. Cautious booksellers, such as Samuel Dancer in the 1660s, might produce only five hundred copies of a play which quickly sold out and a reprint was called for.[55] In a different league was Charles II's 'Gracious declaration', which formed the basis of the Restoration settle-ment, of which nine thousand copies were produced in Dublin, but even this was not enough for an insatiable market demanding to know the shape of the future. Copies were quickly retailing at 2s each, well above their normal price as supply failed to meet demand.[56] For those who specialised in the import trade there was also a problem of stock management. Like printers, book-sellers could not afford to tie up capital for long periods of time by holding stock. Rather than import occasional large cargoes of books, the Dublin book importers tended to ship regularly in small quantities. During the 1680s the larger importers, such as Samuel Helsham, Eliphal Dobson, John North or Patrick Campbell, might ship between six and eight cargoes a year from Chester in an effort to keep markets supplied. In some respects this meant that books published in London would reach Dublin more quickly than if the trade had been conducted with larger, more infrequent cargoes. However, some works published in England could be slow to get to Dublin in quantity, and if sufficiently popular could sell out quickly. When Edmund Borlase's history of the rising of 1641 was first published it was much in demand in Dublin and quickly sold out, with Sir John Temple paying 'perhaps ... something above the common rate that it is sold at' in his anxiety to get a copy.[57] Similarly when the controversial memoirs of the earl of Castlehaven appeared in 1681 in London it took some time for them to reach Dublin, the duke of Ormond having to import his own copy. When it did arrive it sold out almost immediately.[58]

Fluctuating demand and sometimes thin markets meant that the book-sellers worked at a range of levels. At the lower end of the scale, William Winter, who imported nothing in his own name but who appears in a number of imprints as a bookseller, advertised his wares in one of his books in 1685.[59] Most of what Winter advertised were small works. A large amount of stationery, including pre-printed forms, was offered for sale including forms of indentures, bonds of arbitration, letters of attorney, bonds for debt and various types of processes. Moving through the scale there were pamphlets for legal work including Richard Bolton's *Rules for a grand juror*, reprinted from his larger handbook for justices of the peace. There were also sets of instructions for keeping manorial courts. Also included were the steady sellers: a selection of schoolbooks and two popular chapbook romances, the *Seven wise masters* and *Don Bellianis of Greece*, which had presumably been purchased from importers. Other steady sellers such as Bibles and Common Prayers also appear on the list. In the class of small books there were 'the choice of the best collection of plays in this kingdom'. Winter also claimed that there was 'a good choice of histories, novels and romances to be sold or lent at reasonable rates' suggesting that he also operated a lending library. He also dealt in second-hand books. In this list there is little that appears in contemporary library lists as being deemed worthy of preservation by their owners. There were only five books of substance in stock, all of which were Dublin-printed. Three, Robert Ware's *Foxes and firebrands*, Richard Lawrence's *The interest of Ireland in its trade and wealth stated* and Edward Wetenhall's *Judgement of the comet*, had appeared that year and were presumably in local demand. The remaining two were law books, an edition of the Irish statutes and Richard Bolton's manual for justices of the peace which were probably bought by country gentlemen acting as JPs.

By contrast a 1688 advertisement for books sold by William Norman and Eliphal Dobson presents a rather different picture.[60] Dobson was a significant importer of books during the 1680s, and Norman appears in Dublin imprints on eighteen occasions in the same decade. In this list there is some overlap with the contents of Winter's advertisement, including Bibles and Books of Common Prayer, Richard Bolton's edition of the Irish statutes and his manual for justices of the peace and Richard Lawrence's *Interest of Ireland*. Works such as these were the staple of the trade and are also characteristic of Samuel Helsham's bookselling business in the 1680s.[61] The other twelve titles are different from the sort of stock which Winter had. All are imported and they include the sort of works that would happily have graced a gentleman's library. The stock was largely devotional and confutational but there was also one recent scientific work, by William Molyneux, for sale and a biography of the earl of Rochester by Dr Burnett.

Even a city growing as fast as Dublin was in the late seventeenth century could not on its own support a book trade on the scale described above. In order to survive, the booksellers had to broaden their market beyond the capital. How they did this is unclear since almost no evidence has survived as to how they conducted their business. In only one case, that of Samuel Helsham, has any evidence survived. Part of his day book for 1685 shows Helsham supplying customers with paper and other stationery requirements as well as a wide range of books including Bibles, books of Common Prayer, sermons, school textbooks, classics, verse and ephemera such as 'sheets of news'.[62] Most of Helsham's customers seem to have come from Dublin but a number were from outside the city including two bishops, an alderman of Kilkenny and a probable resident of Hospital in County Limerick. However, most of the customers in Helsham's day book are not identifiable and hence a more detailed reconstruction of his business outside the city is not possible. Others may have tried to establish agents outside the city to deal with their wares. A Dublin reprint of a London tract in 1694 was, according to the imprint, 'to be sold at the Treasury Coffee House, at Mr Norman's, Dublin, at Mr Jones's in Cork and Mr Letcher's in Tralee'.[63]

How successful the Dublin booksellers were in penetrating the provincial market for books remains unclear. Some of those outside Ireland certainly complained that they were poorly supplied. In Cashel, Andrew Sall complained in 1680 that 'this place where I live is unfortunate in the want of books and bookish men'.[64] Sall, like Marsh in Dublin, was a particularly demanding customer and his views are far from typical. The customs returns from the late 1690s suggest that a flourishing trade in books had developed not just between Dublin and England but with other ports also. Looking simply at bound books for the period 1697 to 1700 the bulk of the trade was with Dublin but a third of all the trade, by value, between England and Ireland moved through the port of Cork. Adding in the other Munster ports of Kinsale, Youghal and Waterford increases that part of the country's share of the English trade to over 40 per cent.[65] This was not a new development of the 1690s. The port books of Bristol, which was the main entrepot for the

Munster book trade, for the 1670s and 1680s, reveals significant quantities of books shipped from that port to mainly Munster ports.[66] Comparisons with the Chester port books in the 1680s are difficult, since port books are often incomplete, but rough comparisons suggest that in quantity terms the Munster trade might amount to about a tenth of that of Dublin. A significant growth in the provincial trade in the 1680s is indicated by the Bristol port book evidence. Imports grew in the early 1680s, almost certainly because of a desire for news from London in the form of pamphlets as the various scares surrounding the popish plot unfolded. Throughout the late seventeenth century it was Cork that dominated the provincial trade of Munster, with Waterford a poor second. While Limerick, Youghal and Wexford all imported books, none did so on the scale of the other Munster ports. It is difficult to reconstruct what might have been imported. The port books make no mention of titles but if the trade was similar in composition to the sort of books available in Bristol then Bibles and religious works formed the bulk of the trade with a smaller range of geographical and historical works.[67] The port books also suggest that a wide range of printed items other than books were imported. In the 1690s 'printed pictures', for instance, were shipped into Cork and Derry to be sold as cheap decorative items.[68]

In Ulster, perhaps not surprisingly, the pattern was rather different to that in Munster. The rapidly growing port of Belfast took a very small part, about 1 per cent, of the trade in English books with Ireland in 1697–1700. However the Ulster ports had sources of supply elsewhere. Almost all the trade in books from Scotland to Ireland in the 1690s went to the Ulster ports. While the Scottish book trade with Ireland was much smaller by value than that of England – about 15 per cent of the value of the English trade – it was much more focused. The evidence of the Scottish port books, which detail the nature of the Ulster trade, suggests that the bulk of this trade was to support the Ulster Presbyterian community's demand for religious works. In 1671, one Glasgow ship going to Ulster had three dozen Bibles and two dozen copies of the Westminster Confession. Another ship for Derry in 1682 had fifteen dozen Bibles, six gross of catechisms, six gross of pamphlets and two dozen testaments. A further shipment in 1691 contained Bibles, New Testaments, psalters and catechisms.[69] While this formed the mainstay of the trade, the exchange was not exclusively religious. In 1689 almanacs left Portpatrick in Scotland bound for Ulster, and in 1682 'a parcel of books, ballads and pamphlets' went to Ulster from the same port.[70] In addition there are less identifiable books lurking in port book records as 'small books', 'Bruce's histories', 'gestione [story] books' and 'story books'. As a result of this import trade Belfast had a stationer by 1661 and a bookbinder by 1684. By the 1680s inland towns such as Ballymena and Antrim town had bookbinders as well.[71]

One lacuna in this pattern of imports is Connacht. The customs figures for the 1690s record imports to Galway from England only once, in 1699–1700, when books worth £10, a small sum in this context, were imported.[72] That this is not simply a clerical error is suggested by the port books for Bristol. Ships from that port travelled northwards to Ulster and Sligo and southwards to Limerick but do not mention Galway as a port to which books were taken. The Scottish port books do not mention any Connacht port. One Galway woman in the 1640s is listed as a bookseller in 1646 and 1647 but there are no further references.[73] It may be that Galway imported books from other sources such as continental Europe, and books worth only 15s from Holland were listed in the custom return for 1699–1700. Connacht, on the whole, seems to have been an area poorly supplied with print, possibly owing to its low levels of commercialisation and scattered population which made it difficult to market books in the hinterland of Galway.

In both Ulster and Munster the book trade was not, in the main, carried on by specialist booksellers as in Dublin. Rather it was part of the normal stock in trade of general merchants to carry books. A case in point is the Bristol ship *Diligence* which in the 1670s made regular trips to north-west Ireland. In March 1679 it journeyed to Sligo and three months later it had returned to the same port. It was only one of a small flotilla of ships from Bristol which forayed in the late seventeenth century to the apparently isolated ports of Killybegs and Sligo in north-west Ireland. These ships carried a range of goods essential to the survival of those who lived at the edge of Europe. The hold of the *Diligence* contained bottles, window glass, gunpowder, lead, leather, sugar, hops, drinking glasses and wool cards. Other ships bound for Sligo and Killybegs in the 1670s had molasses, oil seed, tobacco, madder, logwood, figs, tobacco pipes, bellows, shot and brass manufactures. The cargoes of these ships contained a wide range of materials but the cargo which most had in common was books, ranging in quantity from 14 lb to a hundredweight.[74] Such general merchants shipped a few cargoes of books as part of their wider trading activities. In some of the larger urban centres small specialist booksellers emerged to deal with these imports. In Cork, for instance, three booksellers can be traced in the late seventeenth century, T. Taylor (a widow) and Richard Plummer operating in the 1650s and David Jones in 1691. In Limerick Richard Wilkins sold books in the town in the 1660s and 1670s and in Waterford there was at least one stationer in the 1600s.[75]

As well as new books some booksellers seem to have branched out into a second-hand trade. The 1596 Dublin library list of Luke Challoner, for example, noted Bible prices between 6s and 10s with New Testaments at 6d, which is very cheap in comparison to ruling prices for Bibles, and this may represent purchases on the second-hand market.[76] By 1685 the Dublin bookseller William Winter was offering 'money for old books'.[77] Some shops, including booksellers, may have had stalls of second-hand books through which customers could browse. In 1681 one correspondent of the earl of Arran claimed to have found a copy of *The third part of no Protestant plot with some observations on the proceedings upon the indictment of the earl of Shaftesbury* (London, 1682) with manuscript annotations by Sir John Davys 'upon the booksellers stall' in Dublin, which does suggest a second-hand trade.[78] By the end of the century some claimed that the best place to sell stolen books was through the second-hand book dealers in Dublin.[79] The second-hand trade may well have thrived in provincial Ireland also, and by the 1690s what the Bristol port books described as 'old books', presumably second-hand, were being imported into Derry, Belfast, Waterford and Cork.[80]

While ports may have been the main ways in which books entered provincial Ireland, there were a number of ways of distributing those works into the hinterland. For some, wishing to spread their own religious or political message, print was cheap enough by the end of the seventeenth century to be scattered about the countryside. William Tisdall, the vicar of Belfast, for instance was told that a Presbyterian woman, the wife of an Elder, was seen in Belfast shortly after the publication of *The parallel or persecution of Protestants* was published 'with a whole apronful of them in order, as must be presumed, to place them in the proper hands'.[81] From a Catholic perspective a convert priest in the 1680s, Neal Carolan, alleged that the archbishop of Armagh, Oliver Plunkett, compelled his clergy to buy from him two books which would be necessary 'to confute protestants out of their own Bible'.[82]

A more orthodox and probably more effective way of distributing books was by using the services of a chapman or pedlar. The Dublin almanacker John Whalley certainly advertised in his almanac that where no such shops were available to buy his goods, as in parts of Connacht, he employed chapmen to carry his books to potential customers.[83] Chapmen were well-established figures. In the 1630s pedlars or chapmen had acted on behalf of merchants in distributing imported salt around the Dublin area, and in Ulster customs officials complained of chapmen entering Ulster from Scotland with their wares and undercutting the shopkeepers.[84] In the 1650s they were such a common sight in the landscape that one priest in Galway wishing to conceal himself adopted the disguise of a Scottish pedlar, and by the 1690s they were so active in Kinsale as to draw complaints from the corporation almost every year.[85] Such chapmen could have substantial businesses. One chapman, Thomas Jones of Tullamore, listed his losses in the rising of the 1640s as £66, of which about 10 per cent was in ready money, and in the 1680s pedlars going to a fair at Antrim were robbed of goods of 'a considerable value'.[86] While many dealt in the sort of small wares which the Rev. Andrew Rowan of County Antrim purchased from them in the 1670s, ribbons, sheets of pins, stockings, calico, linen, cloth, tobacco, buttons and spoons, some dealt also in books.[87] The Dublin guild of St Luke, to which printers and stationers belonged, complained in 1696 of packmen selling 'any bound book or horn book, primer catechism, almanacs, writing paper or jute knives, sizer or any other goods'. Six years later the guild referred to such packmen as 'exposers of news' presumably meaning they sold newsheets also.[88] Being highly mobile, chapmen were able to cover large distances. They were also on the edge of society, which made them ideal figures for disseminating unorthodox material. One Church of Ireland clergyman complained in the late 1690s that he had 'observed that the Scotch strollers and pedlars, who go from house to house all over the country selling small ware have generally a Scotch Directory and Solemn League and Covenant along with them which they still expose for sale among their toys'. Similarly John Toland's *Christianity not mysterious* was 'cried about with almanacs' according to Peter Browne, provost of Trinity College, Dublin.[89] A similar allegation was made by Convocation in 1712, which spoke of seditious books 'handed through the kingdom ... by pedlars and vagabonds'.[90]

The mobility of these figures meant that they could draw stock from a wide range of sources. On occasion there were single-sheet broadsides produced in Dublin which pedlars sold around the city. The execution of John Atherton, bishop of Waterford, in 1640 quickly produced 'scandalous rhyming pamphlets', which were presumably sold by pedlars.[91] Again when John Toland was indicted in Dublin in 1697 for producing *Christianity not mysterious* the Dublin printers quickly ran off a copy of an older English indictment with a new 'emphatical title and cried [them] about the streets'.[92] Such spectacular works were unusual. The mainstay of the pedlars' trade can only be guessed at. It seems that most carried small, easily portable books. One advertisement directed to pedlars in an almanac of 1689 listed a range of schoolbooks, the Church catechism and popular histories such as the *Seven champions of Christendom, Valentine and Orson* and a number of other cheap fictions which pedlars were likely to carry.[93] A substantial part of their stock came, at least initially, from London. One late seventeenth-century London bookseller advertised that at his shop 'English and Irish chapmen ... may be well furnished and have good penniworths'.[94] In 1685 one London bookseller extracted the material on St Patrick from a well-known chapbook, the *Seven champions of Christendom*, and published it separately, presumably with a view to the Irish market through the pedlar trade.[95] By the end of the century the Dublin printers were making inroads on London's dominance of the pedlar trade. An advertisement in an almanac of 1689, addressed to such 'chapmen as deal in books', informed them that, whereas they previously 'had been forced to send to London' for their stock, this was now available from the king's printing house and the Dublin booksellers.[96] Such mechanisms ensured that books arriving in ports did not remain in warehouses or shops but reached readers in rural Ireland.

III

It is possible to observe something of the effect of the growing volume of print available in Ireland in the late seventeenth century through the expansion of libraries. Those professionally involved in print, such as the clergy, accumulated more books than before. In 1661 Bishop Jones of Meath could boast ninety-nine titles in his library but by the end of the century Bishop Samuel Foley of Down and Connor had almost seventeen hundred titles in his library and in the 1680s Bishop Ward of Derry had just over twelve hundred titles.[97] At a lower ecclesiastical level William King, rector of St Werburgh's, had 694 titles.[98] Outside the church, lawyers had substantial collections. The judge Sir Jerome Alexander left 615 titles to Trinity College, Dublin, in 1673.[99] At a lower legal level a list of books made in an almanac by an unnamed lawyer in 1689 named eighty titles which comprised his working library since they were described as being 'in my use'.[100] Gentry also had large libraries which sometimes reflected special interests. According to a 1694 account of his family by William Molyneux he claimed, with due modesty:

> my library consists of but a few volumes (I think at present not much above one thousand) but they are such as are choice and curious on those subjects wherein I delighted, chiefly mathematical and philosophical and miscellanies. I have likewise a good collection of common law books and amongst each kind of these there are some volumes scarcely to be met with.[101]

Others had smaller collections. Sir John Perceval of Burton Hall in County Cork had some five hundred books at his death in 1686.[102] Those of the middling sort were also assembling substantial collections. A list of Coronet Wilkinson's books, possibly in Kilkenny, had over a hundred books and another gentleman from Munster in the 1670s had almost eighty.[103] Both men seem to have had similar interests, classical works, religion (both devotional and controversial works), literary works, and in the case of the Munster list an interest in French language. However, not all of those of the middling sort were book collectors. The 1669 probate inventory of John Hay, a Dublin merchant, recorded only nine books while that of Robert Watts, a Dublin gentleman, made in 1661 listed ten.[104] These did not make for stimulating reading since one book, a folio volume, was in Dutch, another a French dictionary and a third an old Bible with silver clasps. The remainder were described as 'small books'.

While very few library lists have survived for those at the bottom of the social scale, the production of cheap books by the Dublin presses from the 1660s would suggest a market there for such works. The Bible was clearly important in the case of Protestant families. One Quaker shearman in Dublin 1695 owned a number of books worth £2 10s, of which the Bible accounted for a valuation of 10s.[105] Cheap books, such as almanacs, selling for a penny, as well as broadsheets also became more common after 1660.[106] Chapbooks, such as the *Seven champions of Christendom* and the *Seven wise masters*, also appear in Ireland in the late seventeenth century as do criminal biographies, such as that of Redmond O'Hanlon.[107] By the end of the century printers thought there was a sufficient popular market to begin issuing gallows speeches as broadsheets.[108] In this case the initiative seems to have come from Samuel Lee, the printer of the first of these, *The last speech of Mr John Geoghegan*, which appeared in 1694.[109] Lee was a recent arrival in Dublin from London and was clearly interested in the sensational as a way of breaking into the Dublin market. He had, for instance, tried to undercut established printers to produce one of the instalments in the pamphlet war between Bishop King and the Presbyterians, and in the view of John Dunton 'such a pirate, such a cormorant was never before'.[110] Such entrepreneurial drive played a large part in expanding the popular market. It is difficult to assess how important that market was by the end of the seventeenth century. Most of these ephemeral items which made up the trade have not survived, most having simply been worn out by reading or as William Mercer described the treatment of his verse story, *The moderate cavalier* published in Cork in 1675,

> If you don't like their [the moderate cavaliers'] story you may clap them
> By the heels, cashier or tear, or you may wrap 'em
> About your sweetmeats, or they'll light your pipe
> Or at the worst they'll serve your - - - - to wipe.[111]

The fact that a popular market for print developed at all was significant for the future of the Dublin press.

IV

By the end of the seventeenth century most areas in Ireland were being rapidly drawn into the world of print. The output of the Dublin presses had increased dramatically but more importantly imports of books from both England and Scotland were not just passing through the professional world of the Dublin bookseller but were also arriving directly into the world of provincial Ireland as the power of the king's printer to police the book trade weakened. The inhabitants of Gaelic Ireland was also being drawn into this world of print, a development linked to the rise of bilingualism. Native Irish poets and scribes began to take an interest in print. In the 1650s the poet Dáibhí Cúndún listed the books which he had read as part of a poem that he had composed. While some were clearly manuscript works, others, such as the work of Hector Boece, were available in print and it may have been these he consulted.[112] Later in the century the Limerick poet Dáibhí Ó Bruadair explicitly named printed works which he consulted.[113] Less clearly, some literary works in Irish which circulated in manuscript appear to have been modelled on printed works, in English or French, which may have been available and read in Irish-speaking Ireland.[114]

Not all areas were affected equally. Regions closest to ports clearly had easiest access to the printed word through booksellers or chapmen. Some ports, however, particularly those in Connacht, had not yet been much affected by print. While the Munster region absorbed books mainly from England, Ulster took its reading matter from Scotland, leading to a confirmation of cultural trends which were set through seventeenth-century migration and religious practice. Despite such regional differences print culture was firmly established in Ireland by 1700. Expanding literacy, a growing knowledge of the English language and an expansion in the role of writing expressed itself in a growing demand for printed books and ephemera. That demand was supplied in a number of ways from personal contacts, booksellers or chapmen. How the inhabitants of seventeenth-century Ireland would deal with this growing volume of print was a separate issue and it is to this question that the remainder of this book will be devoted.

NOTES

1 H.M.C., *Calendar of the manuscripts of the marquess of Ormonde* (new series, 8 vols, London, 1902–20), v, p. 508.

2 Mary Pollard, *Dublin's trade in books, 1550–1800* (Oxford, 1989), pp. 6–11.

3 J.W. Phillips, *Printing and bookselling in Dublin, 1670–1800* (Dublin, 1998), pp. 28, 39.

4 B.L., Add. MS 41769, f. 35.

5 Raymond Gillespie, 'Irish print and Protestant identity: William King's pamphlet wars, 1687–1697' in Vincent Carey and Ute Lotz-Heumann (eds), *Taking sides: colonial and confessional mentalities in early modern Ireland* (Dublin, 2003), pp. 231–50.

6 William K. Sessions, *The first printers in Waterford, Cork and Kilkenny* (York, 1990), Wesley McCann, 'Patrick Neill and the origins of Belfast printing' in Peter Isaac (ed.), *Six centuries of the provincial book trade in Britain* (Winchester, 1990), pp. 125–38.

7 Pollard, *Dublin's trade in books*, p. 41.

8 P.R.O., CUST 3/1.

9 Scottish Record Office, E72/10/3, 5, 6, 7; E72/19/2, 6, 8, 11 13, 19, 22.

10 Plantin-Moretus Museum, Antwerp, MS AR320, Groteboek A, 1681–1701, pp. 88, 138; Ms AR400, Daybook, 1687–88, f. 34v.

11 P.R.O., CUST 15/3.

12 Mary Pollard, 'Control of the press through the king's printer's patent, 1600–1800' in *Irish Booklore* iv (1980), pp. 83–6.

13 Mary Pollard, *A dictionary of members of the Dublin book trade, 1550–1800* (London, 2000), pp. 479–82.

14 Phillips, *Printing and bookselling in Dublin*, p. 40.

15 Appendix, table 1.

16 Appendix, table 2.

17 Pollard, *Dictionary*, pp. 142–3; Patrick Thomas, *The collected works of Katherine Philips* (3 vols, Stump Cross, 1992), iii, pp. 79, 97. Dancer's stock is listed in Jeremy Taylor, *A discourse of confirmation for the use of the clergy and instruction of the people of Ireland* (Dublin, 1663).

18 Peter Walsh, *The history and vindication of the loyal formulary or Irish remonstrance* (n.p., 1674), p. xlviii.

19 For example T.C.D., MS 883/1, pp. 138, 223, 256; MS 883/2, p. 106; Henry Piers, *A chorographical description of the county of Westmeath* (rpt Tara, 1981), pp. 105–6, 108.

20 Advertisement in [Robert Ware], *The hunting of the Romish fox and the quenching of sectarian firebrands* (Dublin, 1683), p. 250.

21 John Whalley, *A treatise of eclipses* (Dublin, 1701), sig. a2; John Whalley, *Ptolemy's Quadrpartite or four books concerning the influence of the stars* (Dublin, 1701), sig. b4v.

22 For a review of the evidence, though with a different conclusion, see McCann, 'Patrick Neill and the origins of Belfast printing', pp. 125–38; Gillespie, 'Irish print and Protestant identity', pp. 241–2.

23 Raymond Gillespie, 'The circulation of print in seventeenth-century Ireland' in *Studia Hibernica* no. 29 (1995–97), pp. 47–52.

24 N.L.W., MS 9108D, ff. 118–19.

25 T.C.D., MS 2929, ff. 3, 180–1.

26 John Hanly (ed.), *The letters of Saint Oliver Plunkett* (Dublin, 1979), p. 62; B.L., Egerton Ms 1627, f. 30v. For another Catholic bishop buying books in London see H.M.C., *Report on the Franciscan manuscripts* (London, 1906), p. 5.

27 The correspondence is edited in 'Sir Thomas Molyneux' in *Dublin University Magazine* xviii (July–December 1841), pp. 314, 315, 318, 320, 476, 479, 607.

28 Bodl., Smith MS 52, ff. 55, 59, 61, 81.

29 T.C.D., MS 750/1/156; MS 750/3/2/159, 1221; Robert Matteson, 'Francis le Janu's letter to William King' in *Long Room* nos 16–17 (1978), pp. 13–26.

30 P.R.O., E190/1343/3, ff. 21, 24v, 25v; E190/1346/1, ff. 39, 44, 47v; E190/1353/9, f. 12.

31 P.R.O., E190/1346/12, f. 37v; E190/1349/11, f. 34.

32 City of London Records Office, Court of Orphans inventories, nos 1810, 1830, 2743.

33 William Tisdall, *The conduct of the dissenters in Ireland* (Dublin, 1712), p. 67; James Kirkpatrick, *An historical essay upon the loyalty of the Presbyterians* ([Belfast], 1713), p. 526.

34 Olive C. Goodbody (ed.), 'Inventories of five Dublin Quaker merchants in the late seventeenth century' in *Irish Ancestor* x (1978), p. 43.

35 R.J. Hunter, 'Chester and the Irish book trade, 1681' in *Irish Economic and Social History* xv (1988), pp. 90–1.

36 Pollard, *Dublin's trade in books,*, pp. 61–2.

37 Keith Lindley and David Scott (eds), *The journal of Thomas Juxon, 1644–1647* (Cambridge, 1999), p. 125.

38 Copy now in B.L., Thomason tracts, E974(3).

39 Pollard, *Dictionary*, p. 571.

40 T.C.D., MS 883/1, p. 69.

41 H.R. Plomer, *A dictionary of the printers and booksellers who were at work in England, Scotland and Ireland from 1668 to 1775* (Oxford, 1922), pp. 69–70.

42 H.M.C., *Report on the manuscripts of the marquess of Downshire* (5 vols, London, 1924–), i, p. 242.

43 Pollard, *Dictionary*, pp. 564–5.

44 Plomer, *Dictionary*, p. 208. Minshul sent his son to Trinity College, Dublin, again suggesting strong local contacts. Another example of Chester links may be Thomas Tilliard, who, although from Chester, had strong London links and died in Dublin: see Pollard, *Dictionary*, pp. 568–9.

45 *Cal. S. P. Ire., 1663–5*, p. 698.

46 Based on figures in Pollard, *Dublin's trade in books*, p. 41.

47 Corporation of London Records Office, Court of Orphans inventories, no. 957.

48 Corporation of London Records Office, Court of Orphans inventories, no. 2701. Leigh also had among his possessions 'Irish stitcht hangings', suggesting his involvement in the Irish trade.

49 Corporation of London Records Office, Court of Orphans inventories, no. 1810. For Sawbridge see H.R. Plomer, *A dictionary of booksellers and printers who were at work in England, Scotland and Ireland from 1641 to 1667* (London, 1907), p. 161.

50 Appendix, table 3.

51 P.R.O., E190/1360/1; E190/1359/1; E190/1357/4; E190/1355/4; E190/1353/9.

52 For Helsham see Pollard, *Dublin's trade in books*, pp. 42–61.

53 Pollard, *Dublin's trade in books*, pp. 57–8.

54 Bodl., Smith MS 52, ff. 73, 112.

55 Thomas, *The collected works of Katherine Philips*, iii, pp. 79, 97.

56 Mary Pollard, 'Printing costs c. 1620' in *Long Room* no. 10 (1974), pp. 26, 28–9; Bodl., Carte MS 221, f. 152.

57 B.L., Sloane MS 1008, ff. 226, 253v, 271.

58 H.M.C., *Ormonde*, n.s., v, p. 599; B.L., Sloane MS 1008, f. 301.

59 Michael [Boyle], *Rules and orders to be used and observed in the high court of chancery in Ireland* (Dublin, 1685), sigs A3–3v.

60 In Neal Carolan, *Motives of conversion to the Catholic faith as it is practised in the reformed Church of England* (Dublin, 1688), p. 68.

61 Pollard, *Dublin's trade in books*, pp. 60–1.

62 Pollard, *Dublin's trade in books*, pp. 42–61.

63 [Richard Orpen], *The London master or the Jew detected* (Dublin, 1694).

64 B.L., Sloane MS 1008, f. 275v.

65 P.R.O., CUST 15/1–3.

66 This analysis is based on P.R.O., E190/1138/1, E190/1139/3, E190/1140/3, E190/1142/3, E190/1144/1, E190/1149/1; E190/1148/2, E190/1147/2.

67 For the pattern of book ownership in Bristol see Carl B. Estabrook, *Urbane and rustic England: cultural ties and the social spheres in the provinces, 1660–1780* (Manchester, 1998), p. 202.

68 P.R.O., E190/1156/1, f. 83v; E190/1151/1, f. 39; E190/1154/2, f. 12v.

69 Scottish Record Office, E72/19/19; E72/19/22; E72/19/8; E72/19/6; E72/10/7; E72/10/3(1).

70 Scottish Record Office, E72/20/7; E72/20/14.

71 R.M. Young (ed.), *The town book of the corporation of Belfast* (Belfast, 1892), p. 259; *Cal. S. P. dom., May 1684–Feb 1685*, p. 259; P.R.O.N.I., Mic 1P/3/1, 3 June 1679; D1614/3, pp. 3, 10, 12.

72 P.R.O., CUST 15/1–3.

73 Robert Munter, *A dictionary of the print trade in Ireland, 1550–1775* (New York, 1988), p. 91.

74 P.R.O., E190/1138/1, f. 116v; E190/1140/3, ff. 19v, 40; E190/1139/3, ff. 15v, 30v.

75 Munter, *A dictionary of the print trade*, pp. 148, 211, 266, 300; Séamus Pender (ed.), *Council books of the corporation of Waterford* (Dublin, 1964), pp. 6, 9.

76 T.C.D., MS 357, f4; MS 287, f. 194.

77 Michael [Boyle], *Rules and orders to be used and observed*, sig, A3v.

78 Bodl., Carte MS 39, f. 560v.

79 T.C.D., MS 1995–2008/2365.

80 P.R.O., E190/1154/2, ff. 4, 13v; E190/1151, f. 81v; E190/1156/1, f. 40.

81 Tisdall, *The conduct of the dissenters*, p. 75.

82 Carolan, *Motives of conversion*, sig. A2.

83 John Whalley, *Advice from the stars or an almanac for the year of Christ 1697* (Dublin, [1697]), sig. A4v.

84 D.R. Hainsworth (ed.), *The commercial papers of Christopher Lowther* (Durham, 1977), pp. 75, 158; B.L., Harley MS 2138, ff. 179v–80, 182, 184v.

85 P.F. Moran (ed.), *Spicilegium Ossoriense* (3 vols, Dublin, 1874–84), ii, pp. 148–9; Michael Mulcahy (ed.), *Calendar of Kinsale documents* (2 vols, Kinsale, 1988–89), i, pp. 96, 99, 103, 109, 114, 118–19, 122; ii, pp. 3, 7, 9, 13, 17, 19, 23.

86 T.C.D., MS 814, f. 48; Bodl., Carte MS 21, f. 440.

87 P.R.O.N.I., D1614/3, pp. 134, 148, 162, 163, 165, 170, 184, 186.

88 N.L.I., MS 12,123, entries for 4 April 1696 and 7 August 1702.

89 Tisdall, *The conduct of the dissenters*, p. 67; Peter Browne, *A letter in answer to a book entitled Christianity not mysterious* (Dublin, 1697), p. 9.

90 *A representation of the present state of religion ... drawn up and agreed by both houses of convocation in Ireland* (Dublin, 1712), p. 10.

91 Nicholas Bernard, *The penitent death of a woeful sinner* (Dublin, 1641), 'To the reader'.

92 John Toland, *An apology for Mr Toland in a letter from himself to a member of the House of Commons in Ireland* (Dublin, 1697), pp. 5–6.

93 Dom Russell, *A new almanac for the year of our Lord 1689* (Dublin, 1689), [N.L.I., microfilm, p. 4529], 'Advertisement'.

94 Quoted in Margaret Spufford, *Small books and pleasant histories* (London, 1981), p. 111.

95 *The history of the life and death of St Patrick* (London, 1685).

96 Russell, *A new almanac*.

97 R.C.B., MS 25, ff. 98v–100; *A catalogue of the books of the Rt Rev. father in God, Samuel Foley, late lord bishop of Down and Connor* (Dublin, 1695); T.C.D., MS 865, ff. 295v–86v.

98 T.C.D., MS 1490.

99 T.C.D., MUN/LIB/1/5.

100 Notes in Russell, *A new almanac* [N.L.I., microfilm p. 4529].

101 Capel Molyneux, *An account of the family and descendants of Thomas Molyneux* (Evesham, 1820), p. 74.

102 B.L., Add MS 47,038, f. 22. For a partial list see B.L., Add MS 47,024, ff. 81v–3.

103 N.L.I., MS 11048/141; 'A seventeenth-century Anglo Irish library' in *the Irish Book Lover* xxx (1946–48), pp. 31–2.

104 P.R.O, PROB4/25547; PROB4/22126.

105 Goodbody (ed.), 'Inventories', p. 45.

106 Edward Evans, *A historical and bibliographical account of almanacs and directories published in Ireland from the sixteenth century* (Dublin, 1897).

107 Gillespie, 'The circulation of print', pp. 44–6; Niall Ó Ciosáin, *Print and popular culture in Ireland, 1750–1850* (Basingstoke, 1997), pp. 72–5, 91–3.

108 James Kelly (ed.), *Gallows speeches from eighteenth-century Ireland* (Dublin, 2000).

109 Kelly (ed.), *Gallows speeches*, pp. 83–4.

110 Pollard, *Dictionary*, pp. 362–3.

111 William Mercer, *The moderate cavalier or the soldier's description of Ireland* (Cork, 1675), p. 3.

112 Cecile O'Rahilly (ed.), *Five seventeenth-century political poems* (Dublin, 1952), p. 42.

113 Bernadette Cunningham and Raymond Gillespie, 'Lost worlds: history and religion in the poetry of Dáibhí Ó Bruadair' in Pádraigín Riggs (ed.), *Dáibhí Ó Bruadair: his historical and literary context* (Dublin, 2001), p. 25.

114 N.J.A. Williams (ed.), *Paírlement Chloinne Tomáis* (Dublin, 1981), pp. xliv–lx; Brian Ó Cuív (ed.), *Párliament na mBan* (Dublin, 1952) p. xxiv; Tadhg Ó Dúshláine, *An Eoraip agus litríocht na Gaeilge, 1600–1650* (Dublin, 1987); Mícheál Mac Craith, *Lorg na hasachta ar na dánta grá* (Dublin, 1989).

Part III

The strategies of reading

Chapter 5

Reading for power: institutions and print

One of the most significant trends visible across European society in the early modern world was the rise of the state. Increasingly centralised governments made greater financial and other demands of their subjects. Taxes increased, and their collection was improved. In addition rulers claimed the right to determine the religion of their followers through the Treaty of Augsburg principle of '*cuis regio, euis religio*'. Multiple local centres of power were reduced as the growing institutions of central government consolidated jurisdiction at the expense of provincial noble authority. The use of violence and the possession of military power increasingly became the prerogative of central government rather than local magnates and feud largely replaced by legal remedies for disputes. Law too became increasingly standardised at the expense of local custom. All this created centralised bureaucracies to service the emerging state structures. Inevitably the progress down this road to homogeneity was slow and imperfect, but it was real.[1]

Ireland was no exception to these generalisations. The early modern Irish 'political experiment' was principally concerned with creating a uniform commonwealth within the country with one king, one religion and one set of cultural attributes. Regional variations in customs and laws created diversity of allegiance and hence disorder, declared Rowland White, the late sixteenth-century commentator on the state of Ireland.[2] As the 1534 Act for the 'English order, habit and language' expressed it:

> [there is] nothing which doth more contain and keep many of the [king's] subjects of this his said land in a savage and wild kind and manner of living than the diversity that is betwixt them in tongue, language, order and habit, which by the eye deceiveth the multitude and persuadeth unto them that be as it were of sundry sorts, or rather sundry countries, where indeed they should be wholly together one body whereof his Highness is the only head under God.[3]

In the early seventeenth century, one commentator on the role of plantations echoed similar sentiments, declaring that the role of the land settlement was that 'by this means shall that people [the Irish] now grow into a body commoned and into a commonwealth before they wholly consisted of poor, proud gentry'.[4] Throughout the sixteenth and seventeenth centuries various strategies were tried to achieve this aim, with varying degrees of success. After the end of the Nine Years' War in 1603 the royal writ ran across the entire island but that did not solve the problem. The manipulation of the process of granting land and authority meant that a large number of powerful landlords remained in the Irish countryside including the earl of Antrim, the earl of Clanricard and the earl of Cork.[5] Such figures were described by the Irish lord deputy of the 1630s, the earl of Strafford, as 'strange people, their own privates altogether their study without any regard to the public ... I find this kingdom abandoned for these late years to every man that could please himself to purchase what best liked him for his money'.[6] The process of reducing the power of these new local interests began most consistently under Lord Deputy Wentworth in the 1630s and continued through the Cromwellian regime of the 1650s when adverse economic conditions and heavy taxation broke the power of many local interests.[7] In the later seventeenth and early eighteenth centuries the authority of central government penetrated into areas where it had previously been weak. The building of army barracks, for instance, served to control marginal areas where lawlessness had previously been prevalent.[8] Franchisal jurisdictions, such as the duke of Ormond's palatinate liberty of Tipperary, and the presidency courts of Munster and Connacht, were all abolished in the late seventeenth century thereby increasing the power of central government in the localities.

I

The ways in which this long-term process of state-building in Ireland occurred were complex but a central role was played by print. From the perspective of government print had many advantages. First, it could explain to a wide range of people what the administration was doing and what was expected of subjects. It could encourage those who had reservations to comply with government desires and, equally, it could spell out the penalties for those who did not. In 1671, for instance, Dublin corporation, which was then engaged in setting up a poor hospital, resolved:

> forasmuch as it was very necessary that a satisfactory account should be given to all persons how much is subscribed and paid and by whom as well for the building and finishing of the said work as also what is received and disbursed for what, and to whom and what remained unreceived of the subscriptions etc. which cannot be done unless the account was printed and disposed to the several benefactors as

forasmuch as this kind of satisfaction would not only justify the care and honesty of the trustees appointed for carrying out that work but also be a motive and encouragement for others to assist in carrying out the said work.[9]

Secondly, because of its ability to produce large numbers of a fairly standardised texts and using the market and other mechanisms to distribute these, print ensured that a large number of people were exposed to the language and workings of government, both in words and in printed symbols such as the royal arms. It was the desire of the Dublin administration that this process would create common bonds between the different communities who lived on the island of Ireland and hence create a common framework for day-to-day existence or a 'commonwealth'. In that sense the state could be seen as a textual community in which certain crucial, and widely circulated, works could be read within an accepted framework of interpretation by people who would then shape their lives around them. Print could make this ambition achievable by teaching to native Irish and New English alike the language of government and the framework of thought which articulated that language into a culture of government.

Much of the language and ways of reading which the central administration wished to communicate was concerned with the law, articulated through statutes and proclamations. By the end of the sixteenth century print was beginning to make this material both standardised and accessible.[10] By 1610 printed editions of the Irish statutes already existed and new editions appeared in the early part of the century. The most important of these was the Sir Richard Bolton's 1621 edition of the statutes which, he argued, was made for 'the general good of the commonwealth'. A new, updated edition of the work was issued in 1678. It became normal practice to review the legislation at the end of each parliament to ensure that all the new statutes had been printed.[11] In addition an edition of the English statutes applicable to Ireland, in a thematic arrangement with indices to make access easier, appeared in print in 1617. It was edited by John Mericke, a lawyer of the Inner Temple in London and also an official of the presidency court in Connacht. A reprint followed in 1625.[12] Other specialist collections of statutes, such as that relating to the revenue issued in 1684, also existed by the late seventeenth century. In the case of judge-made law, at least one Irish student in Gray's Inn declared that he could 'not rest satisfied with reading' published law reports. He felt that, since they were to be 'specially regarded of all those that shall intend to manner and proceeding of law within the realm of Ireland', an abridgement and index to the volume were necessary to make access easier. These he made himself.[13] In late sixteenth-century Ireland knowledge of the law had been diffused using English printed handbooks but the issuing of a handbook for Irish justices of the peace by Richard Bolton in 1638, with a second edition in 1682, pushed the process further.[14] Bolton's work, with its thematic index to the statutes and formulary for legal documents, quickly became a standard work for those involved in administering the law. Already, by 1639 and throughout the late seventeenth century the parts of Bolton's work relating to the charges to grand juries were available as separate reprints for use with such juries.[15] It seems that a printed document such as this was being referred to by Sir Richard Cox in his charge to the Cork grand jury in the 1690s when he declared that 'it would be very tedious to give you a catalogue of them [the pleas before them] because you have it printed and are well acquainted with this matter'.[16] Bolton's work continued to be supplemented by English published handbooks. In the 1660s, for instance, Kilkenny corporation was using Michael Dalton's *Officium vicecomitum: the office and authority of sheriffs* (London, 1662) as its source for the oath of supremacy which was to be administered to all new freemen of the town.[17]

It was not just at the local level that print was used to disseminate standard rules and language for the Irish administration. Printed rules had been laid down for the workings of the Irish chancery in 1622 as part of the inquiry for the reform of Ireland, and a reprint of this was issued in 1638. There may also be an untraced version of 1632. Changing political and administrative priorities necessitated new rules in printed form to be circulated in 1658 and 1685.[18] The army too came under the discipline of print. Printed regulations for the conduct of Irish military affairs first appeared in the 1590s, as part of the second earl of Essex's military campaign in Ireland, and new printed regulations were issued in 1638, 1641 and 1672. By the end of the seventeenth century larger and more wide-ranging military manuals began to make their appearance in Ireland. In the 1680s a number of these were available in Dublin, leading one newspaper to carry an advertisement by one Dublin bookseller, Robert Thornton, pointing out that there was a choice of such books under similar titles, and incorrect editions 'are frequently sold to the great prejudice of the buyer they being much less and quite different books'. To prevent this problem one was urged to buy only from the official outlet, Robert Thornton himself.[19]

In addition to these substantial books and manuals of practice there also existed a wide range of printed ephemera. Leases, hearth money receipts, forms for debts and court schedules came to have printed forms and circulate widely. Such material had begun to circulate in print from the 1540s when books of legal formulae described as 'chartulae English' were among the works imported into Dublin by one bookseller.[20] By the 1560s Dublin corporation was making use of the printing press on an ad hoc basis to produce such instruments. In 1681 Joseph Ray was appointed as printer to the city, producing administrative documents such as court schedules and mayoral proclamations.[21] By the late seventeenth century, a wide range of printed forms for legal instruments was available from the Dublin stationers.[22] By the 1670s printed rules were issued as to how collectors of customs were to keep their accounts and how their abstracts were to be made up.[23] By the 1690s the Irish Revenue Commissioners had retained the printer John Ray to print blank books and receipts and they also availed themselves of the services of the office of king's stationer, created in 1692 with Robert Thornton, a Dublin bookseller, as its first incumbent.[24] In some respects this was a formalisation of existing arrangements whereby a Dublin bookseller was linked to the king's printer and acted as an agent for official publications. In the 1670s Joseph Wilde was identified on the imprint of most proclamations as the source where they could be purchased and in the 1680s that role was fulfilled by Samuel Helsham. The formalisation of this arrangement marks the seemingly irresistible rise of print in the service of government which is suggested also by the tenfold rise in surviving items produced by the Dublin press for government over the seventeenth century.[25] By the 1690s a printer was so central to the new Williamite government in Ireland that the king travelled to Ireland with a London printer in his entourage.[26]

The importance of print to government was made particularly clear in the 1640s. In the initial session of the parliament of 1640 the press was used by Lord Deputy Wentworth as a way of demonstrating control. Thus the House of Lords declaration complying with the royal wish for a subsidy was to be 'published in print for a testimony to all the world and succeeding ages'.[27] As that control collapsed, the parliament took advantage of its freedom after the fall of Lord Deputy Wentworth to resort to the printing press in order to produce materials setting out its own position. As the Galway lawyer Patrick Darcy put it in the 'Queries', produced for the judges as part of the attempt to redefine constitutional relationships after Wentworth's fall, they were made available in print 'that all in the world may take note of them'.[28] When the Irish Confederates set up their own administration in Kilkenny, one of their earliest priorities was the acquisition of a printing press.[29] By early April 1642, within a month of the formation of the Confederation, it was claimed that the first general assembly had 'passed many and very Christian laws ... which have been printed by order of the parliament'.[30] The importance of the press to the Confederation was emphasised in 1646. When the body split over the excommunications of the papal nuncio a fierce war broke out between the two factions over the control of the press.[31] After the Restoration in the more politically delicate world of the 1660s the Dublin parliament had witnessed the sort of problems which print could create for the social order and it became more cautious about resort to the printing press. Certain approved documents, such as sermons at the opening of parliament, set speeches and king's letters were sent to the press.[32] Parliament did not rely on the existing licensing and print restrictions to keep control over the Dublin presses. The office of king's printer was in dispute between William Bladen and John

Crooke, and early in the parliamentary session Bladen had proved difficult over parliamentary requests. Instead, parliament set up its own supervisor of the press, the first incumbent of the office being Dr John Sterne.[33] They enforced their rules rigidly. In May 1662 the sergeant at arms was instructed to take the Dublin bookseller Samuel Dancer into custody for the unauthorised printing of a parliamentary speech, a move which proved so effective that no further complaints of this sort of activity were registered before 1700.[34] In addition they tried to prevent English news-sheets printing reports of the votes and orders of the Irish House of Commons.[35] Likewise those Irish printers who failed to produce the required work were summoned before the parliament to explain themselves.[36]

A number of printed texts provide important insights into the government's use of print. Perhaps the most significant of these was the proclamation. Proclamations formed the mainstay of government printing and, before the 1620s, were the main business of the Dublin printers. In the late sixteenth century two hundred or three hundred copies of each proclamation might meet government demand, although four hundred copies of an important order might be issued. By the early seventeenth century five hundred copies of an important order were necessary, and by the late seventeenth century one thousand or two thousand of a significant proclamation would be issued. By the 1680s Dublin alone would absorb six hundred copies of a mayoral proclamation, such was the demand for print.[37] Printing was done by the king's printer in Dublin, and copies then dispersed, with a covering letter from the privy council, requiring the texts to be proclaimed locally.[38] The form that this took varied a good deal. In most cases they were read out at markets, usually with some solemnity. In one case at Drogheda proclamations were to be read at the market cross 'with a drum and trumpeter'. They were then often nailed to the market cross for future consultation. In 1641, for instance, when one of the O'Farrells arrived in Longford with a government proclamation issued on the outbreak of the rising, he fixed one on the market cross at Longford and another on the door of the market house at St Johnston in the county.[39] Military proclamations in the 1660s were said to 'be published and fixed up in all the garrisons, market houses and other public places'.[40] Other proclamations, particularly those with religious connotations, were to be read in churches.[41] For more permanent reference some kept their own private collections of proclamations. In Youghal printed proclamations were copied into the corporation book by hand and the provincial council of Munster also copied proclamations into its formal record. In Cork during the 1690s it was resolved because of the 'great inconvenience ... for want of recourse unto proclamations that from time to time come down from the government', copies were to be kept in the town clerk's office.[42] Other institutions also kept copies of proclamations relative to them. The clerk of the Clones vestry, for instance, copied into the parish vestry book the 1704 proclamation for punishing vice and immorality as well as instructions from the quarter sessions and the bishop.[43] Private individuals too made collections of proclamations which in one case were bound together with an index.[44] In another case one Limerick man copied into his notebook proclamations relevant to him.[45]

As a way of spreading information, proclamations were remarkably successful and the method was copied by others. The Quakers in Moate, for instance, wishing to censure one John Roe for his irregular marriage, drew up a paper which, in imitation of a proclamation, was nailed to the door of the market hose in Moate.[46] The reasons for the effectiveness of proclamations are not difficult to find. Proclamations spanned a number of different methods of communication. For those who could read, the printed text was available. For those with less developed literacy skills, the iconography of the document with royal arms prominent as a headpiece alerted them to its importance and it might be read for them by someone in a group. Failing that, the proclamation on a market day, with appropriate ceremonial, meant that illiterate people would none-the-less be aware of its content. The passage of the text into manuscript ensured that it would continue to circulate even when the flimsy broadsheet had been destroyed.

Proclamations were at least as important for the messages they conveyed indirectly about the commonwealth as for the information they imparted directly. The layout of proclamations, with the use of the royal arms and the authority of the king's printer, all helped in this area. The language of the proclamation, with phrases such as 'commonwealth', 'king's peace' and various legal terms, all helped, with other institutions, to establish a basic political vocabulary among the inhabitants of early modern Ireland.[47] Proclamations were not the only way of doing this and government issued works which conveyed these messages more overtly. A proclamation of 1616 required that a book entitled *God and the king*, explaining the powers of the king, was to be printed in Dublin for the use of schools and it was to be available at no more than 6*d*. There is no evidence it ever was published in Dublin although since this work related to the proposed oath of loyalty for Catholics in England it may have been seen as having little relevance in Ireland.[48] Again in Dublin during the Jacobite regime of the 1680s a weekly printed propaganda sheet 'to rake together all the little stories that might reflect on Protestants' was introduced and at the same time, it was claimed, all other newsletters and gazettes were banned from the Dublin coffee houses leaving only the official *Dublin Gazette*, 'which is a legend of their [the Jacobite regime's] own composition'.[49]

The use of print in this process of legitimation was not confined to substantial works. Printed ephemera also had an important role to play. In the years after 1660 the lord lieutenant of Ireland, the duke of Ormond, attempted to make a reality of the idea of the kingdom of Ireland, as sixteenth-century legislation had described it, rather than the colonial world which many early seventeenth-century commentators saw the country as. One part of that process was an enhanced status for the office of lord lieutenant, a process begun by Lord Deputy Wentworth in the 1630s. One aspect of this involved increasing the pageantry and ritual surrounding the office. The staging of dramatic pageants at the arrival and departing of the lords lieutenant was one manifestation of this.[50] Part of these pageants was the composition of verse praising the new holder of the office. Initially these were in manuscript form but increasingly throughout the century they appeared as printed broadsheets which were sold through the city.[51] It was not necessary for such works to be great art. The poems composed by William Mercer for the entrance of Lord Robartes in 1669 were short works, some composed as acrostics. This was clearly intended to make them memorable, and possibly recited later. Their poetic brevity may suggest they were to be distributed freely as handbills.[52]

More subtly, governments realised that the manner and timing of publication could influence the messages contained in printed works. Texts bound together could influence how each was read in the context of another. In this way potentially seditious messages could be defused with a correct arrangement of works. For example in 1683 when the Dublin printers, with an eye to profit, were planning to issue the last speech of Lord William Russell, who had been executed for his complicity in the Rye House plot, Ormond was strongly urged by the archbishop of Armagh that a document whose meaning could potentially glorify rebels should be carefully controlled. The archbishop suggested that the speech should be printed with some observations on it by Sir Roger L'Estrange, the licenser for the English press, already in print in England, 'so that the kingdom may be undeceived by the pretended innocency an integrity of that suffering nobleman'. L'Estrange's work was popular in England, going through three editions in quick succession in London, as well as one in Edinburgh. The aim of the exercise was to ensure that the meaning of a potentially disloyal work was explained to readers and not left to their own vivid imaginations, with the potential of creating further trouble. Unfortunately for the government, L'Estrange's work was a substantial one of fifty-two pages in quarto, and the economics of reprinting this in Ireland did not commend the book to printers looking for quick profit and so it was never produced.[53]

The timing of the release of printed works, as well as their contents, was significant. In January 1649, for instance, when implementation of the terms of the second Ormond peace was running into difficulties, Lord Inchiquin arranged to have the Cromwellian tract by Henry Ireton, *Remonstrance of the army*, reprinted at Cork. He used the Confederate press that had been moved from Waterford, which, according to Ormond, 'put a speedy end to our contestations about the conditions of the peace, for it gave me and all others such horror that we judged it a very unseasonable thing to spend time in disputing about the circumstances of government, whilst the whole frame of it was so near subversion'.[54] It may also have been to strengthen the peace that Charles I's *Eikon basilike* was printed in Cork later that year. Unfortunate release of printed material could have significant implications. In 1679, for instance, the duke of Ormond, hoping to break an alleged conspiracy, was frustrated by the publication of discovery since, as Ormond noted, 'the publishing of it in print will in a great measure frustrate the success of our further enquiry, instruct such as may be guilty what defence to make, and perhaps warn them to fly from justice'. That the resort to print was politically motivated Ormond had no doubt.[55] An important example of the use of timing in the release of print to gain maximum political effect is provided by the publication during the Jacobite government of Dublin in the late 1680s of a controversial work by Peter Manby, the dean of Derry who had converted to Catholicism. This appeared in two Dublin editions in 1687 both produced by the Jacobite bookseller Christopher Jans.[56] According to the title page the work was licensed on 11 March 1687. However, it may have been written some time earlier since Manby's conversion had taken place before July 1686. In that month he was granted a royal dispensation to continue to hold the deanery of Derry notwithstanding his Catholicism. According to a later reply to Manby by William King, rector of St Werburgh's, the work had already been circulating in manuscript for some time.[57] The practice of circulating controversial works in manuscript before releasing them to a wider world through print was common. One of Manby's later replies to King was said to have been 'dispersed about [in] a sheet of paper' before being printed. Likewise the contribution of the Presbyterian Joseph Boyse to the debate was in the form of an open letter which may have first circulated in manuscript form.[58] The move from scribal publication to the world of print was determined by the growing Catholicisation of Ireland after the arrival of the earl of Tyrconnell as lord deputy in February 1687. One Protestant diarist certainly drew a connection between the two trends, noting in his diary for April 1687 the appointment of Catholic judges, the surrender of urban charters, Tyrconnell's open attendance at mass and that 'about this time Dean Manby turned papist and writes for popery'.[59] However, the immediate context of Manby's resort to print may well have been the failure of the Catholic administration to engage the Church of Ireland in oral forms of controversy as a means of using such events for propaganda purposes. The failed attempt by the Catholic authorities in Dublin to arrange a formal disputation on 26 February 1687 prompted the Church of Ireland archbishop of Dublin to forbid his clergy taking part in any such public disputations.[60] The publication of Manby's tract shortly after may be seen as a substitute for the preferred drama of live debate.

Given the importance of print as a tool for conveying both information and the language and ideas of loyalty, the Dublin government was concerned to exercise a monopoly over the use of print. In the 1660s Ormond filtered carefully what was to appear in the English news-sheets and decreed that 'nothing of public concernment' was to be printed without his approval.[61] As the bookseller Samuel Dancer observed in his news-sheet, *Mercurius Hibernicus*, of one of the rumours of a plot in Dublin in 1662, 'you can have no information concerning the plot, or upon what score the people now in hold were secured, it being not thought fit by the council as yet to divulge any reason concerning it'.[62] As the first Jacobite licenser of the Irish press, Thomas Sheridan, commented in his 1677 tract *A discourse on the rise and power of parliaments*, there was a need

> to take the printing of books into the state, it is as necessary as the mint. False coinage of books having done England more mischief than ever money did, or will do, the licensing of printing or importing from beyond sea, will not otherwise prevent a great evil to church and state. Let there be but a convenient number of booksellers permitted; those to be under an obligation to vend no other books than such as are printed in this allowed printing house where foreign books, with advantage to the public, may be reprinted.[63]

The Irish press was highly selective in what it was prepared to print. As Sir Christopher Sibthorpe, one of the justices of king's bench, replied to one of his opponents in a religious dispute who had complained at not being given access to the press, 'Yea the very name of a Protestant press (if there were no more) might have been sufficient to tell you that it were utterly unmeet for popish works to come into it'.[64] Control of the printing press, of itself, was not unusual, and this clearly paralleled attitudes in Stuart England. In Ireland, however, the issue was even more pressing, arising from the numerical predominance of Catholics and, by the late seventeenth century, the high concentrations of dissenters in Ulster. This meant that censorship was not confined to Catholics. The godly preacher Faithful Teate claimed that his sermon at the funeral of Sir Charles Coote in 1642 was 'first intended for the press as well as the pulpit but till this day [1658] hath lain dormant ... [because] here was something spoken against the cessation [of 1643] which was then so vigorously prosecuted'.[65] Items which slipped through were quickly dealt with. In 1661 all copies of a Bible printed by a man describing himself as 'printer to the lord protector' had the title pages torn out and replaced with new ones.[66]

The way in which the Irish administration chose to control the Dublin press was through the office of king's printer in Dublin.[67] The office of king's, or queen's, printer in some form would seem to date back to the coming of print to Ireland since Humphrey Powell described himself as such in 1551 on the first book printed in Ireland, the Book of Common Prayer. However the powers of the office become clear only at the beginning of the seventeenth century when it was granted by royal patent to John Franckton in 1604 and again in 1609. The terms of the patent gave Franckton a complete monopoly in the right to print, bind, import and sell in Ireland all printed matter, while no other stationer could operate without the King's printer's licence.[68] In 1618 the patent as king's printer passed to the Stationers' Company and in 1639 it seems to have passed from the Stationers to William Bladen, who by 1642 was describing himself on proclamations as king's printer. In the chaos of the 1650s the Irish council was to act as censor, controlling what could be printed on the Dublin press. After the Restoration in 1660 John Crooke, a Dublin bookseller from the 1640s, acquired the patent but the position of the patentee was not as strong as it had been earlier in the century. As commercial opportunities expanded, the monopolistic practices of the king's printer were resented and the formation of the guild of St Luke in 1670 provided an alternative way of regulating the print trades. Two attempts were made to break the monopoly of the king's printer after 1660, and the state's response was to attempt to tighten the system. An order in council of 1664 explicitly set out the state's role as licenser of the press, requiring that copy be submitted before publication and approved by either the lord lieutenant, one of the principal secretaries of state, the archbishop of Dublin or Armagh or their chaplains.[69] In the early 1670s the Crooke family and Benjamin Tooke, who then held the patent, petitioned to have a rival press, run by Dr Thomas Bladen a son of the patentee holder in the 1640s, closed down. Again in the early 1680s Joseph Ray attempted to break the monopoly with the king's printer, pleading reasons of state for his monopolistic control.[70] Whatever the outcome Ray continued to print, possibly under licence. The king's printer's patent seems to have been renewed in 1693 although by that stage the growing number of printers in the city made it difficult to enforce. The state, presumably, had to rely on the licensing system to control the output of the press.

Given the important of print in conveying attitudes and ideas, those who did not accept the rulings of the Dublin government on access to the press turned to other means of subverting such arrangements. The circulation of manuscript, and later printed, 'libels', for instance, was a well-established feature of Irish political life from the sixteenth century. According to Edmund Campion, in Dublin in 1572 during the controversy over taxation in the pale, 'a seditious libel entitled Tom Troth [was] let fall in the streets of Dublin, nipped by name divers honourable and worshipful of the realm and certain officers of the deputies' household for grieving the land with impositions of cess'.[71] In fact the 'bill', signed by Thomas Truth and John Justifier, was directed against John Thomas, the chief remembrancer of the exchequer. It accused him of being 'the rankest knave and vilest briber, extortioner and bloodsucker' and threatening to inform the queen of his knaveries.[72] Sir Henry Sidney was likewise troubled on campaign by libels and leaflets thrown into his camp by rebels and in the 1590s the earl of Tyrone, then in rebellion, arranged for 'writings' to be spread around the streets of Dublin.[73] Such libels, in manuscript and in some cases printed, became a standard feature of Irish political and religious life. In the early 1640s the execution of John Atherton, bishop of Lismore, was said to have given rise to 'divers scattered written papers' as well as scandalous rhyming pamphlets in Dublin.[74] Quakers too distributed such pamphlets, with one Independent clergyman in Limerick in the 1640s complaining of 'multitudes of pamphlets, libels and papers full of their sad stuff' nailed to church doors or scattered about in the city.[75] Again in the 1660s libels were spread about in Derry by Presbyterians after the visit of the assize judges, and in the 1680s one Presbyterian bookbinder in Belfast was also active in dispersing seditious libels.[76] Scattering of libels remained a feature of Irish political life into the eighteenth century.[77]

Such libels were meant to fulfil the same function for their own part as proclamations and statutes did for government. In 1637 Malachy Queely, the Catholic archbishop of Tuam, found himself in dispute with Walter Lynch of Galway over accusations that Lynch was interfering with one of the city's institutions, the wardenship. Queely wrote to a correspondent, probably another ecclesiastic, sending him

> the copy of a kind of libel he [Lynch] published in giving a copy of it to everyone of his faction in town and abroad without putting his hand to it as I heard. I was advised to write an answer to it which I could not do for many reasons ... After this gag or libel came to light the inhabitants of this place began to chafe so far *ruri et hic* that they resolved commonly to withdraw their love and benevolence from me as *de facto* they did, and not only that but some ill willers among them do swear to bring me in for foreign jurisdiction. [78]

Clearly the context of this dispute was a personal and local one but the attempts at libels against the state adopted a similar strategy. They aimed to bind together those of like mind who might read the document. It taught them the grounds of the dispute and the language in which it was to be conducted and so convinced themselves of the legitimacy of the position of the author of the libel. In that sense such documents helped define and articulate political opposition. Reaction to such libels varied a good deal according to the political context in which they were spread. In the 1630s the advice of the Irish lord deputy, Thomas Wentworth, was simply to ignore them so that 'no noise of them at all went abroad'. If ignored the issue might well fizzle out. In the 1660s the duke of Ormond expressed a similar view, simply ignoring libels.[79] Others reacted more violently. In the politically uncertain climate of 1661 the earl of Orrery claimed that the author of a seditious republican libel needed to be tracked down since 'such little seeds if not rooted out often bring forth quantities of ill fruit and such pamphlets are the forerunners of greater evils'.[80] Overall it was the view of Ormond rather than of Orrery that prevailed.

Subversive ideas which formed political subcultures were not confined to the printed word. Ballads and songs could convey politically subversive messages and might even make it into print. The sort of heterodox ideas set out in pamphlet form by a Catholic priest in a Dublin dispute in the 1620s were spread also by 'his songs and other speeches' according to the reports of his opponents.[81] More professional ballad sellers and singers moved between fairs 'bawling ballads and shivering with the cold' according to one Irish poem of 1692.[82] Ballad singers could convey seditious messages over long distances. One singer, Thomas Cooper, who sold seditious ballads printed by the Cork printer William Smith in 1670, was active in places as far apart as Cork and Drogheda.[83] One did not have be literate to appreciate the messages conveyed by such singers, although they were also available in print. Some seditious ballads were clearly imported. In 1593, for instance, a proclamation was issued prohibiting the importation of Catholic ballads into Ireland. Presbyterian political messages were also conveyed in ballads to judge from the cargo one ship, seized at Belfast in 1682, which contained a gross of ballads valued at 1s 6d as well as Bibles, psalters, some pamphlets and other small books.[84] Precisely what messages these ballads may have conveyed is impossible to reconstruct since almost none has survived from an Irish context. One, 'Mount Taragh's triumph', of 1626 is not a seditious ballad but rather one expressing loyalty to the king in the face of a possible Spanish invasion.[85] Yet this may not have been as straightforward as it seems. Internal evidence suggests that it may have been written by a Catholic, Old English, author and, as events over the next three years would show, such outward show of loyalty was used to demand concessions from the king.

If it was possible to undermine the controls on the press through ballads or manuscript libels, it was equally possible to manipulate the controls on the press to one's own ends. As the power of the king's printer declined in the late seventeenth century the Jacobite administration in the 1680s enforced more strictly the system of state licensing for the publication of books, the first Jacobite licenser being Thomas Sheridan.[86] This resulted in a spilt of authority within the licensing system. One element was a Catholic-controlled mechanism, through Sheridan, and the other the episcopal licensing system, in the hands of the Church of Ireland archbishops of Armagh and Dublin. In early 1688, as tensions between the Protestant Church of Ireland and the Catholic government grew rapidly, both sides used their own agents of legitimacy to issue propaganda, on the issue of conversions, from the Dublin presses. On 22 April 1688 a reprint of a London work by the Benedictine John Huddleston was licensed in Dublin, in which it was claimed that Charles II had been received into the Catholic church on his deathbed.[87] The Church of Ireland replied in August of the same year by providing an imprimatur for a conversion narrative of a Catholic priest, Neal Carolan, which presumably referred to events earlier but was now issued for propagandist reasons.[88] The use of the two licensing systems by the different parties ensured that propaganda items cancelled each other out but also provided material to encourage their own adherents.

Some, perhaps rather naively, hoped that they might get access to the Dublin press by covert means. In June 1679, in the wake of the murder of Archbishop Sharpe and the Covenanter rising in Scotland, a member of the Church of Ireland from Ballymoney in County Antrim sent to Mary Crooke, the king's printer in Dublin, the text of an anonymous letter describing the Presbyterians of north Ulster in unflattering terms. He asked that she would 'print the enclosed letter (which is a true account of matters in these parts) and gain yourself some pence thereby any new thing being acceptable at this time. Let it be well done which is all the requital [your correspondent] expects for the copy'.[89] The writer's motivation can only be guessed at but it was certainly not financial. It is more likely that his purpose was to use print to foment discontent among the disillusioned Presbyterians. At any rate the work was not printed but handed to the government, who, concerned with the possibility of disorder in Ulster, suppressed it. Despite this the growing number of Dublin printers in the late seventeenth century meant that some were prepared, presumably for the right price, to print material for use by dissenting political and religious groups. From the mid-1670s the Quakers, who placed great reliance on print, began to print material in Ireland whereas before they had relied on English imports. They produced both religious and political works, one by William Stockdale claiming that the aim of producing his book 'is to make known to the rulers and magistrates and others the oppression and great suffering which we endure'.[90] As Lord Chief Justice Scroggs lamented during the early stages of the popish plot in Dublin, there were 'many libellous pamphlets which are publishing against the law to the scandal of ... government and public justice'.[91] A 'scandalous and invective' pamphlet entitled *Ireland's sad lamentation*, probably produced in Dublin, was certainly circulating in the city in 1681.[92]

For most people with dubious intent, access to a press might have been denied in Ireland but it was available elsewhere. In 1664, for instance, Elizabeth Warren, the wife of one of those implicated in a failed Presbyterian plot against the government, was considering using stationers in London to have items of propaganda printed for import into Ireland.[93] The result of this was that most subversive printing in Ireland was smuggled into the country. Catholic works, including books by Edmund Campion, were already making their way into Munster in the 1580s and Catholic works printed in Douai or Rheims were smuggled into Ireland in the early seventeenth century.

However, England seems to have been the main routeway for such smuggled works.[94] In 1641 one Dublin deponent claimed that three or four years previously many books had been brought to Limerick from 'foreign parts' and had been seized by the bishop as prohibited works.[95] Certainly in the 1640s there seems to have been little difficulty in smuggling contentious works printed in Europe into Ireland.[96] In some cases individuals with prohibited Catholic works were clearly indulging in once-off sales. In 1663, one Patrick Rothe was said to be selling copies of a work by R.S. detailing atrocities against Catholics in the 1640s despite the banning and public burning of the book.[97] Rothe had no known connections with the Irish book trade but in 1685 the established Dublin bookseller William Weston was found to be selling Bishop Nicholas French's seditious *Settlement and sale of Ireland*, which had been reprinted in London, from where Weston claimed to have got his copies.[98] Again in the 1690s the Catholic bookseller James Malone, one of the largest importers of books into Ireland through Chester, was retailing seditious Catholic books.[99] In the late seventeenth century there seems to have been no shortage of books regarded as seditious by the authorities but which feature in the list of confiscated Jacobite libraries after the Williamite victory in Ireland.[100] From another perspective dissenting Protestants also smuggled potentially seditious works and distributed them.[101] By the end of the century there were enough dissenting Protestants involved in the book trade to provide a smuggling and distribution mechanism for books. Two of the largest players in the Dublin book trade during the 1690s, Patrick Campbell and Eliphal Dobson, were Presbyterians, although, according to John Dunton, Dobson was not 'a jot precise'.[102] Perhaps more serious as a smuggler may have been the Quaker Amos Strettle, who imported large quantities of books into Ireland in the 1690s, some of which may have been Quaker works.[103]

The importance which the central government attached to print in shaping the Irish commonwealth in the early modern period clearly led to attempts to regulate access to the world of print. Like most aspects of early modern government, the administration might hope to curtail the subversive use of print but their limited enforcement powers meant they could never eliminate it. Instead others devised ways of subverting and even using the press for their own ends. Libels, ballads and other mechanisms spread alternative messages about the nature of the Irish commonwealth and its inhabitants.

II

The creation of a recognisably modern Irish commonwealth with common language of loyalty and recognisable administrative structures was not exclusively the work of a secular centralising government. A second, and equally important, institutional element was the churches. As an institution, the established Church of Ireland also used print in the straightforward task of ensuring increasing administrative uniformity. Like the machinery of central government, the established church also required a network of quasi-judicial and administrative institutions which needed rules and procedures within which they could operate. Certainly by the 1660s a consistory court in Galway was using an English printed manual of procedures entitled *The clerke's practice*.[104] Again the circulation of the sort of rules contained in the canons of 1634 or the articles of belief of the same year was greatly enhanced by print. According to one petition to the lord deputy from the Irish House of Commons in 1641, 'in the diocese of Waterford and other places every churchwarden must buy a book of articles of the registrar and pay 2*s* 6*d* for it, no more worth than 3*d*'.[105]

Administrative convenience, however, was not the main way in which the early modern churches of Ireland used print. Like government, each religious group, Church of Ireland, Catholic, or from the late seventeenth century a range of dissenting churches, wished to create a religious culture of language and practice that would allow its followers to define and maintain confessional identities and allow the institution to ensure doctrinal uniformity within those groupings. The earliest Irish printings, the first Edwardian Book of Common Prayer (1551), the Articles of Religion (1566) and the Irish-language catechism of John Kearney (1571), were all aimed at defining belief and worship so that uniformity within Protestantism could be maintained. Furthermore, the language of belief and worship of the Church of Ireland was enhanced by the fact that most of the printed liturgical books in use in Ireland were imported from England. Print, through devotional and practical works such as the *Whole duty of man*, could exercise a powerful cohesive influence on the established churches throughout the British Isles and thereby reinforce confessional identities.

One of the most important techniques in creating confessional identities, through establishing uniformity of belief, language and organisation, was the effective use of the printed catechism. Catechisms were cheap works. They were often advertised in almanacs, which suggests they were aimed at a wide social range. Moreover, this appeal extended even into the world of the illiterate since catechesis was an oral activity in which the contents of a printed book could be made known even to those who could not read. It also portrayed in a vivid way the relationship between spiritual master and pupil, emphasising ministerial authority. As Anthony Dopping, in the late 1670s rector of Summerhill in County Meath, and later bishop of Meath, claimed, people of 'inferior capacities' were to come to catechising 'with submission and willingness to be instructed'.[106] Dopping fully appreciated the importance of the catechism in shaping confessional solidarity. As he wrote of Presbyterian catechisms in 1670 since Christianity hath been broken into parties and divisions the heads of [the] catechism are swollen into too intense a bulk and they do not so much labour to inform their proselytes in the principles of religion as to make them speak the language of their own parties and suck in the principles which are peculiarly adapted to the shibboleth of every communion.[107]

By such means the young learned words and phrases from the catechism that could create shared bonds of religious language. In the case of the Church of Ireland, for instance, it ensured a close identification between that church and the Church of England. Until 1699 Ireland lacked an English-language catechism written specifically for members of the Church of Ireland. There had been earlier catechisms written by those living in Ireland, such as Edward Wetenhall, bishop of Cork, but these had been aimed at the wider British Isles market. In that year Narcissus Marsh, the archbishop of Dublin, composed a catechism which he 'thought convenient to have printed for the more easy dispersing of copies in private families'.[108]

Catechisms, however, taught more than confessional language. They also laid down the parameters for how one read within a confessional tradition. Most importantly the catechism conveyed the rules within which that highly charged political text, the Bible, had to be read correctly. Individualistic interpretations of scripture posed problems for both church and state. Thus the satirical account of the reformation by the Catholic bishop of Ferns, Luke Wadding, portrayed 'the cobbler with his great black thumb / Turning the Bible will have it done'.[109] The problem of how to control this subversive use of scripture and to assert particular confessional readings of the text was solved by forming an interpretative community around it which instructed readers on how to understand their Bibles. Sermons were one way of presenting approved interpretations of scripture, and seventeenth-century Presbyterians were urged to bring their Bibles with them to church and to turn to the texts of scripture as they were cited by the preacher so that they could follow how diverse passages were used to make a coherent, and approved, narrative. They were also encouraged to make notes of this and to read these over.[110] In this process of constructing approved frameworks for reading, the catechism was of prime significance. As Edward Wetenhall, bishop of Cork and the author of a catechism, observed:

> it [the catechism] will teach you the same things in a different form and besides convince you of their truth and otherwise affect you with them. But when plain reason meets with hard places in their Bibles not relating to these necessaries I would have them pass such difficulties over, and not interpret them on their own heads without a teacher but content themselves commonly to know, to believe, to be affected with and practice these necessary points thus summarily comprised by our church.[111]

Other churches took the same message to heart. Within Catholicism great stress was placed not on reading the Bible early in life but rather on using the catechism to shape the elements of belief that would guide any subsequent contact with the text. Emphasis was placed on catechesis and prayer, and parents were warned that the first books children encountered at school should convey simple Catholic ideas in a catechetical form.[112] The Bible was rarely, if ever, intended to be used as an unmediated text but was to be read in a guided way within a community of readers nurtured on sermon and catechism.

Perhaps the body which made the greatest use of the catechism in the process of establishing confessional discipline and a religious culture was the Presbyterian church. In the Presbyterian ministry catechesis was held to be the most fundamental of the ministerial functions since it laid the foundation for an approved reading of scripture later in life.[113] In the 1650s the conduct of catechising was held to be one of the markers of the faithfulness of an Ulster Presbyterian minister to his congregation.[114] The Dublin Independents were so convinced of the merits of catechesis in the 1650s that they performed it publicly at Christ Church.[115] Baptists, with a less well-developed theology and, depending to a greater extent on the inspiration of the Spirit, were slow to develop catechisms. In late seventeenth-century Baptist memoirs, such as that of Ann Fowke, there is no mention of catechesis. Quakers, of course, lacking a formally articulated set of doctrines, could not rely on the catechism. Among Presbyterians and Independents in the later half of the century the importance of catechesis did not decline. As Joseph Boyse observed in the 1690s, 'the ministers of the north of Ireland ... do (speaking generally) outstrip all others that we know of in the Christian world as to their unwearied diligence in catechising those under their charge'. Likewise the minister at Larne, Thomas Hall, described catechising as 'one part of my work'.[116] Parishes were divided into districts, often called quarters, and each district was catechised at least once a year, usually at the house of an elder. Knowledge of the catechism was a requirement for admission to communion on the first occasion.[117]

In late seventeenth-century Dublin catechesis seems to have worked in a slightly different way. Boyse noted that catechising there was done publicly on Sundays and the catechism was gone through at least once a year.[118] The catechism used was not necessarily the *Shorter catechism of the Westminster Assembly*, although the Independent ministers in the Dublin area during the 1650s had recommended the *Shorter catechism* 'unless some particular brother shall think some other catechism more convenient for his congregation'.[119] Before the 1680s there was a lack of printed catechisms in Dublin. The early seventeenth-century catechism of James Ussher, the archbishop of Armagh, was the main one in use, and some clergy composed their own. By the 1680s there were a variety of catechetical resources in the city, including reprints of

English catechisms by Thomas Lye and John Wallis undertaken by the strongly anti-Catholic bookseller Joseph Howes. By 1700 others had been reprinted in Belfast.[120]

Something of how these works were used to achieve the desired effect can be traced in the activities of Robert Chambers. According to John Cooke, one of his congregation, Chambers 'did so constantly and earnestly apply himself to [catechising] and that in so peculiar a method that he always had before him publicly in that exercise a number of very ripe years and understandings, many standing in the rank to their very marriage day'.[121] Chambers's technique was to distribute each week 'papers' containing the questions and answers to those who were to respond the following week. These 'papers' were eventually assembled into his 1679 'Explanation of the Shorter Catechism' which, it seems, he intended for publication.[122] On the basis of that text the papers contained not only the relevant question and answer from the *Shorter catechism* but a host of subsidiary questions which expanded on the earlier questions and developed the bare questions and answers into a systematic theology. That this method was widely used is suggested also by the format of a catechism composed by the minister of Larne, Thomas Hall. Here too there is the text of the *Shorter catechism* but also 'questions raised from the answers of the catechism', although these were probably of lesser importance, to judge from the typography. The largest font was reserved for the text of the *Shorter catechism*, with smaller type sizes and italics being used for the subsidiary questions.[123] Thus catechesis became not simply a bare repetition of simple question and answer but the setting out of a complex confessional position. It is likely that those of 'ripe years and understandings' who appeared before Chambers were expected to master the finer points of theological debate rather than merely acquire the basis of belief.

Presbyterians had yet another perspective on the importance of print in shaping confessional identities. It was through print that the Solemn League and Covenant became known in Ulster. Some Scottish preachers declared it to be 'the pathway to heaven' and declared, 'the Covenant is as necessary as is the sacrament'.[124] The text of the Covenant certainly circulated widely in Ulster in the seventeenth century. Copies printed in Scotland flooded into Ulster as an integral part of the catechism and were distributed throughout the province by chapmen.[125] By 1680 the duke of Ormond commented of the Covenant, 'I find great industry is used in dispersing them through this kingdom especially through the northern counties'.[126] Archbishop King of Dublin later claimed that by 1694 there was a Belfast printing of the text, and such was the demand by the early eighteenth century that printers 'let their frames at Belfast stand unbroken and print them as they find occasion as printers do often do with the almanacs'.[127] As a result the printed word became a central defining element in Ulster Presbyterianism.

III

Both central governments and churches regarded print as an important tool in shaping the idea of commonwealth or confession but readers who engaged with the sort of printed material which governments or churches issued did not necessarily extract from the printed word the meaning that was intended. The Bible, for instance, was a complex text which could be read in ways that neither the clergy nor the government would have approved of. Notwithstanding attempts through catechism and sermon to control such ways of reading, they still took place on a wide scale. Political readings of the biblical text, for example, were common. In 1662 a miller on the Clandeboy estate in County Down, William Fury, revealed to James Phillips of Ballymaconaghy his interpretation of Micah 5.5–6 and Jeremiah 4.20 and 6.23: this involved a Spanish invasion of Ireland and the Scottish army, which had recently been in Ulster under General Munroe, together with some elliptical statements about the king. The Dublin government were not impressed and clamped down on Fury, who was clearly frightened, for

> being demanded whether he thought he himself a prophet or had the interpretation of the scriptures or if what he said were by revelation or inspiration or by his own imagination and conception of the text, he sayeth only by his own imaginations and conception of the text and that be both believes his interpretations of them to be true but if this be passed by in silence he will never interpret again.[128]

Administrators took a dim view of such actions, especially after the explosion of strange interpretations of scripture in the 1650s. Roger Boyle, earl of Orrery, writing in the aftermath of this free interpretation of scripture, observed:

> I confess an aversion from the late custom of our age for every private hand as it serves to draw all stories and expressions of scripture into the consequence for the conduct of our lives and the framing of our opinions. I have observed this to be of mischievous effect and destructive in a great measure to the respect and obedience we owe to civil authority. I revere the scriptures but esteem them given to us for other use than to fortify disputes concerning state affairs.[129]

Others urged theological caution. Thomas Halsam, the schoolmaster of Lisburn in the 1630s, condemned in a sermon those who wrestled with scripture to interpret it, since 'the wrestler becomes a new judicer of scripture and takes upon himself the person of God'. In the later part of the century Robert Craghead, the Presbyterian minister at Derry, warned those who 'wrestled with scripture to your own destruction' to desist.[130] Devotional works were likewise subject to many readings, orthodox and unorthodox.[131]

The church was not the only body that faced the problem of how people read the printed works they issued. Proclamations may have left the Dublin press in a standard form but when it came to their formal reading at the markets of the county towns, their performance could introduce unwelcome interpretations of their meaning. The printed word of the proclamation when read, either publicly or privately, was given meaning from the context in which it was read. This context of its proclamation at the market cross with trumpeters was usually intended to emphasis the solemnity of the state. However the effect of this could be negated by the events surrounding its performance. In 1629 a soldier reading a proclamation in Drogheda 'made it seem like a May game', according to the lord deputy, since he was drunk while reading it.[32] Again, the proclamation of James I at Waterford in 1603 should have been an occasion for the demonstration of loyalty to the new king but the effect of the performance was negated by 'disloyal speeches' shouted from the crowd and a refusal to recognise the king's style until after Catholic mass houses had been established.[33] The proclamation of the accession of James II at Downpatrick was similarly mocked by 'traitorous words' shouted by a man who was later discovered to be drunk.[34] A clear example of this undermining of the authority of the printed word of the proclamation comes from the description by Richard Bellings of the proclamation of the first Ormond peace at Limerick in 1646. The proclamation was being read from the market cross, as was normal, by a herald 'vested in the coat of his office' together with the mayor and corporations in their gowns when

> the multitude and meaner sort of people ... fell on the sudden to flinging of stones at the herald, at the mayor, and those of the better sort, who assisted to countenance that solemn action; and having disordered their ranks with so unexpected a volley they flew among them wounding the herald and tearing his coat of arms off his shoulders, beating the mayor and some of the aldermen and without any reverence to their scarlet gowns or the badges of magistracy, drove them for shelter into the next door that stood open.

That such actions were intended to be nothing short of a social revolution is suggested by Bellings's comment that 'with a popular suffrage, without consulting any charter or any ancient custom' they elected a new mayor.[35] The effect had been to totally negate the intended impact of authority and its symbol, the printed word.

The construction of the printed word of government could intermesh with elements of popular protest when forms of official documents were imitated but their meaning inverted. Thus in the late 1680s objections to the religious innovations of James II appeared nailed to the door of Christ Church cathedral, Dublin, in the form 'to publish the banns of matrimony between that church and the see of Rome, bidding any that could forthwith to show cause why they should not be joined together'.[36] Again printed proclamations might be deliberately imitated although necessarilly in manuscript rather than print. In 1662, for instance, after the departure of the justices of assize from

Derry, the Presbyterians in the city scattered about 'libels' and according to the bishop of Derry 'a large one set up at a market place in ugly (Scotch) verse'.[137] While its content was no doubt scurrilous, its size and location resemble that of a proclamation and by this strategy it undermined the authority of the printed word. Others, rather than subverting printed works which they did not wish to read, simply avoided any contact with them. Some simply refused works with which they did not agree. It was claimed in 1577 that the Jesuit James Archer had sworn not to uphold Queen Elizabeth's jurisdiction 'and to read not in no English book'.[138] A variant on this was reported in the 1580s when it was claimed that some Catholic clergy who had nominally conformed, when forced to go to church 'they carry with them a book in Latin of the Common Prayer set forth and allowed by your Majesty. But they read nothing of it or can well read'.[139] Others might go further and not simply refuse to read what they objected to but destroy it also. Proclamations might simply be torn down, as at Longford in 1641 or in Dublin in 1678.[140] In Belfast in 1685 the proclamation informing the inhabitants of the town that James II had succeeded to the throne was also torn down much to the 'displeasure' of the sheriff.[141]

If the state had problems with how its printed words were spread, the church had similar difficulties. Ministers might well hold catechesis using printed catechisms in high regard because it presented to the laity a systematic view of confessional positions and because it provided a quick way in which the illiterate might be brought into contact with the written word which was held to be central to belief. In practical terms lay men and women were less keen to follow the scholarly approach of their pastors. In the 1690s Bishop King and the Presbyterians debated the importance of the catechism in the formation of faith with rather disappointing results. Even the Dublin Presbyterian Joseph Boyse had to admit that out of 2,400 people in the Derry congregation of Templemore only about a quarter could repeat the *Shorter Catechism*.[142] This reflects not a lack of interest in religion among the laity but rather a rather different perception of what belief constituted, most being more interested in devotion than in doctrine.[143]

IV

From the institutional point of view, print made possible the extension of the central government's idea of a 'commonwealth' into the provincial world with very considerable social consequences. At one level this was a practical exercise. With secular government, printed statutes, proclamations, manuals of justice and blank forms all helped to ensure that its rules could be more effectively enforced. In the case of the churches, books also helped the ecclesiastical courts of the Church of Ireland follow a similar trend. Within the churches, however, a rather different sort of printed documents was important, the catechism, which led the drive for theological and confessional conformity. It was now possible, though perhaps not practicable, to give standard answers to key questions over large geographical areas from a confessionally approved perspective. However institutions wanted to achieve more with print than merely the mechanical process of administration. They saw the possibility of shaping a political or confessional culture with its own language and symbols. In this, the documents of the Dublin government were remarkably successful in spreading the language and attitudes of monarchy and the common law throughout Ireland. A letter from Ireland published in London in 1643 recorded that

> there was a friar taken in the last expedition unto Connacht about whom was found a collection of all your votes, ordinances and declarations in England, very carefully perused and marked with short marginal notes by him and out of them a large manuscript entitled 'An apology of the Catholics of Ireland ...' in truth so unhappily penned and with so little variation of language that but for the alteration of Ireland for England and some great persons of this kingdom in the places of some named by you, your clerk would hardly know it from one of your own declarations.[144]

Within the churches too, confessional language became increasingly impor-tant as the seventeenth century developed. Within the mainstream churches, catechisms achieved this end but in other religious groups, such as the Quakers, other forms of print were used to maintain religious cohesion and validate their position. For example the Quaker sufferings, recording the persecutions of the group, became increasingly structured and available in print to record their own beliefs and to demonstrate to that social and religious group the validity of their position against others.[145] Through the shaping of such political and confessional micro-societies, or textual communities, print was potentially an important force in creating the political and religious cultures of early modern Ireland.

Government and the churches may have had some success in creating a language which provided commonalities in that world. All talked of courts and the law, God and the supernatural. However there were competing interpre-tations, or readings, of some of the central texts in this discussion. The very public nature of the differences between groups aired in print perhaps tends to overstate their importance in daily life but they were significant at the level of the commonwealth or confession. For this reason the central government and church tried to restrict access to the press by what it regarded as sub-versive groups or to use it against them. Attempts to close off the Dublin presses to such groups led only to illegal printing and, more particularly, smuggling. Moreover, the power of print was not an irresistible force. The authority of print could be undermined by setting it in a ritual context which inverted or discredited the meaning which the printed words were meant to convey. The meaning of print was thus not as straightforward as institutions wished it was and usually had to be negotiated between the government or church as producer and the subject, or adherent, as consumer. The inter-actions thus promoted meant that print was a major force in reshaping the social worlds of early modern Ireland.

NOTES

1 For a broad overview of the process see Charles Tilley (ed.), *The formation of national states in western Europe* (Princeton, 1975).

2 Nicholas Canny (ed.), 'Rowland White's "The dysorders of the Irishery"' in *Studia Hibernica* no. 19 (1979), p. 155.

3 Philomena Connolly (ed.), *Statute rolls of the Irish parliament, Richard III–Henry VIII* (Dublin, 2002), p. 237.

4 B.L., Harley MS 3298, f. 30.

5 Raymond Gillespie, *Colonial Ulster: the settlement of east Ulster, 1600–41* (Cork, 1985), pp. 85–94, 206–12.

6 Sheffield City Library, Wentworth Woodhouse papers, Strafford letter book viii, no. 11.

7 Raymond Gillespie, 'Landed society and the interregnum in Ireland and Scotland' in Rosalind Mitchison and Peter Roebuck (eds), *Economy and society in Scotland and Ireland, 1500–1939* (Edinburgh, 1988), pp. 38–47.

8 Sean Connolly, *Religion, law and power: the making of Protestant Ireland, 1660–1760* (Oxford, 1992), pp. 198–217.

9 J.T. and R. Gilbert (eds), *Calendar of the ancient records of Dublin* (19 vols, Dublin, 1889–1944), iv, p. 542.

10 D.B. Quinn, 'Government printing and the publication of the Irish statutes in the sixteenth century' in *Proceedings of the Royal Irish Academy* xlix sect. C (1941), pp. 45–129.

11 For example, *Journals of the House of Commons of the kingdom of Ireland* (19 vols, Dublin, 1796–1800), i, p. 47.

12 John Merrick, *A brief abstract of all the English statutes which are now in force within the realm of Ireland* (Dublin, 1625).

13 Robert Barnwall, *Syntomotaxia del second part de roy Henrie le sixt* (London, 1601) bound as an appendix to *Les reports de les cases conteinus in le and vint primer et apres in temps del roy Henry le siz* (London, 1610).

14 Quinn, 'Government printing', pp. 60–1; Richard Bolton, *A justice of the peace for Ireland* (Dublin, 1638).

15 Listed among the items available from William Winter, stationer, in Michael [Boyle], *Rules and orders to be used and observed in the high court of Chancery in Ireland* (Dublin, 1685), sig. A3.

16 T.C.D., MS 1181, f. 97.

17　Kilkenny Corporation Archive, CRO/3, Liber Albus, f. 56.

18　G.J. Hand and V.W. Treadwell, 'His majesty's directions for ordering and settling the courts within his kingdom of Ireland, 1622' in *Analecta Hibernica* no. 26 (1970), pp. 177–212; *Rules and orders to be observed in the proceedings of causes in the high court of Chancery* (Dublin 1659), [Boyle], *Rules and orders*.

19　*The Newsletter*, no. 85, 9 Feb. 1686. Advertisements for the same work also appeared in no. 67, 20 Dec. 1685; no. 68, 29 Dec. 1685; no. 76, 16 Jan. 1686; no. 92, 25 Feb. 1686.

20　L.M. Oliver, 'A bookseller's account book, 1545' in *Harvard Library Bulletin* xvi (1968), p. 150.

21　Gilbert and Gilbert (eds), *Calendar of the ancient records*, v, pp. 192, 227, 258, 330, 444, 489; vi, pp. 126, 176, 227.

22　Dublin City Archives, MR/35, pp. 206, 662. The range of instruments is clear from the bookseller's stock list of William Winter printed in [Boyle], *Rules and orders*, sigs A3–3v.

23　*Instructions for the collection of customs and imported excise in the kingdom of Ireland* (Dublin, 1677); *Instructions for the collection of inland excise with directions how to keep their books and make up their abstracts* (Dublin, 1677); *Instructions for gaugers of excise with the form of their pocket book and vouchers* (Dublin, 1677).

24　P.R.O., CUST 1/3, 9 Sept. 1696, 19 Nov. 1696, 29 Dec. 1696, 21 Mar. 1697; Mary Pollard, *A dictionary of members of the Dublin book trade, 1550–1800* (London, 2000), pp. 566–7.

25　Appendix, table 2.

26　William Sessions, 'Edward Jones: the travelling printer with William III in 1690' in William Sessions, *Further Irish studies in early printing history* (York, 1994), pp. 24–52.

27　*Journals of the House of Lords [of Ireland]* (8 vols, Dublin, 1779–1800), i, p. 111 .

28　*Commons jn.* i, pp. 146, 198, 219, 242, 293–4.

29　For examples Sessions, *The first printers in Waterford, Cork and Kilkenny pre-1700* (York, 1990), pp. 218–54.

30　H.M.C., *Report on the Franciscan manuscripts* (London, 1906), p. 134.

31　Micheál Ó Siochrú, *Confederate Ireland, 1642–1649: a constitutional and political analysis* (Dublin, 1999), pp. 183–4.

32　*Commons jn.* i, pp. 387, 394, 399, 406, 687, 695, 737; ii, pp. 13, 24, 45, 243.

33　*Commons jn.* i, pp. 389, 393, 647; *Lords jn.* i, pp. 272, 236, 302, 377.

34　*Commons jn.* i, p. 638. Dancer, perhaps unwisely, had advertised the fact that he was going to produce the speech within two days in his newsheet *Mercurius Hibernicus* no. 5, 15–17 Feb. 1663.

35　*Commons jn.* i, pp. 536, 538.

36　*Commons jn.* ii, p. 116.

37　Raymond Gillespie, 'The circulation of print in seventeenth-century Ireland' in *Studia Hibernica* no. 29 (1995–97), pp. 46–7; Northampton County Record Office, Northampton, Fitzwilliam of Milton MSS, Irish no. 68, f. 133; R.R. Steele (ed.), *Tudor and Stuart proclamations* (2 vols, Oxford, 1910), ii, Ireland nos 603, 644, 646, 646a; Gilbert and Gilbert (eds), *Calendar of the ancient records*, vi, p. 126.

38 John Bradley (ed.), *Treasures of Kilkenny: charters and civic records of Kilkenny city* (Kilkenny, 2003), pp. 114–15.

39 Steele, *Tudor and stuart proclamations*, ii, Ireland no. 425; Nicholas Bernard, *The whole proceedings of the seige of Drogheda in Ireland* (London, 1642), p. 60; T.C.D., MS 817, f. 235v.

40 Bodl., Carte MS 144, f. 26v.

41 Steele, *Tudor and Stuart proclamations*, ii, Ireland nos 552, 627, 634; B.L. Add MS 25287, ff 15, 19.

42 Richard Caulfield (ed.), *The council book of the corporation of Youghal* (Guilford, 1878), pp. 46–7, 55–6, 70–1, 75–6, 79–81, 82–3, 97, 103–4, 107–8, 109–117 for example; B.L. Harley MS 697, ff 106–6v, 171–99; Richard Caulfield (ed.), *The council book of the corporation of Cork* (Guilford, 1876), p. 251.

43 R.C.B., P804/1/1, pp. 199–201, 201–2, 209–11.

44 N.L.I., MS 1793.

45 N.L.I., MS 16085, p. 140.

46 Friends Historical Library, Dublin, MMIV A1 8c, f. 29.

47 For this process see Raymond Gillespie, 'Negotiating order in early seventeenth-century Ireland' in M.J. Braddick and John Walter (eds), *Negotiating power in early modern society* (Cambridge, 2001), pp. 199–205.

48 P.R.O., SP63/234/36. For the English context of the publication see W.W. Greg, *A companion to Arber* (Oxford, 1967), pp. 157–61.

49 William King, *The state of the Protestants of Ireland* (Dublin, 1744), pp. 251–2, appendix pp. 121–2, *An account of the present miserable state of the affairs of Ireland* (London, 1689).

50 Raymond Gillespie, 'Political ideas and their social contexts in seventeenth-century Ireland' in Jane Ohlmeyer (ed.), *Political thought in seventeenth-century Ireland* (Cambridge, 2000), pp. 123–7.

51 For examples, *Upon the arrival of his excellency Henry, earl of Clarendon and his entering upon the government of Ireland* (Dublin, 1686); John Wilson, *To his excellency, Richard earl of Arran ... lord deputy of Ireland: a poem* (Dublin 1684) printed with a contemporary manuscript reply in James Maidment and W.H. Logan (eds), *The dramatic works of John Wilson* (Edinburgh, 1874), pp. xii–xiv.

52 William Mercer, *A welcome in a poem to his excellency John Lord Robartes* (Dublin, 1669).

53 Bodl., Carte MS 40, ff 98, 106; Roger L'Estrange, *Considerations upon a printed sheet entitled the speech of the late Lord Russell to the sheriffs together with the paper delivered by him to them at the place of his execution on July 21 1683* (London, 1683).

54 Bodl., Carte MS 23, f. 291.

55 H.M.C., *Report on the manuscripts of the marquess of Ormonde* (new series, 8 vols, London, 1902–20), v, p. 224.

56 Peter Manby, *The considerations which obliged ... to embrace the Catholic religion* (Dublin, 1687).

57 William King, *An answer to the considerations which obliged Peter Manby ...* (Dublin, 1687). A shorter version of the work seems to have existed and was sent to the archbishop of Armagh, H.M.C., *Report on the Laing manuscripts* (2 vols, London, 1914–25), i, p. 451.

58 B.L., Add MS 4312, f. 21; T.C.D., MS 1121, p. 68, which adds that it was 'dispersed among the common people'; [Joseph Boyse], *Some impartial reflections on D[r] Manby's considerations etc.* (Dublin, 1687), p. 66.

59 H.M.C., *Ormonde*, n.s., viii, p. 350.

60 H.M.C., *Ormond*, n.s., viii, p. 349.

61 Bodl., Carte MS 49, ff. 127–9.

62 *Mercurius Hibernicus* no. 8, 3–10 Mar 1663.

63 Sheridan's tract is reprinted in Saxe Bannister, *Some revelations in Irish history* (London, 1870), p. 102. For Sheridan's background see John Miller, 'Thomas Sheridan (1646–1712) and his "Narrative"' in *Irish Historical Studies* xx (1976–77), pp. 105–28.

64 Christopher Sibthorpe, *A reply to an answer which a popish adversary made in two chapters contained in the first part of that book which is entitled A friendly advertisement* (Dublin, 1625), sig. C3, p. 115; Christopher Sibthorpe, *A surreplication to the rejoinder of a popish adversary* (Dublin, 1627), pp. 8–9.

65 Faithful Teate, *The soldier's commission, charge and reward* (London, 1658), sig. A2, A3v.

66 *Lords jn.* i, p. 272.

67 Mary Pollard, 'Control of the press in Ireland through the king's printer's patent, 1600–1800' in *Irish Booklore* iv (1980), pp. 79–95.

68 The full text is in Pollard, 'The control of the press', pp. 79–95, to which much of what follows is indebted.

69 Pollard. 'Control of the press', pp. 85–6.

70 Pollard, 'Control of the press', pp. 86–9.

71 Edmund Campion, *Two bokes of the histories of Ireland*, ed. A.F. Vossen (Assen, 1963), p. [142].

72 P.R.O., SP63/35/11 no.1.

73 Ciarán Brady (ed.), *A viceroy's vindication?: Sir Henry Sidney's memoir of service in Ireland, 1556–78* (Cork, 2002), pp. 64–5, 67; *Cal. S. P. Ire., 1599–1600*, p. 253.

74 Nicholas Bernard, *The penitent death of a woeful sinner* (Dublin 1641), sig. A2v.

75 Claudius Gilbert, *The libertine schooled* (London, 1657), p. 56; *A journal of the life, travels, sufferings of William Edmundson* (Dublin, 1820), pp. 55, 82.

76 Bodl., Carte MS 45, f. 117; *Cal. S. P. dom., May 1684–Feb. 1685*, pp. 258, 259, 261; H.M.C., *Ormonde*, n.s., vii, pp. 293–4.

77 *An account of the public affairs in Ireland since the discovery of the late plot* (London, 1679), p. 8; H.M.C., *Ormonde*, n.s., iv, pp. 361–4.

78 Edward MacLysaght (ed.), 'Report on documents relating to the wardenship of Galway' in *Analecta Hibernica* no. 14 (1944), p. 24.

79 Sheffield City Library, Wentworth Woodhouse MSS, Strafford Letter books, vii, f. 55; Bodl., Carte MS 143, f. 52.

80 H.M.C., *Report on the manuscripts of R.R. Hastings* (4 vols, 1928–47), iv, pp. 117, 124–5.

81 Brendan Jennings (ed.), *Wadding papers, 1614–38* (Dublin, 1953), p. 456.

82 Hugh Shields, *Narrative singing in Ireland* (Dublin, 1993), pp. 43–4.

83 *Cal. S. P. Ire.*, 1669–70, pp. 279, 286; Seamus Ó Caiside, 'Cork printing in the seventeenth century' in *Irish Book Lover* xxi (1933), p. 90.

84 Shields, *Narrative singing*, p. 43; George Benn, *A history of the town of Belfast* (Belfast, 1877), pp. 316–17.

85 Shields, *Narrative singing*, p. 43.

86 H.M.C., *Ormonde*, n.s., viii, p. 345.

87 John Huddleston's claims are in John Huddleston's *A short and plain way to the faith and church* (Dublin, 1688). That this was a quasi-official publication may be deduced from the fact that its publisher, William Weston, described himself on the title page as printer and stationer to the lord deputy.

88 Neal Carolan, *Motives of a conversion to the Catholic faith* (Dublin, 1688).

89 Bodl., Carte MS 45, ff. 431, 433–3v.

90 William Stockdale, *The great cry of oppression* ([Dublin], 1683), sig. A4; Richard Greaves, *God's other children: Protestant nonconformists and the emergence of denominational churches in Ireland* (Stanford, 1997), pp. 300–7.

91 *Lord Chief Justice Scroggs, his speech in the King's bench the first day of this present Michaelmas term* (Dublin, 1679).

92 *Cal. S. P. dom.*, 1680–1, p. 281; Gilbert and Gilbert (eds), *Calendar of the ancient records*, v, pp. 216–17; *An act of the lord mayor, sheriffs, commons and citizens of the city of Dublin, 14 May 1681* (Dublin, 1681).

93 Bodl., Carte MS 33, f. 663.

94 *Cal. S. P. dom*, 1601–3, p. 146; *Cal. S. P. Ire.*, 1574–85; *Cal. S. P. Ire.*, 1608–10, p. 192; Sibthorpe, *A reply*, sig. C3; Gillespie, 'Circulation of print', pp. 47–9.

95 T.C.D., MS 809, f. 1.

96 For example J.P. Conlan, 'Some notes on the "Disputatio apologatica"' in *Publications of the Bibliographical Society of Ireland* vi (1955), pp. 69–77.

97 Bodl., Carte MS 60, f. 612; *Cal. S. P. Ire.*, 1663–5, pp. 151–2.

98 H.M.C., *Ormonde*, n.s., vii, pp. 398, 399.

99 Mary Pollard, *Dublin's trade in books, 1550–1800* (Oxford, 1989), p. 18; Gilbert and Gilbert (eds) *Calendar of the ancient records*, v, pp. 137–8. For imports see P.R.O., E190/1342/10, ff. 29v, 37v; E190/1343/3, ff. 28v, 40, 48; E190/1344/6, f. 28; E190/1345/16, f. 36.

100 T.C.D., MS 2160/21a, 23.

101 Gillespie, 'Circulation of print', pp. 48, 49–50.

102 Pollard, *Dictionary*, pp. 84, 157.

103 For Strettle's imports see P.R.O., E190/1360/1, June (two shipments); E190/1357/4, June, Dec.; E190/1353/9, Feb., July, Oct., Nov.

104 Bodl., Carte MS 60, f. 707.

105 Printed in H.F Hore, *History of the town and county of Wexford* (6 vols, London, 1900–11), vi, p. 317.

106 T.C.D., MS 2467, ff. 7v, 9.

107 T.C.D., MS 2467, f. 14v.

108 *The church catechism explained and proved by apt texts of scripture* (Dublin, 1699).

109 [Luke Wadding], *A small garland of pious and godly songs* (Ghent, 1684), p. 51.

110 Joseph Eyres, *The church sleeper awakened* (London, 1659), pp. 48–9, 52, Robert Craghead, *An answer to a late book entitled a discourse concerning the inventions of men in the worship of God* (Edinburgh, 1694),, pp. 98, 145.

111 Edward Wetenhall, *Collyrium: a sense of the destructive ignorance and saving knowledge preached in Christ Church, Dublin, August 4 1672* (London, 1672), pp. 17–18.

112 Cainneach Ó Maonaigh (ed.), *Seanmónta chúige Uladh* (Dublin, 1965), pp. 39–40; Cuthbert Mhag Craith (ed.), *Dán na mBráthar Mionúir* (2 vols, Dublin, 1967–80), i, pp. 45–7.

113 Union Theological College, Belfast, Robert Chambers, MS 'Explanation of the shorter catechism', sigs C1v, A4.

114 P.R.O.N.I., D1759/1A/1, pp. 1, 32, 123, 131, 141, 156.

115 N. A., M2817, pp. 41, 42.

116 Joseph Boyse, *Remarks on a late discourse of William, lord bishop of Derry* (Dublin, 1694), p. 85; Thomas Hall, *A plain and easy explication of the assembly's shorter catechism* (Edinburgh, 1692), sig. A2v.

117 Presbyterian Historical Society, Belfast, Larne session book, 1701.

118 Boyse, *Remarks*, p. 86.

119 *An agreement and resolutions of the ministers of Christ associated with the city of Dublin and the province of Leinster* (Dublin, 1659), p. 6.

120 Ian Green, '"The necessary knowledge of the precepts of religion": catechisms and catechising in Ireland, 1560–1800' in Alan Ford, James McGuire and Kenneth Milne (eds), *As by law established: the Church of Ireland since the reformation* (Dublin, 1995), pp. 85–6.

121 Presbyterian Historical Society, Belfast, Diary of John Cook, 1698.

122 Union Theological College, Belfast, Robert Chambers, MS 'Explanation of the Shorter Catechism' sig. B2.

123 Hall, *A plain and easy explication*, sig. A2v. The same is true of Thomas Lye, *A plain and familiar method of instructing the younger sort* (Dublin, 1683): p. 6 explains the rationale for the typography, the most important words being those in bold print.

124 Bodl., Carte MS 8, f. 478; Carte MS 10, f. 336.

125 Scottish Record Office, E72/10/3(1), 7, E72/19/2, 6, 19, 22; Gillespie, 'The circulation of print', pp. 43–4.

126 Bodl., Carte MS 45, f. 554

127 T.C.D., MS 750/5/171–2.

128 Bodl., Carte MS 32, ff. 216–16v, 276.

129 Roger Boyle, earl of Orrery, *The Irish colours displayed* ([London, 1662]), p. 16.

130 P.R.O.N.I., Mic1/5; Robert Craghead, *An answer to a late book entitled a discourse concerning the inventions of men in the worship of God* (Edinburgh, 1694), p. 88.

131 Gillespie, *Devoted people*, pp. 153–8.

132 C.E. Elrington and J.H. Todd (eds), *The whole works of the most reverend James Ussher* (17 vols, Dublin, 1847–64), xv, p. 438.

133 *Cal. S. P. Ire., 1603–6*, p. 33.

134 T.C.D., MS 1178, ff. 18–20.

135 J.T. Gilbert (ed.), *History of the Irish confederation and the war in Ireland* (7 vols, Dublin, 1882–91), vi, p. 18.

136 *Ireland's lamentation: being a short but perfect, full and true account of the situation, natural constitution and produce of Ireland* (London, 1689), p. 12. For another 'libel' nailed to the door of the cathedral in the 1680s see Andrew Clark (ed.), *The life and times of Anthony Wood, antiquary of Oxford, 1632–95* (4 vols, Oxford, 1891–95), iii, p. 255.

137 Bodl., Carte MS 45, f. 117.

138 W.M. Brady (ed.), *State papers concerning the Irish church in the time of Queen Elizabeth* (London, 1868), p. 23.

139 Brady (ed.), *State papers*, p. 118.

140 T.C.D., MS 817, f. 236; H.M.C., *Ormonde*, n.s. iv, pp. 220, 479.

141 T.C.D., MS 1178, f. 20; H.M.C., *Report on the manuscripts of the late R.R. Hastings* (4 vols, London, 1928–47), ii, p. 395.

142 Joseph Boyse, *A vindication of the remarks of the bishop of Derry's discourse* (Dublin, 1695), p. 2; William King, *An admonition to the dissenting inhabitants of the diocese of Derry* (Dublin, 1694), pp. 5–6.

143 This is argued in Gillespie, *Devoted people*, passim.

144 *A letter from a Protestant in Ireland to a member of the House of Commons of England* (n.p., 1643), p. 5.

145 Greaves, *God's other children*, pp. 358–64.

Chapter 6

Reading for salvation

The religious impulse in early modern Ireland generated a wide range of responses. For some, religious affiliation was simply a matter of custom, the result of the circumstances of birth or cultural background. For others it was a political statement. Allegiance to the established church, nonconformist churches or Catholicism all had implications for one's political loyalties. For yet others it was the result of genuine religious experience which brought deeply felt convictions about the reality of sin and the need for repentance, conversion and salvation.[1] Whatever perspective lay contemporaries took on the role of religion, they began with the idea that God existed and was at work in the world. How they gave meaning to that conviction was shaped by their own experiences of the world and their cultural backgrounds, including their reading.[2] There were various tools for forging religious belief. In some cases the formularies of the institutional churches satisfied, although clergy were often needed to explain them, but in other cases the process was a more complex one.

The world of print had an important role in shaping, and being shaped by, spiritual movements. Within the Catholic tradition mass and a range of sacramentals helped individuals to put form on their religious impulses. Godly books, particularly within the spiritual tradition encouraged by the Tridentine movement, were not ignored but were seen only as part of that wider process. Protestants laid the stress rather differently, emphasising the central role of books in achieving salvation, and especially the importance of the Bible, which formed the standard by which all things were judged. As the Protestant polemicist Barnaby Rich told his fellow Irish Protestants, 'when thou hearest tell of a vision or miracles ... bring them to the touchstone and compare them with the word of God'.[3] Protestants paid particular attention to the various ways of reading the text and of understanding it aright. As a result their religious language was heavily influenced by that of the biblical text.[4]

Sermons, catechisms and other godly books provided doctrinal frames within which the biblical text was to be understood.

For contemporaries, to read for salvation was not necessarily to approach works of religion uncritically or with the same view that clergy held. Rather they used books and printed religious ephemera as tools to understand, and in some cases harness, the power of God at work in the world. Most importantly the Bible provided all religious groups with a diverse range of ways of viewing the world, depending on how one read the text. Such readings could be highly subjective and individualistic. Some, it was claimed by one bishop, read the Bible only as a set of fabulous stories, while another suggested that some of his adherents did not read the Bible since it 'possesseth them with strange fears and fills them with incredible terrors'.[5] The Bible alone did not contain unambiguous answers on all points of salvation and so various denominations provided their own works setting out approved modes of, and frameworks for, reading. Salvation, for many Protestants and some Catholics, became tightly tied with spiritual models presented by the printed word, whether read or heard.

I

Of all the books with which early modern Irishmen and women came into contact, the most widespread and potentially the most important for all confessional groups was the Bible. There were a number of forms in which contemporaries might be exposed to the text. For those learning to read for the first time the Bible was often the first book they encountered. The Dublin printer Thomas Gent described how, when he was young, his mother 'Made me read, betimes each sacred page' and Jonathan Swift claimed that by the age of four he 'had learnt to spell and by that time ... could read any chapter in the Bible'.[6] Quakers, too, taught their children to read the Bible according to one Waterford testimony of the 1690s.[7] At a more elementary level the basic readers, hornbooks and primers, that flooded into southern Ireland from that late sixteenth century were constructed around a mastery of biblical verses and short texts.[8] Later in the seventeenth century reprints of English schoolbooks also brought children into contact with selected psalms and the ten commandments.[9]

Once reading had been mastered there was little difficulty in purchasing a Bible. In the 1620s a full Bible could be had for 8s in Dublin and a New Testament for 3s. Such prices were high by English standards, and in the 1690s William King, bishop of Derry, observed that many families in his diocese had problems in obtaining a Bible despite its availability in print. There were further complaints in early eighteenth-century Ireland about the cost. Cheaper versions, however, were also in circulation. In 1614 four Bibles and four psalters imported into Derry were valued at 15s and in the late seventeenth century the Catholic Bishop Luke Wadding of Ferns could purchase Bibles for between 5s and 6s and a New Testament for 1s.[10]

The market was not the only mechanism for the supply of Bibles. They were a common and fashionable gift, and the earl of Kildare certainly felt it was an appropriate present for his father-in-law, the earl of Cork, in 1633. By the end of the century this custom was recognised with the Belfast printing of John Taylor's *Verbum sempiternum: the Bible the best new year's gift.*[11] This sort of giving extended beyond fashionable society, and some Protestant clergy gave Bibles to those who were too poor to buy their own.[12] Such gift-giving extended beyond the grave as contemporaries specifically identified Bibles in their wills to be left to appropriate persons. The Catholic lawyer Richard Hadsor left his Bible to William Clarke, while in Clonmel one man left his son 10s to buy a Bible.[13] Through the market and gift giving the Bible became a commonly available work in seventeenth-century Ireland which was well known to many. As Katherine Perceval from County Cork wrote to her brother, when she began to learn Latin in 1680, she wanted a Latin copy of a text she knew well and asked for the Book of Common Prayer and the New Testament.[14]

The distribution of the Bible was not even across society. As a very broad generalisation Catholics were less likely than Protestants to own Bibles. However, there were many exceptions, and Catholics of the upper social ranks were quite likely to own the text of scripture, but usually a Vulgate for which a knowledge of Latin was required. Although the English Douai–Rheims translation existed in Ireland, according to the Dublin priest Cornelius Nary at the end of the seventeenth century copies were 'so scarce and dear that the generality of the people neither have nor can procure them for their private use'.[15] The Catholic landowner of the Upper Ards, Henry Savage, was described as 'loyal and moderate in his Romish religion and read the Holy Scriptures'.[16] By the early eighteenth century it was certainly claimed by Catholic bishops that the demand for Bibles in Ireland among Catholics was insatiable.[17] Within the native Irish tradition there also seems to have been a good knowledge of the biblical text at the upper social levels, and poets complained of those who read 'foolish senses' into Scripture or 'pulled it to pieces.[18] While there was no translation of the Catholic text of scripture into Irish in the early modern period, two Protestant scholars William Daniel, archbishop of Tuam, and William Bedell, bishop of Kilmore, did complete a translation into Irish. The New Testament part of the translation was in print by 1608 but Bedell's translation of the Old Testament had to wait until the 1680s before it appeared in print. There is a strong possibility that these translations were used by Catholics as well as some Protestants.[19]

For most contemporaries, the Bible was not simply a volume to be owned but a book that was meant to be read. When George Wilde, bishop of Derry, bequeathed Bibles of the 'largest octavo' bound with the Book of Common Prayer to his grandchildren in 1665, it was 'for them to use not to look upon'.[20] This emphasis on reading the book came from an understanding of the Bible as the revealed word of God which had an application to everyday life as well as the world beyond. Katherine Boyle, the daughter of the earl of Cork, owned a Bible in which the English poet and divine Thomas Pestel had written verses which argued that the Bible was the best revelation of God:

> All books in one, all learning lies
> This is your first ABC, the best primer is
> Whence having thoroughly learnt the [chris]tcross row
> You may with comfort to out Father go
> Who will to you that higher lesson bring
> Which seraphims instruct his saints to sing.[21]

At a lower social level the notebook of a Limerick gentleman, Edmund Sexton, carried a similar message:

> Two truths there is the scripture saith
> Two testaments, the old and new
> We must acknowledge them to be true.[22]

Before the end of the seventeenth century few would quibble with that view.

Despite all this, the Bible was a deeply ambiguous text which had to be read carefully and in many different ways. One Munster settler of the early seventeenth century, Robert Marshall, suggested that the Bible had to be read in at least three ways: literally, figurally (which required the drawing of a series of universal types from the biblical text which had universal applications) and consignually (which allowed for the symbolic content of the text and the interpretation of difficult and contentious phrases such as 'this is my Body').[23] These three types of reading are all present in the notes made by the Killileagh Presbyterian merchant James Trail at the beginning of the eighteenth century.[24] Literally, he made notes of what the text actually said and tried to place it in its historical context. Thus he commented that 'the book of Genesis which was writ by Moses contains the history of the world to the death of Joseph and comprehends the space above 2,400 years'. Figuratively, he saw in I Peter 'superstition is figuratively styled Babylon here and in Rev[elation] 17.18'. His reading of Isaiah as one who 'spoke most clearly of the coming of Jesus Christ, of His suffering, of His Kingdom and of the calling of the gentiles' reveals his view of Old Testament figures as types of the New Testament revelation. Chapters nine and ten of the book of Hebrews he saw as consignual or symbolic of the nature of legal ceremonies and the sufficiency of Christ's sacrifice.

This rather sophisticated variety of ways of reading the Bible, all of which might be in play simultaneously, points to the complexity of reading the Bible. On the basis of a literal reading the reader might understand the Bible as a chronological narrative. In the early seventeenth century the Irish judge Sir Charles Calthorpe filled his commonplace book with genealogies constructed from the Old Testament on the basis of reading the Bible as narrative. Some in the late seventeenth century, such as James Bonnell, the comptroller general, and an anonymous Irish poet in the early eighteenth century might try to splice together the gospels to produce one narrative from many.[25] This sort of reading of the Bible as narrative was particularly important where the text was transmitted orally, which was a feature of Catholic access to the Bible. Catholics were dissuaded from a verse-by-verse examination of the text but were urged to concentrate primarily on the meaning of the narrative. Such an approach did not require a written or printed text. In 1642 Friar Malone on discovering a number of Bibles at Skerries in County Dublin had them burnt explaining that 'it was fitting for every man to have the Bible by rote and not to misinstruct them which should have it by rote'.[26] Indeed the primer composed in the 1680s by the Cavan priest Thomas Fitzsimons suggests that where parts of the biblical text were destined for lay hands they were printed as a narrative without verse divisions.[27] Many Catholic laymen seem to have read the Bible in this way. When the Meath Catholic John Cusack composed his commentary on the government of Ireland in 1629 he sprinkled it liberally with his own translation of passages from the Vulgate giving chapter numbers but not verses, and when the Limerick doctor Thomas Arthur quoted Job 8.8 at the beginning of his fee-book he did not provide a verse reference.[28] For Irish Catholics the important division in reading the Bible was the chapter or narrative section rather than the verse.

By contrast, Protestant readers of the Bible were more orientated to the printed text, read the detail of the narrative more closely, and took advantages of the various divisions into which the story was broken down, especially the verses. As William Sheridan, the Church of Ireland bishop of Kilmore, stressed in 1685, 'every distinct sentence of holy scripture does command and require our belief as much as the whole or any part of it'.[29] One of the obituary poems composed on the death of Katherine Boyle, Lady Cork, in 1630 by Daniel Spicer of Trinity College, Dublin, claimed:

> That I heard a revered man profess
> If of the Bible you could but express
> A sentence as't was writ (such was her skill)
> She could denote the chapter and verse.[30]

Others, such as the late sixteenth-century divines Luke Challoner and Ambrose Ussher, made detailed verse-by-verse summaries of parts of books of the Bible as a finding aid for verses.[31]

Such close reading of the biblical text sometimes confused as much as it enlightened. The meaning, and relevance, of many texts was not immediately obvious to readers, and the Bible often had to be read in conjunction with other works before it could be understood as a meaningful narrative. Sometimes that explanatory context was supplied by the text itself. One Dublin Presbyterian minister urged his catechumens to 'be very diligent in comparing one text with another'. In the case of ministers their access to biblical concordances brought verses on similar subjects together.[32] The sort of notes printed as part of the sixteenth-century Geneva Bible, still in use in Ireland until the late seventeenth century, or in the Catholic Douai–Rheims translation into English may also have helped some individuals to interpret the text appropriately. Some, such as the late seventeenth-century Dublin doctor Duncan Cummings, read his Bible daily with the aid of a commentary, while others, such as Christopher Sexton of Limerick, had biblical commentaries in their libraries.[33] Biblical commentaries were also available in more popular forms. At least one broadsheet was circulating in Dublin in 1624 which was ruled into five columns each of which had theological headings such as 'the certainty of our faith and salvation' and 'against merits and righteousness' with corresponding proof texts which could be verified in a Bible and their meaning made clear.[34]

While commentaries were certainly important, the more common way of contextualising disparate verses of scripture was to adopt a figurative reading of the text and treat it as a series of types which could be related to the reader's personal experience. Some saw in the life of the nation parallels with the biblical narrative. In 1587, for instance, Andrew Trollop saw parallels between the sins described in Ezekiel 16 and those of contemporary Ireland; and in 1633 the Cork settler Vincent Gookin saw yet further parallels between his world and that of Isaiah 5 and 6. Again in the 1680s the godly comptroller general, James Bonnell, meditated on the image of the beast of Revelation, seeing an immediate parallel with the Jacobite regime.[35] From a Catholic perspective too this was possible though it was done using narratives rather than specific verses. The parallels between Ireland and the elect nation of Israel was commonplace in seventeenth-century Irish poetry, and in the 1640s events from the Old Testament would be imported into the contemporary Irish world.[36] Such types could be even simpler, and one Dublin man made notes of 'predictions of weather according to sacred scripture' paralleling climatic portents with scriptural verses.[37]

However the types sought were not usually so impersonal. The Bible was more often read for universal solutions to personal dilemmas, and many texts had personal associations. The pious Kilkenny Baptist Anne Fowke throughout her life latched on to individual scriptural verses, whether heard or read, as ways of finding solutions to problems as they presented themselves to her. Once a verse was read or heard, a concordance could be used to find other, linked, verses that might explicate its meaning.[38] The admittedly rather eccentric Walter Gostellow in Cork in the 1650s attempted to divine the meaning of his dreams by reading his Bible in this way. On 11 March 1655 he opened his Bible at the prophet Haggai, a part of the Bible with which he was unfamiliar, and read a chapter 'directed and over-ruled (as I then and now believe) by God almighty' which referred to the rebuilding of God's house. This, Gostellow believed, referred to the rebuilding of the church at Lismore, and he then badgered the earl of Cork until he agreed to rebuild the church. Dipping further into his text Gostellow encountered Psalms 84 and 85, which he believed had been brought to his attention by God 'who for my further confirmation gave me those psalms of scripture to strengthen me and dispose others to their duty'.[39] In a rather less exalted way one Dublin man, on seeing a great fish washed ashore at Dingle in 1673, concluded that it was one of the beasts depicted in the book of Revelation and wrote a detailed account of the biblical parallels of his experience.[40]

The reading of the Bible was therefore a pursuit in which readers actively engaged all their emotions and reason. Such readings could produce many and diverse results. In the 1630s Alice Wandesford, the twelve-year-old daughter of the Irish lord deputy, described how she read Luke 2.49 in which Jesus disputed with the doctors in the Temple. According to her account,

> In the reading of which passage ... I fell into a serious and deep meditation of the thoughts of Christ's majesty, divinity and wisdom, who was able to confound the learned doctors and confute their wisdom who were aged, he being so young himself but then twelve years of age. And then I considered my own folly and childish ignorance that I could scarce understand mean and low things without a great deal of teaching and instruction; and although I read the word of God, yet was of a weak capacity to know the way of salvation and therefore in my heart begged my dear Saviour to give me knowledge, wisdom and understanding to guide all my days.[41]

Other meditative readings produced less dramatic through still significant responses. Ann Southwell, the wife of the Cork planter, wrote a long verse meditation on the text of the commandments, expanding their meaning by drawing in verses from other places in the Bible.[42] Later in the seventeenth century Elizabeth Freke, who moved happily between England and the family's Irish estates, was clearly a Bible reader and owned a Bible, which had been her mother's, a testament and a psalter 'with [wood]cuts'. As she read she composed a number of 'emblems' or poems based on biblical texts. In these she selected a text and in some cases teased out its meaning by constructing a dialogue around that text. The dialogue was an attempt to explain the meaning of the text for her by using other verses of scripture, woven around the central verse, to develop the meaning of the text.[43] A more emotive reader was Elizabeth Chambers, a members of an Independent congregation in Dublin in the 1650s, who told that congregation how, after hearing a sermon by John

Rogers, 'with sighs and tears I took the Bible and looked for Christ there, and looked out and turned to the proofs that master Rogers mentioned and examined them'.[44] Yet another reader was curious. One judge on the 1627 assize circuit in County Down approached Robert Blair, the preacher at the assize, with questions about what he had said in his sermon. In response Blair noted, 'he opened his Bible and I mine. We considered all the points and proofs, turning to the places and reading them over.'[45] These various experiences are not mutually exclusive. Reading the Bible was a complex undertaking and required the blending of many strategies on a number of levels to make sense of the text. Reading in this context was not a simple exercise.

II

The Bible was certainly the most important book that Christians in early modern Ireland were likely to read but it did not exist in isolation. There were other works which supplemented and explained it. A web of books and advice was spun around the Bible which helped to shape particular ways of reading. In the early seventeenth century James Ussher, archbishop of Armagh, offered advice on how, when, and to what effect the Bible was to be read. He urged the laity to read church history, the Church Fathers and the history of the Jews, Greeks and Romans in order to understand the Bible story better.[46] Later in the century Jeremy Taylor, bishop of Down and Connor, likewise spun a web of works of Church of Ireland divinity around the Bible. Significantly he saw this list not as an end product but as a starting point, telling the two Dublin men to whom it was directed, 'in reading these authors I have recommended to you pray observe what quotations they have that thereby you may perceive what authors they made use of and especially read for 'tis likely that they are the best books. Many books are not useful.'[47] In this way distinctive patterns of reading, at an elite level at least, could be established. Within the Church of Ireland context, for example, the liturgical and private use of the Bible served to place it within a wider Protestant tradition in which the supremacy of the Bible was opposed to the corporate tradition of the Catholic church. However the experience that convinced many that they were not simply Protestants but members of the Church of Ireland, with links to the Church of England, was their encounter with another book, the Book of Common Prayer, which, together with a wide range of devotional works, was urged on the laity as a way of building shared reading experiences.

The text of the Book of Common Prayer was identical to that used in the Church of England and its history was similar.[48] The prayer book seems to have had a wide distribution in Ireland. The visitation returns of the 1630s suggest that most functioning churches had a copy. Again reports of its destruction by rebels in the 1640s in Waterford, Cavan, Kilkenny and

Westmeath indicates a wide distribution.[49] Unlike the Bible, which was a privileged book, the Irish press could produce editions of the Book of Common Prayer and they did so in 1551, 1621, 1637, 1665, 1666, 1668, 1680 and 1700. An Irish translation appeared in 1608 and this was still in use among Highland Scots in Ulster in the 1690s.[50] Since the text was identical to that of the English Book of Common Prayer, imports from England were an important way of supplementing local production, and according to Archbishop King in 1715 'our Prayer Books are generally printed in England'.[51] The size of Irish editions and the scale of English imports, however, can only be a matter for speculation. In the 1560s there are indications that there was a significant trade in books of Common Prayer between Ireland and England. In 1560 863 copies were sent to Ireland and by 1566 another six hundred had been consigned to Humphrey Powell, the queen's printer in Dublin.[52] Even in its Latin form the prayer book seems to have been accessible to many in the sixteenth century. One observer, Andrew Trollop, commented in the 1580s that many Catholic clergy forced to go to the established church 'carry with them a book in Latin of the Common Prayer' which they used as a prop for their sermons but whether or not it was read is unknown.[53]

As distribution mechanisms for print developed in the seventeenth century so the availability of the Book of Common Prayer improved. One indication of this is that early seventeenth-century churches, such as St John's in Dublin, repaired their copies of the Bible and Book of Common Prayer on a number of occasions whereas in the latter half of the century they simply bought new ones when the old copies wore out.[54] As with the Bible, economies of scale ensured that the volume could be made available cheaply. About 1620 the communion book, probably containing the weekly services, was available in Dublin in three formats, quarto, octavo and sextodecimo. Such formats lent themselves to portability and cheapness, prices ranging from 2s 4d to 5s.[55] Larger formats also existed in churches in a bewildering range of styles and costs. The cathedral church at Cloyne paid £1 2s 0d for two Common Prayer books in 1667 but the Dublin parish of St Michael could get two copies for 4s 6d in 1670. The more normal cost for a church copy of the Book of Common Prayer in the late seventeenth century lay between 6s and 10s depending on the edition and the quality of the binding.[56] While price trends are difficult to gauge on the basis of a small sample of prices, it does seem that, as with the Bible, real prices fell over the seventeenth century as books of Common Prayer became more readily available. As with the Bible the market was supplemented by the giving of gifts of the text and bequests through wills. Bishops, such as Dives Downes of Cork, dispensed copies of the Book at confirmations and parochial visitations.[57]

The distribution of copies of the Book of Common Prayer is a poor measure of its impact. As with the Bible the varied contexts within which it was used meant that it reached an audience much wider than simply the literate who could read the text. Those contexts of reading the text in different types of interpretative communities ranged from liturgical performance, accessible to both literate and illiterate, to personal devotional reading which provided the context for other readings. The widest context was the liturgical use of the Book of Common Prayer both on a Sunday basis and also for occasional services such as baptisms, marriages and funerals. Most members of the church witnessed these uses of the book regularly. Such hearing of a text read was clearly what the Dublin polemicist Barnaby Rich envisaged when he referred to the Irish translation of the Book of Common Prayer as 'that as well the lettered sort can read their own language as also the unlettered sort that can but understand what they hear others read'.[58]

These liturgical contexts were important since it was here that oral and textual worlds crossed and the meaning of the printed text was provided by the context of the performance of the text, which was carefully watched by at least some of the congregation. These were contexts which were highly sensitive and in which words were important. Thus Catholics objected to the use of the words of the Book of Common Prayer at the burial of James Barnwell's mother at Balrothery in 1608. They assaulted the minister reading the burial service and 'struck the Book of Common Prayer from his hand and trod it disdainfully under foot'.[59] A similar episode seems to have taken place at Kilmallock in 1685 when a Church of Ireland minister was assaulted by a young Catholic priest as he was reading the burial service.[60] As the dissenting community grew more confident in the late seventeenth century and entered into controversy with the Church of Ireland, the matters at stake were the rituals prescribed by the Book of Common Prayer rather than formal doctrinal positions. Thus at the public debate between the Presbyterians and Bishop Leslie at Belfast in 1636 the issues for discussion included kneeling at communion and the rituals of the Book of Common Prayer.[61] The same issues were to reappear, together with other matters enjoined by the Book of Common Prayer, in the debate between William King, bishop of Derry, and the Presbyterians in the 1690s.[62]

The importance of these contexts meant that those who witnessed the use of the Book of Common Prayer were alive to the sort of readings and editings which were employed by those who used it in these liturgical contexts. In Dublin Castle at the beginning of the seventeenth century, according to Sir John Harrington in his description of Ireland, 'interpretation' allowed the replacement of the reading of the text entirely, permitting the chaplain simply to pray extempore.[63] In other cases where words or phrases could cause difficulty new interpretations were offered. In 1638 it was alleged that one native Irish minister in County Cavan, Murtagh King, had used not the words of the Book of Common Prayer in his administration of Holy Communion but the phrase 'eat this according to our Saviour's meaning'.[64] A similar problem of belief lay behind the omission of part of the printed text by one clergyman in 1709.[65] In another case additions were made to the text in order to explicate its meaning more clearly. The Rev. Dr John Yarner, minister of St Bride's in Dublin, in the 1660s included in his notebook a series of supplementary prayers to be used in the office of the visitation of the sick.[66] In such ways the meaning of the Prayer Book text could be negotiated or in some cases subverted.

There were constraints on the extent to which the text could be modified. Where the wider community did not approve of the deviation from the printed text complaints could result. In one instance in 1634 a minister in Wicklow refused to bury his parishioners with the appropriate service, arguing that 'they [the dead] need not any such ceremony in their burial, that prayers were for the living not for the dead'. The consequence of this behaviour was that 'divers English Protestant have forborne their habitations within that parish saying they desire to live where they may be buried like men and not like dogs'.[67] After 1660 the practice of clergy deviating from the text of the Prayer Book was less tolerated by the church authorities. The spread of the ideas of the Caroline divines with their concern for liturgical exactitude required the full text of the Prayer Book to be adhered to.[68] Increasingly awareness of the importance of the text of the Book of Common Prayer was urged on members of the Church of Ireland. William Beveridge's 1681 English sermon *A sermon concerning the excellency and usefulness of the common prayer* was reprinted in Dublin in 1698 and again in 1700 and 1719. This guide to the Prayer Book, which provided a commentary on the service, explained the layout of churches and enjoined devout behaviour in church, probably received a wide distribution within Dublin at least. According to the Dublin printer

> his grace the archbishop of Dublin, having approved of the design, it's hoped he will be pleased to recommend to his clergy the buying of some dozens of them to be distributed among their poor parishioners so that they, as well as the rich, may not be without so useful a book in their families.[69]

Whether or not the scheme succeeded is not known, but given the subsequent reprints of the work it is likely that it had some measure of success, especially since the technique of passing out free samples of religious literature was well established in Dublin.

The second context within which the printed text of the Book of Common Prayer could be read was to hear it being used at family prayers led by the head of a household. Family prayers seem to have grown in popularity in the late seventeenth century as the Prayer Book became more widely used. Thomas Pollard's 1696 sermons on family prayers in St Peter's in Dublin certainly urged the practice and provided examples of families who engaged in the such devotion.[70] In the duke of Ormond's 1680s library list, one cluster of Common Prayer books may represent the location of the domestic chapel for such prayers.[71] Evidence of what occurred at these events has not survived so it is difficult to measure their impact. For some it may well have been a genuine engagement with the book while for others it may simply have been custom.

The third context within which the Book of Common Prayer might be understood was meditative reading by an individual, usually alone. Such an introspective engagement with the book leaves little trace in the surviving evidence. Only occasionally are glimpses of this activity possible, as in 1641 when a number of Galway rebels threatened to kill a Tuam merchant 'because he read a Prayer Book on the Sabbath day'.[72] There is, however, some indirect evidence for this sort of activity. The prayers composed by Jane Bingham, the wife of the landlord of Castlebar, in 1693–4, contain phrases from the Prayer Book, as do some of the prayers of the duke of Ormond composed in the late seventeenth century.[73] Again the meditations of Elizabeth Freke on the death of her brother in 1696 echoed the words of the burial service when she noted, 'it pleased God to take to himself my dear brother Austin'. Later, in 1709, she echoed the words of the Litany when noting 'from such friends and friendship, good Lord deliver us'.[74] Phrases such as this may well have been remembered from formal liturgical settings or from family prayers but it is also possible that they represent an attempt to individualise a text intended for corporate worship and personalise it, adapting the book to their own circumstances.

One further element in the individual appropriation of the Prayer Book may lie in the use of illustrations. The Dublin stationer William Winter advertised that he had for sale 'Common Prayers of all sizes, with or without [wood]cuts' and the duke of Ormond also had illustrated books of Common Prayer in his library.[75] Edward Wetenhall, bishop of Cork, complained of this practice of illustrating the prayer book, asking 'What is the meaning of filling people's common prayer books with pictures. Our church books have none. How came these into the hands of Protestants at their devotions?'[76] Such books were clearly for private devotional use. For Wetenhall, the practice of using such images in the context of prayer was popish but for at least some of the readers of the text images may have helped to give meaning to what they read.[77]

While the Book of Common Prayer and the Bible may have been the main books that early modern members of the Church of Ireland read for salvation, there was also for those who wanted to read them a wide range of sermons and other devotional books. From the 1590s Francis Seager's *School of virtue*, a small didactic work for children dealing with religion, morals and social behaviour, was available in the Munster port towns.[78] The lists of libraries of members of the Church of Ireland, such as the Limerick lawyer Christopher Sexton, contained a substantial proportion of godly books, about a third of his library in the case of Sexton.[79] Lady Anne Hamilton, in Dublin in the 1630s, had fourteen books, mostly religious, and all bestsellers of a godly variety. These including Lewis Bayly's *The practice of piety* (then in its thirty-sixth edition), Nicholas Byfield's *The marrow of the oracles of God* (in its tenth edition), John Hayward's *The strong helper* and Daniel Fealtey's *Ancillia pietatis or the handmaid to private devotion* (then in its sixth edition).[80] In Sexton's collection of books, Bibles and sermons are prominent, as are Lewis Bayly's *The practice of piety* and the late medieval work of Thomas à Kempis, the *Imitation of Christ*. Both works were popular with Church of Ireland readers throughout the seventeenth century, and the godly accomptant general James Bonnell was deeply affected by Bayly's work, which he read when young.[81] *The practice of piety* was particularly important in the early part of the seventeenth century. Its moralistic tone together with prayers for use on particular occasions ensured its popularity. In the latter half of the century Bayly's work was edged out by a more modern text, *The whole duty of man*, which explained to an individual his duty not only to God but to neighbours and superiors also, suggesting a rather different view of social organisation. In the 1670s Robert Perceval of Cork was forced to read the book as a way of amending his life, and Samuel Ladyman of Clonmel left his son 20s in his will to buy copies of Bayly's work and also *The whole duty of man*.[82] The book was clearly popular in Ireland and there was an attempt to pirate it there in 1663.[83] When it was finally published in Dublin in 1700 in an abridged form, it was attractively priced at 6d bound presumably to sell at the lower ends of the market.

Over the seventeenth century, religious works such as these were easily available, at least in eastern Ireland or near ports. Unlike personal items, such as Bibles and prayerbooks, they were likely to be lent and borrowed. As print became more common in the later seventeenth century, Irish bishops and other clergy began to use printed works as part of their pastoral mission by distributing cheap pious books to their flocks. In particular as the campaign for moral reformation speeded up in the 1690s print began to play a more significant part in godly living. Archbishop Marsh of Dublin had 2,500 copies of one of Archbishop Tillotson's sermons printed which he gave away within the diocese.[84] On visitation in Cork also in the 1690s Bishop Downes scattered a hundred copies of Ashton's *Devotions* and Tillotson's sermons as well as 'little books' and 'small prayer books'.[85] Pious laymen followed their example. James Bonnell, for example, according to his contemporary biographer 'was continually dispersing good books among young people, his clerks and poor families'.[86]

The influence of such godly books was probably less than that of the Bible and the Book of Common Prayer. Such pious books did not receive the sort of oral performance which the Bible and liturgies did. One exception to this generalisation may be found among the resolutions of Bishop Dopping of Meath, who on entering into his first living read a chapter of *The whole duty of man* to his congregation and urged them to buy the book for themselves.[87] At the other end of the social scale reading aloud too might be important. Steven Jerome, the chaplain to the earl of Cork in the 1630s, recorded of the children in the family under his care that 'no day being permitted wherein besides domestic prayer with the family and private in your chambers within the best sermons and theological tractates were not read by you or to you'.[88] The result was that the earl's children proved to be very pious in later life.

If access to godly books by the Church of Ireland laity was relatively easy, they needed to acquire particular skills to read those books in an approved manner. As one early seventeenth-century Irish judge, Sir Charles Calthorpe, noted in his commonplace book on the subject of 'reading godly books',

> by reading and hearing these godly books and exhortations God speaketh and talketh to us as by preaching and prophecy we speak and talk to God but this reading and hearing must be with sincerity, attended and abounded with godly grace, His spirit dressed our understanding with due regard to the matter which we hear or read.[89]

Later in the century Bishop Wetenhall of Cork also set out his expectations of the godly reader. According to Wetenhall one was to read with a heart 'so accommodated and disposed to these employments that the several parts of each office makes suitable impressions on him and naturally drew forth his soul towards God in acts of resignation, humility, faith, hope, joy, love and gratitude'.[90] The expectations which some had of this sort of godly meaning are suggested by the preface to a Dublin reissue of Francis de Sales's *Introduction to the devout life* written by the Anglican Henry Dodwell, who had also suitably Protestantised the text. His preface was intended to 'prepare the reader for the book' so that the reader would approach the task of reading this pious work not as he or she would approach the reading of other works, giving them only a cursory glance. This, according to Dodwell, would be unfruitful and 'endeavours of a practical persuasion and suitable affections' were required since readers were to be more concerned with the 'edification of their affections' than with 'informing their understanding'. Godly books needed to be read slowly and frequently so that the various meanings, moral and meta-physical, of the stories presented would be understood along with their literal meaning. The godly reader was to be an attentive reader rather than a casual one, deploying not only the intellect but the emotions also.[91]

In one case it is possible to see something of this process of godly reading at work. In the middle of the 1660s James Barry from Dublin, then a youth of fifteen, began to take religion seriously as a result of reading the Bible. Brought up in the Church of Ireland, he turned to books as a way of revealing God's will. He observed, 'I became very bookish, looking into almost every book where ever I came to try whether I cold meet with any help which might forward me in my new trade of religion'. Daily he retreated into seclusion to read and meditate on what he read. His stock of reading matter included most of the classic devotional works of the early seventeenth century. He soon found a copy of Richard Baxter's *Call to the unconverted*, 'the which I did no sooner open but its title page invited my fancy to make choice of it for my chief companion ... the more oftener I read it the more I was enamoured with it'.[92] Barry's reading has all the marks of the godly reader at work with his immersion in a text which was read frequently, new insights being found on each reading. The impact of his reading was dramatic, since, comparing the spiritual models he found in the reading with his own experience, he drew the conclusion that he could no longer remain within the Church of Ireland. Despite being urged by a bishop to read *The whole duty of man* as a statement of the church's theological and social position he had found no comfort there and defected to Independency.

If the Church of Ireland laid great stress on its liturgical works as a way of promoting faith and encouraged lay men and women to read those works, the books advocated by the gathered churches of dissent, which lacked formal liturgies, were rather different. It is true that both established and dissenting churches held a great number of devotional works in common reverence and this may explain why so many of the books promoted by many elements of dissent were readily available in Dublin and appear in a number of late seventeenth-century Irish libraries. In the early 1690s John Cooke in Dublin noted that dissenting works, such as those of Richard Baxter, were easily available in the city.[93] However, dissenting congregations did have their own uses for print. One of the characteristics of dissenting communities, with the exception of Quakers, in the late seventeenth century was their fondness for singing. As Edward Wetenhall, the precentor of Christ Church cathedral, Dublin, observed in 1679, singing 'is better approved (indeed strangely doted upon) by those of our nation which dissent from our church'.[94] According to the Dublin Presbyterian minister Joseph Boyse singing was a 'delightful duty' which had 'a genuine tendency (even above all the other duties) to engage their [the people's] attention, to quicken their devout affections, to raise and vent their spiritual joys and give them some relish of the inward pleasures of serious religion'. Hymns and psalms were therefore directed 'to the common people ... whose affection to this part of the public worship deserves all the helps we can give to further it'.[95]

The 'helps' which were to be provided to further singing were texts. The most important was certainly the Scottish psalter of 1650 which was a common text for all dissenters within the British Isles and was used almost exclusively by the Ulster Presbyterians. In Dublin there were other texts such as William Barton's editions of the psalter produced by Presbyterian book-sellers in the city. There were also other alternatives. In 1693 in Dublin Joseph

Boyse produced his *Sacramental hymns collected (chiefly) out of such passages of the New Testament as contain the most suitable matter of Divine praise in celebration of the Lord's supper* which was to be sold by Mathew Gunn, one of a group of Dublin Presbyterian booksellers operating in the city.[96] Gunn was also responsible for producing Boyse's second venture in dissenting hymnody, *Hymns for morning and evening worship with some for the Lord's day and several others for particular occasions* which appeared in 1701. The first work, given its sacramental thrust, was largely based on passages from the New Testament, while the second was based largely on the psalms. We can only guess at how people responded to these printed texts. The books themselves marked Dublin dissenters out as a distinctive group since neither Ulster Presbyterians nor the Church of Ireland had such a hymnbook. The definitions of the church which ran through the hymns in the *Sacramental hymns* was of the church as a collection of gathered saints, a theme which clearly reinforced the messages of the communion service at which the saints did indeed gather and the church was made visible. Just as a sacramental community was created by the liturgy so a textual community was created by the book, since Boyse seems to have envisaged that all those at the service would own or be provided with such a book. The *Family hymns* of 1701 focused on different series of messages related to individual religious identities and their relation to daily life. Two themes are important here, the power of God as creator of the world and the importance of God's providence in ordering daily life. Thus the godly were to be protected while the evil were punished as God intervened in the world. The hymns themselves, when sung, also provided rituals for coping with crises such as sickness and death. In this way oral and print traditions interacted in the popular activity of singing which also articulated group identity by focusing on congregations and families in the dissenting world while at the same time conveying messages about correct ways of interpreting experience and scripture.[97]

III

If Protestantism in all its forms used printed books as a way of giving shape to the religious impulse, Catholicism used a wider range of devotional aids. Saints' cults and sacramentals supplemented the main devotional activity of the mass but at least some saw print as an important cohesive force in creating a particular type of spirituality. Some Catholics urged the godly reading of pious books, and the rules for a Catholic sodality in Dublin in 1703 emphasised the important of not only reading pious books but meditating on them frequently.[98] Obtaining such pious works was, of course, a problem. Since printing was controlled by the king's printer it was the 1640s before the printers of the Catholic confederation were in a position to produce Catholic works. Certainly there was the possibility of illicit printing. There were certainly rumours of secret Catholic printing in the area around Dublin at the beginning of the seventeenth century but such printing never seems to have materialised.[99] The main locus of Irish Catholic printing was continental Europe. Certainly by 1617 it was claimed that a work was being printed in Douai concerning the difficulties of Irish Catholics.[100] Only in the 1640s with the presses of the Catholic Confederation in Kilkenny and Waterford was there the possibility of publishing Catholic works in Ireland. However, those presses limited their output to administrative, political and confutational works. One exception occurred in 1647 when the Waterford press produced a small volume of forty-eight pages containing the lives of St David and St Ciaran edited from John Colgan's much larger collection of saints' lives, the *Acta sanctorum Hiberniae*, recently published in Louvain. The editor was William Swayne, then recently appointed parish priest of St Mary's parish, Gowran, County Kilkenny.[101] The lives may have been produced on the initiative of the Catholic bishop, David Rothe, since he was the owner of the life which Colgan had printed and Swayne claimed to be 'near kin' to Rothe. It may be that Rothe intended the work to be distributed gratis throughout the diocese to promote piety.

In the case of scholarly Latin texts of theology and church government the sort of books Catholic Ireland needed were freely available in Europe. In other cases, particularly in the area of catechetical and devotional texts, when material in the vernacular was required this had to be specially prepared. The Louvain Franciscans operated a press which had a font of Irish type and from the beginning of the seventeenth century produced books in Irish, and in the late seventeenth century Propaganda Fide in Rome also had a press which could fulfil the same need. This meant that the bulk of the Catholic works which arrived in early modern Ireland were smuggled works sometimes brought by merchants or clergy returning to Ireland from Europe.[102] Not all were. Even in the Dublin bookshops some Catholic works were available for the curious or the disputatious. A Jesuit work, *Mariana*, was sought by some from the Dublin booksellers in 1641 and was, presumably, still available in 1679 when it was attacked in the visitation sermon of a Church of Ireland bishop.[103]

By its nature, smuggling was a furtive activity. The lack of documentation means that it is very difficult to provide an overview of the sort of works at the disposal of Irish Catholics. Occasionally as a result of the seizure of ships it is possible to catch a glimpse of the sort of works that were smuggled. In 1578 the Catholic bishop of Emly, Maurice MacBrien, whose baggage was seized at Waterford, was found to be carrying six Latin primers.[104] An Irish student at Lincoln's Inn on his way home to Dublin in 1608 was found to have hidden among his law books 'a number of catechisms' and in the following year a Dublin merchant was found with 'sundry popish books, printed and manuscript' in a cargo as part of a scheme to smuggle Catholic books into Ireland.[105] In 1619 a French ship from Spain which was seized in Cork was found to contain a range of Catholic books including catechisms, a Catholic *Rituale*, a copy of the *Maleus malificorum*, Richard Stanihurst's *Vita St Patricii* and his *De rebus in Hibernia gestis*, a tract on penance and a wide range of Catholic statuary and images.[106] Again a ship from Calais bound for Waterford in 1625 carried not only wine, tobacco and sugar but also 'certain books of St Patrick' for Ireland.[107] This book seems to have been Robert Rochford's *The life of the glorious bishop S. Patricke apostle and primate of Ireland together with the lives of the holy virgin S. Bridgit and of the glorious abbot Sainte Columbe, patrons of Ireland* published at St-Omer in 1625. It circulated widely in Catholic Ireland. Geoffrey Keating in the 1630s referred to the same work as 'a book in which were written in English the lives of Patrick, Columcille and Brigit'.[108] Again in 1641 an Enniskillen schoolmaster, Richard Bourke, reported that in Limerick the Irish insurgents had 'an English book printed in the Low Countries imparting another prophecy of St Patrick' which seems to be the same text.[109] Rochford's text appears in another form in the library of Thomas Arthur of Limerick in the early seventeenth century which contained a copy of the *Lives of the saints* by the Spanish Dominican Alfonso de Villegas to which Rochford's work was attached as an appendix in the 1627 and 1636 editions.

In the late 1680s the sorts of books which Catholic might have access to are somewhat easier to discern. In 1688 as the Jacobite revanche moved towards its zenith the Dublin Catholic bookseller William Weston issued a reprint of *A short and plain way to the faith and church* by the English Benedictine John Huddleston, who had been credited with reconciling Charles II to Catholicism. Weston used the last page of the tract to advertise other titles which were available in his High Street shop.[110] The seventeen titles listed are all works of Catholic theology. Although they were described as 'printed and sold' by Weston it is unlikely that he printed any of them. Most of them can be identified as works that had been published in London during the previous year or at Douai, Paris or Ghent over the previous five years. It seems likely that they represent a consignment of books brought to Dublin by Weston in 1688. He had certainly imported politically dubious works from a London bookseller in the recent past and in 1684 he also imported quantities of books on his own account through Chester.[111] There are considerable difficulties in interpreting lists of books such as that of William Weston. It is not clear, for example, whether these works were available only in Dublin or whether Weston also carried on a trade with customers in the countryside as other booksellers did. He certainly sold small works and other cheap printed items to Bishop Luke Wadding for Ferns, but how the transaction was carried out is not specified.[112] Again all the works are in English, which clearly limited their circulation in some parts of Ireland. Despite such difficulties the list does provide a window into the sort of books that shaped the spirituality of some Irish Catholics. Weston was engaged in commercial activity and his stock was intended to be sold and so represents at least one man's judgement of what Catholics in Dublin, and possibly further afield, both lay and clerical, wanted to read.

The books which Weston offered were the sort of books that the clergy read and wished the laity to read also. Some are to be found in the libraries of clergy. Bishop Daton of Ossory, for instance, possessed a copy of Dominique Bouhours's *Christian thoughts for every day in the month* which was on Weston's list, while Bishop Wadding of Ferns owned Henry Turberville's *Abridgement of Christian doctrine* and W.C.'s *A little manual of the poor man's daily devotion*.[113] One of Weston's offerings, C.J.'s *A net for the fishers of men* (n.p., 1687), was so appreciated by one Irish Franciscan that he copied the entire text into his commonplace book.[114] Other clergy expressed their approbation for the sort of books which Weston held by distributing copies of the same works to their flock in an effort to promote piety. Bishop Wadding handed out 144 copies of Henry Turberville's *Abridgement of Christian doctrine*, 1,200 copies of Pedro de Ledesma's *Christian doctrine*, at least three dozen copies of Dominique Bouhours's *Christian thoughts for every day in the month* and copies of *The most devout prayers of St Brigitte* as well as 'little books of the mass' which may correspond to a book in Weston's stock entitled *The mysteries of the holy mass*.[115]

Categorisation of such works is problematic but in broad terms three of the titles on the list can be described as doctrinal, one as confutational and the remaining thirteen as devotional works. Of these thirteen, three were concerned with what might be described as public devotions, in particular commentaries on the mass, while the remaining ten were prayerbooks for private use. There is some overlap between these two groups as prayerbooks often contained commentaries on the mass or prayers for use before or after mass. Even allowing for this overlap, the main thrust of Weston's stock was towards books of private devotion. Such books helped to shape the devotional world associated particularly with the reforms of Trent. Works such as Turberville on doctrine, usually known as the Douai catechism since it had been composed there in the late sixteenth century, or that of Ledesma were intended to ensure that belief was underpinned by an understanding of the doctrines of Catholicism. Turberville's work, for instance, expounded the creed, the commandments, the precepts of the church, the sacraments, the four last things and the works of mercy. Early modern Irish Catholics were becoming increasingly familiar with such works. Synods enjoined priests working in Ireland to acquire such catechisms and to use them in educating their flock. Those clergy who could not read, or could not obtain a printed text, were to be taught to memorise the text and then pass it on.[116] Weston's stock was also intended to shape practice. Both Turberville's work and W.C.'s *A little manual of the poor man's daily devotion* offered detailed commentaries on the mass, including an explanation of the ornaments and ceremonies used at mass and a commentary on the actions of the priest from his entrance on the altar. They also included prayers for use before and after mass but not during mass as had been customary before. Now the world of print guided readers through the actions of the mass and they were expected to follow and understand the symbolism of those actions rather than perform their own devotions by reciting traditional prayers during the liturgy.

To understand the role which books, such as those stocked by Weston, were intended to play in the promotion of devotion it is necessary to understand not only the texts but the ways in which they were read. Some insight is provided by the texts themselves. One of the works on Weston's list, *Christian thoughts for every day of the month*, carried a preface which explained how it was to be used. It was a work, the preface explained, for the laity and contained 'plain thoughts, short and easy which may be understood without difficulty and read with less than a minute's expense'. It was to be resorted to after prayers in the morning when the owner should 'read the thoughts of that day but read them leisurely that you may understand them thoroughly'. Like Protestant readers, one was not to be content with a simple comprehension of the truth contained in the work but one was also to consider how it might be applied.[117] Clearly this was a text which was to be read privately and in a meditative mood, in the context of prayer, and was to be absorbed slowly and fully. Weston had other books of a similar nature. The *Most Devout prayers of St Brigitte*, which was sold by Weston and given away by Bishop Wadding, is based on the fifteen traditional prayers of St Brigitte of Sweden, to be said in honour of the wounds of Christ, and was meant for personal meditative private prayer rather than for communal recital. This was an interiorised form of devotion that relied heavily on the response of the individual to the written or printed word rather than the communal assent to the meaning of the work or its performance in liturgy.

The world of the Catholic reader reflected in the stock of William Weston's bookshop was a multi-faceted one. It was a world of faith which concentrated on an individualised devotion inspired by meditation on the mysteries of Catholicism. It encouraged active, informed participation in the sacraments rather than the performance of communal rituals such as pilgrimage to the local holy well. It advanced Counter-Reformation ideas and devotions at the expense of traditional practice. In particular it demanded not simply knowledge that one was a Catholic but rather an understanding of why one had adopted that confessional position. However, there are dangers in generalising from Weston's stock. As with Catholic religious reading across Europe it is necessary to distinguish between regions, town and countryside and different social milieux.[118] The world of books required specialist skills to enter fully. One needed to be sufficiently literate to read such works easily and one had to have a sufficient command of English to understand them. Such education for the bulk of Irish Catholics in the seventeenth century was not available, given the limited educational facilities available, and this accounts in some measure for the differential literacy rates between natives and newcomers noted in Chapter 2. One also needed enough free time to practise the discipline such religious books advocated. By the end of the seventeenth century such books as Weston stocked were probably readily accessible to only a minority of Irish Catholics within reach of a good bookseller.

While in Ireland the structures of Catholic reform spread relatively rapidly, attitudes towards how religious ideas were spread altered more slowly. The conservative ways of spreading religious ideas by sight and hearing, rather than by reading, tended to continue well into the seventeenth century. Thus, perhaps more important was the world of printed ephemera, which has left less trace than Weston's book stock. Included in the contents of a ship from Spain seized at Cork in 1617 was a range of Catholic books and 'divers printed pages with pictures'.[119] Similar items reappeared in 1632 when the archbishop of Cashel complained that a Franciscan in his diocese was distributing printed sheets brought from the Low Countries and almost certainly printed on the Franciscan press at Louvain.[120] These included a printed image of St Francis and an English text which promised that no one wearing the Franciscan habit should die an unhappy death, declared that the Franciscan order would last until the Judgement Day, asserted that the persecutors of the order would be punished and promised that anyone who loved the order, no matter how bad a sinner, would receive the mercy of God. Cistercians were also issuing similar pages.[121] These printed sheets did not have to be entirely devotional works. John Parrie, captured by the Catholic Irish early in the 1641 rising, was taunted by friars in Caledon friary who 'brought forth a picture of Fr Phillips [the queen's confessor] hanging, telling his audience that for the Catholic cause that great prelate was so executed by the heretics and with an admonition to them to stick fast to the cause and to fight so just a quarrel otherwise they could expect no other than the like'.[122] This combination of words and pictures was a particularly powerful one since it appealed to both the literate and the illiterate, it catered for those who could see the image and have the text read to them by a friend as well as those who could read it themselves. Images also transcended the language barrier between English and Irish. While these works were primarily devotional, in a few cases they may have acted as a confutational weapon, fitting with the wider European tradition of confraternities issuing similar printed items which were displayed on the walls of the members of the confraternity.[123] However, in many cases the message of the broadsheet was a conservative one, concerned with salvation rather than confessional division. As such they may actually have reinforced older ideas rather than changing them.

IV

Throughout the early modern period there was a growing reliance on print by those who looked for models for salvation or simply to explain their everyday experiences in religious terms. In search of salvation one Dublin Protestant made an index in his copy of Samuel Mather's *The figures or types of the Old Testament*, which appeared in Dublin in 1683, which he thought would help him to know 'whether thou art under the first or second Adam'.[124] For those looking for experiences to match their own, or to fit into typologies, and provide conviction of being among the elect, the printed spiritual testimony was of considerable importance. For those of a less enthusiastic religious bent, the Bible or Book of Common Prayer provided enough spiritual comfort. Catholics might still turn to their own saints or sacramentals but even for them print came to play a greater part in their spiritual lives. For those who visited St Patrick's Purgatory, one of the most important of the Irish pilgrimage sites, the experience was transformed during the seventeenth century. At the beginning of the century the rituals of the pilgrimage were sanctioned by custom and transmitted by experience and oral tradition. A hundred years later, arriving at the site, pilgrims were confronted by a printed text which prescribed the standard form of the pilgrimage and explained its significance in theological terms understandable to the Catholic clergy.[125] Print was thus one element in the shift in how religious experiences were understood in early modern Ireland. Customary observances came under attack from a new, orderly spirituality exemplified by the orderly presentation of experience in print. What exemplifies this tradition most clearly is the rise of *The whole duty of man* as a central religious text in Protestant Ireland in the late seventeenth century. Here religious belief was marshalled under well-defined heads of social relationships with prayers, scriptural passages and moral instruction underpinning a clear set of ideas about social hierarchy. Perhaps more important than simply providing information for the religiously enthusiastic or the curious, books on salvation helped shape religious cultures. They formed the centres of textual communities as those who agreed to read the Bible or prayerbook in particular ways gathered round those texts and explored them according to confessional norms. As such, print helped to created reading styles which, when added to ways of preaching, singing and hearing, went a long way to creating the cultures of Irish dissent, Anglicanism and Catholicism.

In practice however the power of print to create new types of religious experience or to marshal those experiences into denominational reading patterns was limited. The availability of books and problems of language and literacy were clearly limiting factors but by the end of the seventeenth century these were no longer as important as they had been earlier. More important was simply the diverse ways of reading books which existed and which were used by lay men and women, both literate and illiterate. Since Bibles and liturgical works were available to the illiterate through public reading, what mattered was the experience of those books as things heard rather than seen. Individuals could make up their own minds about what such texts meant. They did so by applying not only the literal meanings to words but also a series of other forms of understandings, some of which came from with the textual community's understanding of the book but some of which did not. In some ways the illiterate Protestant who only heard the Bible read had an experience closer to a Catholic, who concentrated on narrative, than one of his literate co-religionists who dissected the meaning of the works by close comparison of verses. Again the easy availability of books which crossed Protestant traditions, such as the works of Richard Baxter, encouraged the curious to read of other experiences and compare them with their own. If print had the potential to make the search for salvation conform to the ideas of theologians, the act of reading made it impossible to transform society that easily.

NOTES

1 For some examples see Raymond Gillespie, 'The religion of the Protestant laity in early modern Ireland' in Brendan Bradshaw and Dáire Keogh (eds), *Christianity in Ireland: revisiting the story* (Dublin, 2002), pp. 110–11.

2 This is argued in Raymond Gillespie, *Devoted people: belief and religion in early modern Ireland* (Manchester, 1997).

3 Barnaby Rich, *Short survey of Ireland* (London, 1609), p. 55.

4 Prayers, for instance, often drew heavily on biblical phrases: Raymond Gillespie, '"Into another intensity": prayer in Irish nonconformity, 1650–1700' in Kevin Herlihy (ed.), *The religion of Irish dissent, 1650–1800* (Dublin, 1996), p. 38.

5 Samuel Foley, *An exhortation to the inhabitants of Down and Connor concerning the education of their children* (Dublin, 1695), pp. 19–20; *The works of the reverend and learned Ezekiel Hopkins, lord bishop of Londonderry* (London, 1710), p. 710.

6 C.S. King (ed.), *A great archbishop of Dublin* (London, 1908), pp. 3–4; *The life of Mr Thomas Gent, printer of York, by himself* (London, 1832), p. 23; T.C.D. MS 1050, p. 14.

7 Friends Historical Library, Dublin, Portfolio A2, f. 22.

8 Raymond Gillespie, 'The book trade in southern Ireland, 1590–1640' in Gerard Long (ed.), *Books beyond the pale: aspects of the provincial book trade in Ireland before 1850* (Dublin, 1996), pp. 4, 13. For illustrations of these see Margaret Spufford, *The world of rural dissent, 1520–1725* (Cambridge, 1995), pp. 69–76. The only surviving Irish-language primer is [William Bedell], *The ABC or the institutes of a Christian* (Dublin, 1630) in which he used a number of scripture passages described as 'the sum of the gospel' to teach reading. Others clearly existed since one book entitled *The ABC with the church catechism* was on sale in Dublin in 1695: list of books for sale by Richard Wilde, bookseller in William Sherlock, *A sermon preached at the Temple church, December 30 1694* (Dublin, 1695).

9 Edward Coote, *The English schoolmaster* (42nd edn, Dublin, 1684), pp. 41–50.

10 Raymond Gillespie, 'Irish printing in the early seventeenth century' in *Irish Economic and Social History* xv (1988), p. 88; Leeds City Library, Temple Newsham MSS, Irish Customs records I(4)a, Derry port book, 1641, f. 3; William King, *A discourse concerning the inventions of men in the worship of God* (Dublin, 1694), pp. 89–90; Scott Mandelbrote, 'John Baskett, the Dublin booksellers and the printing of the Bible' in A. Hunt, G. Mandelbrote and A. Shell (eds), *The book trade and its customers* (Winchester, 1997), p. 117; P.J. Corish (ed.), 'Bishop Wadding's notebook' in *Archivium Hibernicum* xxix (1970), pp. 63, 64, 69, 72. For even lower prices in Belfast see George Benn, *A history of the town of Belfast* (London, 1877), p. 316.

11 A.B. Grosart (ed.), *Lismore papers* (10 vols, London, 1886–88), 1st ser. iv, p. 5; Wesley McCann, 'An unrecorded edition of John Taylor's *Verbum sepiterum*' in *Linen Hall Review* vi no. 2 (1989), pp. 14–15. A work entitled *The best new year's gift or an epitome of the Bible dedicated to King William and Queen Mary* was being sold by Richard Wilde in 1695: Sherlock, *A sermon preached.*

12 Robert Craghead, *An answer to a late book entitled a discourse concerning the inventions of men in the worship of God* (Edinburgh, 1694), p. 86.

13 Marsh's Library, Dublin, MS Z3.2.6, no. 58; John Ainsworth, 'Abstracts of seventeenth-century Irish wills in the prerogative court of Canterbury' in *Journal of the Royal Society of Antiquaries of Ireland* lxxviii (1948), p. 24; W.P. Burke, *History of Clonmel* (Waterford, 1907), p. 327.

14 B.L., Add. MS 46957, f. 36.

15 C[ornelius] N[ary], *The New Testament of our Lord and Saviour Jesus Christ* ([Dublin], 1718), sig. a2v.

16 George Hill (ed.), *The Montgomery manuscripts* (Belfast, 1869), p. 328.

17 Patrick Fagan, *Dublin's turbulent priest: Cornelius Nary* (Dublin, 1991), pp. 83–4.

18 Lambert McKenna (ed.), *Iomarbhágh na bhfileadh* (2 vols, London, 1918), i, pp. 54–7.

19 Nicholas Williams, *I bprionta í leabhar: na Protastúin agus prós na Gaeilge, 1567–1724* (Dublin, 1986), pp. 131–3, argues this on the basis of similarities of phrasing in Gaelic Catholic devotional works and the Protestant translations.

20 N.A., Dublin Prerogative will book, 1644–84, f. 80.

21 Hannah Buchan (ed.), *The poems of Thomas Pestell* (Oxford, 1940), pp. 2–3, 105. Her brother Viscount Dungarvan also wrote a short poem on the divine inspiration of the Bible: Folger Library, Washington DC, MS V.a.125, f. 7v.

22 N.L.I., MS 16085, p. 136.

23 B.L., Royal MS 17 A xviii, f. 3v. While Marshall's theology is undoubtedly Protestant he also owned a number of Catholic devotional objects which he used: see Brian Donovan and David Edwards (eds), *British sources for Irish history, 1485–1641* (Dublin, 1998), p. 43. For other examples of this see Gillespie, *Devoted people*, pp. 9–10.

24 These are contained in his autobiography in P.R.O.N.I., D 1460/1.

25 T.C.D., MS 676, pp. 323–9; William Hamilton, *The exemplary life and character of James Bonnell* (London, 1703), p. xiii; Áine Ní Chróinín (ed.), *Beatha Chríost* (Dublin, n.d.).

26 T.C.D., MS 834, f. 63v.

27 Thomas Fitzsimons, *The primer more ample and in a new order* (Rouen, 1684), sigs c3v–d6, pp. 390–420.

28 Folger Library, Washington DC, MS G.a.10; B.L., Add. MS 31885, f. 14.

29 William Sheridan, *St Paul's confession of faith or a brief account of his religion* (Dublin, 1685), p. 18.

30 *Musarum lacryamyra* (Dublin, 1630), sig. D3v.

31 T.C.D., MS 287, ff. 200–4, 229, 275v–6; MS 357, ff. 25–9.

32 Joseph Boyse, *Remarks on a late discourse of William, lord bishop of Derry* (Dublin, 1694), pp. 93, 95; Union Theological College, Belfast, MS Robert Chambers, 'An explanation of the Shorter Catechism', p. 28.

33 *The works of the reverend and learned Joseph Boyse* (2 vols, London, 1728), i, p. 316; B.L., Add. MS 19865, f. 74.

34 Society of Antiquaries, London, Broadsides, no. 30.

35 *Cal. S. P. Ire., 1586–8*, p. 424; *Cal. S. P. Ire., 1647–60*, p. 182, Hamilton, *Life of Bonnell*, p. 47.

36 Marc Caball, 'Providence and exile in seventeenth-century Ireland' in *Irish Historical Studies* xxix (1994–95), pp. 175–88; J.T. Gilbert (ed.), *A contemporary history of affairs in Ireland* (3 vols, Dublin, 1879), i, pp. 174, 210, 214; ii, 126; iii, pp. 123–4.

37 Dublin Public Libraries, Gilbert Library, Bound volume of pamphlets 183/1/7F.

38 Stokes (ed.), *Memoirs of Ann Fowke*, pp. 42–3, 44, 48, 53.

39 Walter Gostellow, *Charls Stuart and Oliver Cromwell united* (London, 1654), pp. 17–22, 34–5, 45.

40 Letter bound with pamphlet in N.L.I., Thorpe Tracts, p. 11.

41 Charles Jackson (ed.), *The autobiography of Mrs Alice Thornton* (Durham, 1875), p. 13.

42 Jean Kleine (ed.) *The Southwell–Sibthorpe commonplace books* (Binghamton, 1997), pp. 51–87.

43 Raymond Anselment (ed.), *The remembrances of Elizabeth Freke* (Cambridge, 2001), pp. 173–6, 133–9.

44 John Rogers, *Ohel or Beth Shemesh* (London, 1653), p. 407.

45 Thomas McCrie (ed.), *The life of Mr Robert Blair* (Edinburgh, 1848), p. 79.

46 Elizabethanne Boran, 'Reading theology within the community of believers: James Ussher's "Directions"' in Bernadette Cunningham and Máire Kennedy (eds), *The experience of reading: Irish historical perspectives* (Dublin, 1999), pp. 39–59.

47 Colin McKelvie (ed.), 'Jeremy Taylor's recommendations for a library of Anglican theology' in *Irish Booklover* iv (1978–80), p. 102.

48 The standard history remains William Reeves, *The book of Common Prayer according to the use of the Church of Ireland: its history and sanction* (Dublin, 1871).

49 T.C.D., MS 820, f. 211; MS 832, f. 69; MS 812, f. 213v; MS 817, f. 148v.

50 T.C.D., MS 1995–2008/366, 407.

51 Richard Mant, *History of the Church of Ireland from the restoration to the union of the Churches of England and Ireland* (London, 1840), p. 254.

52 D.B. Quinn, 'Information about Dublin printers, 1556–1573, in English financial records' in *Irish Booklover* xxviii (1942), p. 113; Northampton County Record Office, Fitzwilliam of Milton MSS, Irish, no. 64, f. 133.

53 W.M. Brady (ed.), *State papers concerning the Irish church in the time of Queen Elizabeth* (London, 1868), pp. 39, 118.

54 Raymond Gillespie, 'The circulation of print in seventeenth century Ireland' in *Studia Hibernica* no. 29 (1995–97), p. 31.

55 Gillespie, 'Irish printing', p. 88.

56 R.C.B., MS C12/1/1, account for 1667; P118/5/1, f. 74; P328/5/1, accounts for 1667–68 and 1678–79; P117/5/1/, pp. 25, 27, P327/4/1, f. 19v; P351/4/1/, f. 60.

57 T.C.D., MS 562, ff. 41, 51v, 56v, 69.

58 Barnaby Rich, *A new description of Ireland* (London, 1610), p. 34.

59 H.M.C., *Report on the manuscripts of the earl of Egmont* (2 vols, London, 1905–9), i, p. 33.

60 H.M.C., *Calendar of the manuscripts of the marquess of Ormonde* (new series, 8 vols, London, 1902–20), vii, pp. 346–7, 355, 364.

61 J.S. Reid, *History of the presbyterian church in Ireland* (3 vols, Belfast, 1867), i, pp. 523–42.

62 Phil Kilroy, *Protestant dissent and controversy in Ireland, 1660–1714* (Cork, 1994), pp. 175–80.

63 John Harrington, *Short view of the state of Ireland written in 1605* ed. W.D. Macray (Oxford, 1879), p. 16.

64 *Cal. S. P. Ire., 1633–47*, p. 206.

65 H.M.C., *Egmont*, ii, p. 243.

66 Raymond Gillespie (ed.), 'Rev. Dr John Yarner's notebook: religion in Restoration Dublin' in *Archivium Hibernicum* lii (1998), pp. 36–8, 40.

67 B.L., Harley MS 4297, f. 111v.

68 Gillespie, *Devoted people*, pp. 97–8.

69 William Beveridge, *A sermon concerning the excellency and usefulness of the common prayer* (Dublin, 1698), sig. A2v.

70 Thomas Pollard, *The necessity and advantages of family prayer in two sermons preached in St Peter's, Dublin* (Dublin, 1696).

71 H.M.C., *Ormonde*, n.s., vii, p. 526.

72 T.C.D., MS 830, f. 172.

73 T.C.D., MS 4468, N.L.I., MS 19465.

74 Anslement (ed.), *Remembrances*, pp. 66, 260.

75 Michael [Boyle], *Rules and orders to be used and observed in the high court of Chancery in Ireland* (Dublin, 1685), sig. A3v; H.M.C., *Ormonde*, n.s., vii, p. 526.

76 Edward Wetenhall, *A plain and practical discourse of the form of godliness visible in the present age* (Dublin, 1683), p. 178.

77 These books were clearly imports since none of the surviving Irish prayer books has illustrations and so it is impossible to know what these illustrations were.

78 Gillespie, 'The book trade in southern Ireland, 1590–1640', pp. 5–6, 13.

79 B.L., Add MS 19,865, ff. 74–8.

80 Dublin City Archives, C1/J/2/4, p. 228.

81 Hamilton, *The life of James Bonnell*, pp. 7–9.

82 H.M.C., *Egmont*, ii, p. 74; Burke, *History of Clonmel*, p. 333.

83 Mary Pollard, *Dublin's trade in books, 1550–1800* (Oxford, 1989), p. 68.

84 Pollard, *Necessity and advantages of family prayer*, sig. B1; Bodl., Smith MS 52, f. 73.

85 T.C.D., MS 562, ff. 51v, 52v, 56v, 59.

86 Gillespie, 'Circulation of print', pp. 51–2; Hamilton, *Life of James Bonnell*, p. 213.

87 Cambridge University Library, Add MS 711, p. 232.

88 S[teven] J[erome], *The soul's sentinel ringing an alarm against impiety and impenitency* (Dublin, 1631), dedication.

89 T.C.D., MS 676, p. 493.

90 Wetenhall, *A plain and practical*, p. 58.

91 Francis de Sales, *An introduction to the devout life*, ed. Henry Dodwell (Dublin, 1673) sigs a5v–f4v.

92 James Barry, *A reviving cordial for a sin-sick, despairing soul in the time of temptation* (2nd edn?, Edinburgh, 1722), p. 23.

93 Presbyterian Historical Society, Belfast, Diary of John Cook, 1691.

94 Edward Wetenhall, *Gifts and offices in the public worship of God* (Dublin, 1679), p. 404.

95 Joseph Boyse, *Family hymns for morning and evening worship* (Dublin, 1707), sigs A3–A3v.

96 Mary Pollard, *A dictionary of members of the Dublin book trade 1500–1800* (London, 2000), pp. 263–4. There was a London printing of the text later in the same year.

97 For a much fuller analysis of these texts see Raymond Gillespie,'"A good and godly exercise": singing the word in Irish dissent, 1660–1701' in Kevin Herlihy (ed.), *Propagating the word of Irish dissent, 1650–1800* (Dublin, 1998), pp. 28–45.

98 *Rules and instructions for the sodality of the immaculate conception of the most glorious Virgin Mary, mother of God* ([Dublin], 1703). The text is clearly drawn from an English exemplar but is assigned to Dublin by ESTC on the grounds of typography.

99 H.M.C., *Salisbury (Cecil) MSS at Hatfield House* (24 vols, London, 1883–1976), xvii, pp. 351, 363.

100 H.M.C., *Report on the manuscripts of the duke of Buccleuch and Queensberry* (3 vols, London, 1899–1926), i, p. 189.

101 [William Swayne], *The lives of the glorious Saint David, bishop of Menevia, patron of Wales and master of many Irish saints and also Saint Kieran, the first born saint of Ireland, first bishop and principal patron of the diocese of Ossory* (Waterford, 1647). For Swayne see Brendan Jennings, 'Ecclesiastical appointments in Ireland, August 1643–December 1649' in *Collectanea Hibernica* no. 2 (1959), p. 39.

102 Benignus Millett, 'Irish Franciscans ask *Propaganda* to give them books for their pastoral ministry in Ireland, 1689–96' in *Collectanea Hibernica* nos 44–5 (2002–3), pp. 63–75; Gillespie, 'Circulation of print', pp. 48–9 for further examples.

103 T.C.D., MS 820, f. 266v; Richard Tennison, *A sermon preached at the primary visitation of ... [the] archbishop of Armagh* (Dublin, 1679), pp. 29, 66.

104 Benignus Millett, 'Maurice MacBrien, bishop of Emly, and the confiscation of his baggage, March 1578' in *Collectanea Hibernica* no. 35 (1992–93), p. 13.

105 Chester City Archive, Quarter sessions examinations, QSE/8/11,12; *Cal. S. P. Ire., 1574–85*, p. 286; *Cal. S. P. Ire., 1608–10*, p. 192.

106 Grosart (ed.), *Lismore papers*, 2nd ser., ii, pp. 116–17.

107 John Appleby (ed.), *A calendar of material relating to Ireland in the High Court of Admiralty examinations, 1536–1640* (Dublin, 1992), pp. 303–4.

108 Geoffrey Keating, *Foras feasa ar Éirinn*, eds David Comyn and P.S. Dinneen (4 vols, London, 1902–4), i, pp. 78–9.

109 T.C.D., MS 835, f. 206.

110 Pollard, *Dictionary*, p. 602.

111 Pollard, *Dictionary*, p. 602; P.R.O., E190/1346/12, f. 21v, 30v, 36, 40, 41v.

112 Corish (ed.), 'Bishop Wadding's notebook', p. 90.

113 Hugh Fenning (ed.), 'The library of Bishop William Daton of Ossory, 1698' in *Collectanea Hibernica* no. 20 (1978), p. 41; Corish (ed.), 'Bishop Wadding's notebook', pp. 63, 65.

114 T.C.D., MS 1375.

115 Corish, 'Bishop Wadding's notebook', pp. 88, 89, 90.

116 Michael Olden, 'Counter-Reformation problems: Munster' in *Irish Ecclesiastical Record* 5th ser. civ (July-Dec. 1965), p. 45.

117 *Christian thoughts for every day of the month* (n.p., 1698), sigs A2–A3v.

118 See, for instance, the comments in Dominique Julia, 'Reading and the Counter Reformation' in Guglielmo Cavallo and Roger Chartier (eds), *A history of reading in the west* (Cambridge, 1999), pp. 257–68.

119 Grosart (ed.), *Lismore papers*, 2nd ser., ii, p. 116.

120 Benignus Millett, 'Calendar of vol 1 of the collection *Scritture riferite nei congressi, Irlanda* in Propaganda archives' in *Collectanea Hibernica* nos 6–7 (1963–64), p. 47.

121 Edward MacLysaght (ed.), 'O'Grady papers' in *Analecta Hibernica* no. 15 (1944), pp. 39–41.

122 T.C.D., MS 836, f. 62v.

123 Roger Chartier, *The cultural uses of print in early modern France* (Princeton, 1987), pp. 159–61. For English Protestant equivalents see Tessa Watt, *Cheap print and popular piety, 1550–1640* (Cambridge, 1991), pp. 131–53.

124 This copy in now in the Dix collection in N.L.I.

125 John Richardson, *The great folly, superstition and idolatry of pilgrimage in Ireland* (Dublin, 1727), p. 61.

Chapter 7

Reading for profit and pleasure

For a good part of his life James Butler, twelfth earl and after 1661 first duke of Ormond, was engaged in reading. Much of what he read might be comprehended in the areas already discussed in the preceding two chapters of this book. As lord lieutenant for two prolonged periods in the late seventeenth century he read large quantities of political correspondence and intelligence gathered through gazettes and the information of informers. He read, and sometimes made notes on, political works then currently circulating in Ireland. In 1681, for instance, he noted that he had just received a 'whole cargo of printed matter', mainly political tracts from England which needed to be read and digested.[1] He was also a reader of godly works. In the early 1680s he noted that he had read all the publications of John Tillotson, then dean and later archbishop of Canterbury, especially his sermons.[2] He was also steeped in religious texts such as *The whole duty of man*, the Bible and the Book of Common Prayer. Quotations from and allusions to these works appear in his prayers.[3] However, the list of the duke's library suggests that he had contact with a much greater range of works than these. In the library at Kilkenny there were, for example, atlases, classical works, volumes of history and law, military handbooks and works of literature, including the plays of Shakespeare.[4] Some of these books Ormond undoubtedly purchased himself. Indeed one man, setting up as a bookseller in Dublin in 1663, claimed that he had been a bookseller in Bristol and had furnished Ormond with books in the 1650s. On being discharged from the army at the Restoration he asked that he be appointed as Ormond's bookseller and stationer.[5] Other books which Ormond had in his collection were gifts from those who were either political admirers or aspirants hoping for patronage or favour. One English clergyman sent him a copy of a sermon in 1668 motivated, he claimed, by the duke's patronage of the 'church of God in England and Ireland'.[6] Others had less self-interested motives. Throughout the 1660s the surveyor general, Sir Alan Broderick, sent

Ormond books and news from literary London. Among others he included poems by John Dryden, John Denham and Katherine Philips as soon as they issued from the press. On occasions when he could not obtain the printed book he forwarded copies of the most select poems. These works Broderick described as 'books of diversion' intended to distract Ormond from the worries of state.[7] The duke's friend John Fell also sent him a history of the university of Oxford which Fell had recently completed.[8] In another case Ormond himself commissioned the future earl of Granard, then travelling with his mother in France, to send him French books.[9] Ormond was by no means a typical reader but his diverse interests provide clear evidence that at least some of those who read in early modern Ireland did so for motives other than purely religious or administrative ones.

Perhaps the most vivid picture that exists of one man's reading habits in seventeenth-century Ireland comes from a life of Thomas Wentworth, earl of Strafford and Irish lord deputy in the 1630s, written for his son. According to this Wentworth's reading was eclectic:

> his learning was such as gentlemen use to apply themselves to, chiefly histories wherein he read besides the old Roman [histories], wherein he had taken very good pains, the modern Turkish, French and English stories. Amongst the Latin poets he was always very diligent to be reading Perius in his younger days and in his later times Ovid's Metamorphosis which he liked for his easy vein and good speeches and disciplines. He was able to give a good account of our English poets, especially Chaucer and Spenser. He had taken great pains to inform himself in the controverted points of religion, to which purpose he diligently read Du Plessis's works given him by the author which style he used to commend. For his devotion, besides the liturgy of the church ... [he] used Gerard's meditations and two little books ... He was studied in the part of the English law which concerned criminal justice and the office of a justice of the peace ... He took delight in some French authors, De Vair especially whose elegant and witty expressions so stuck with him and made him take great care of his style ... I must not forget his skill on architecture wherein Vitruvius was his master.[10]

Wentworth's reading was clearly wide and related to his public office but it also varied over the course of his life. This was not unusual for many in Ireland. At the level of landowners, events which were part of the normal life cycle, such as journeys to continental Europe on the grand tour, led some to buy books useful for those circumstances. Samuel Waring, the son of the County Down landowner, for instance prepared himself for this experience in the 1680s by buying forty-seven books, mostly histories of Italy, Geneva, Rome and Venice and works on the architecture he was to see. As he travelled he also collected pamphlets and plays. In this case print shaped the way in which Waring saw some of the places he visited but it also provided models when he kept his own travelogues and later when he wrote an account of his travels in imitation of those already in print.[11] In another case, this time in Richard Head's play about Dublin in the early 1660s, *Hic et ubique*, one Dublin landlady claimed to 'have read much'. On inquiry as to what she had read she replied, 'In my youthful days the most part of the *Garland of good will*, the *Seven wise masters* and there was not a godly ballad that 'scaped my hands'. Since that time her reading had progressed to 'that good Mr Patience his works and what else the Brethren published'. She also claimed to have read works of grammar and 'multiplication'.[12] This development in reading from simple works to more complex ones, often relevant to the reader's current social and economic situation, probably characterised most reading.

I

One of the earliest sorts of books that a reader might encounter were the popular stories which circulated in early modern Ireland and which were aimed at all social levels. From the late sixteenth century Ireland was well supplied with cheap chapbook romances which aimed to provide entertainment and instruction. Printers, with an eye to the market, reproduced what was familiar and what they thought would sell. Stories were both popular and profitable. As Henry Dodwell put it in the 1670s, stories were significant 'for raising the attention of the vulgar who are usually much delighted with stories and strange occurrences however fabulous and trivial, how plain and easy and intelligible to the weakest and grossest capacities'.[13]

What seems to have been the first piece of non-government printing in Ireland was such a work, probably produced about 1558, by Francis Edderman, of which only a few sheets have survived. It was entitled *A most pithy and pleasant history wherein is the destruction of Troy gathered together of all the chiefest authors turned into English metre.*[14] The decision to print such a volume was not accidental. The story of the fall of Troy was well known in late medieval Ireland. The earl of Kildare, for instance, had an English book in his library in the 1520s on 'The destruction of Troy'.[15] Moreover the story had been translated into Irish and had been circulating for some time in Gaelic manuscripts.[16] In many cases, however, these popular histories were imports. In the late sixteenth century, ships from Bristol included among their cargoes 'fable books' and 'small books for children'. Some are specifically mentioned by title, including *The seven wise masters*, *The right pleasant and very tragical history of Fortunatus* and the *Gesta romanorum*. These were all cheap books. In the port books the *Gesta romanorum* were valued as 1d and five dozen 'small books' arriving at Youghal in 1612 were valued at 1s 2d or about a farthing at wholesale rates.[17] By the 1630s they were being condemned as 'fabulous and unprofitable books and stories' by those who wished to call into question the effectiveness of the Stationers as king's printer in Ireland. The godly preacher

Stephen Jerome adopted a similar stance claiming that the lives of those who slew dragons were celebrated and honoured as 'St George, Bevis of Southampton, Guy of Warwick and others amongst us'. Moreoever, the exploits chronicled in the fabulous histories 'are received as gospel truth by credulous papists (I doubt too much too of the Protestant) laity'.[18]

These small romances had considerable power and influence in the world of reading although few copies have survived since the cheap productions were worn out through frequent and intensive reading. Small romances derived their influence from a number of factors. They were, for instance, owned by a very wide social range of readers. The *Seven champions of Christendom*, for example, was owned not only by those at the bottom of the social order but in the 1650s by the godly Provost Winter of Trinity College, Dublin.[19] From the other side of the confessional divide Luke Wadding, the Catholic bishop of Ferns, also owned a copy in the 1680s.[20] Even earlier, in the 1520s, at the pinnacle of the Irish social order the earl of Kildare had a copy of both the *Gesta romanorum* and the *Seven wise masters*.[21] The same texts were often used in Irish schools as readers. Samuel Pepys claimed of the *Seven wise masters* that 'of all histories of this nature it exceeds, being held in much esteem in Ireland that it is of the chiefest use in all the English schools for introducing children to the understanding of good letters'.[22] His contemporary Francis Kirkman claimed also that it 'was held in such estimation in Ireland that it was always put into the hands of young children after the hornbook'.[23]

Cheapness and a good narrative were clearly important to the success of these works but simplicity of language also gave them a wide appeal. Some, at least, appreciated the importance of this point. When Robert Craghead, the Presbyterian minister at Derry, wrote his work on preparation for communion in 1698 he noted, 'it hath sometimes grieved me to see some excellent practical books thrown away by some readers for no other reason but that the words were above their reach which I humbly conceive should be conscientiously prevented for knowing readers can understand the plainest but the ignorant cannot understand words for which they had no education'.[24] The chapbooks concentrated on simple words, making them accessible to a wide audience. All this suggests that these chapbook romances were a group of texts that were widely diffused throughout Irish society, crossing social, linguistic, ethnic and confessional boundaries, and thus may have helped to establish some common bonds among a wide range of such groups.

The second reason why the stories contained in these small books had a greater than usual impact was because they circulated in more than one medium. Many stories apparently migrated into drama form. Some of the late seventeenth-century mummers' plays in southern Ireland seem to have been based on the *Seven champions of Christendom*. A description of Cork in 1685, as preserved in a nineteenth-century copy, noted that

Mumming and masking ... have we daily upon our new green. Last evening there was presented the drollest piece of mummery I ever saw out of Ireland. There was St George and St Denis and St Patrick in their buff coats and the Turk was there likewise and Oliver Cromwell and a doctor and an old woman ... and there came a little devil with a broom to gather up the money that was thrown to the mummers for their sport. It is an ancient pastime, they tell me, of the citizens.[25]

A seventeenth-century description, now lost, of a mummers' play in Wexford has a similar account.[26] The source of this play, with more contemporary accretions and some deletions, seems clearly to be the *Seven champions of Christendom*. Some characters have been dropped and others added. Even the plots have been rewritten but the recurrence of at least some of the saints from the chapbook text certainly suggests that this was their origin. Less obviously there are echoes between chapbook stories and dramatic presentations. A verse recorded in the 1680s in County Down linked St Patrick and St George and may have its origin in such plays.[27] Another example may be the pageant of the 'Nine worthies' which was well known in late medieval Ireland. It was performed in the late fifteenth century on the streets of Dublin and in the early seventeenth century in Kilkenny.[28] Traditionally the 'Nine worthies' comprised three pagans, three Jews and three Christians. When the Limerick man Edmund Sexton noted the names of the 'Worthies' in his notebook in the late sixteenth century, possibly after seeing the pageant in Limerick, he omitted the traditional name of Geoffrey of Boulogne from the Christians and replaced it with the chapbook hero Sir Guy of Warwick.[29] The history of Guy was certainly well known in Ireland. In the middle of the sixteenth century the compiler of the Book of Howth had come across him but in Fabyan's English chronicle.[30] The story was also available in Irish from the fifteenth century.[31] What seems highly likely is that the traditional shape of the pageant had been modified to give it a local flavour by including a character people were familiar with through hearing or reading such chapbook stories.

Finally, the chapbook stories were available in more than one language. While the printed versions of the texts circulated in English, the stories also circulated in Irish. Chapbook stories such as 'Guy of Warwick' and 'Bevis of Hampton' had been translated into Irish by the fifteenth century and were circulating probably both in manuscript form and orally.[32] Certainly by the 1520 the copy of the 'Seven wise masters' owned by the earl of Kildare was in Irish.[33] By the 1630s Geoffrey Keating was aware of many of these tales, noting, 'for there was no kingdom in the world in which there were not written tales called fabulae in Pagan times, for example, the Knight of the Sun, Bevis of Hampton, Huon of Bordeaux, and other such like, which were written even in the time of the faith' and Barnaby Rich claimed that the Irish knew these tales better than godly books.[34]

Readings of such popular works are ephemeral, often purely for entertainment, and hence almost impossible to recover. However, attempts to control such readings do suggest something of that process. The presentation of St Patrick in the *Seven champions* is not that of a saint in the mould of a medieval hagiographical text. In its most developed form St Patrick redeems six Thracian ladies from satyrs before proceeding with the other champions to Greece, Portugal, Jerusalem and Egypt. he then returned to Ireland where he dies, after digging his own grave. However his character retained some of the miraculous and quasi-magical features which were associated with late medieval hagiography, the reading of which was popular among early modern Irish Catholics, and as such saints' lives and chapbook stories may have silently elided into one another. Such miraculous stories would not merely be tolerated but would be celebrated in the context of these popular histories. Yet they were not acceptable to some, who regarded these stories as mere fables and felt that measures had to be taken to prevent them being read as devotional works. That hagiography and histories were read in this way is suggested by a 1685 London reprint for the Irish market of the part of the *Seven champions* dealing with St Patrick. In this case it was prefaced by a short account of the traditional hagiographical story of St Patrick, suggesting that both were to be read together as part of a seamless story.[35] Again the burlesque life of the Tory Redmond O'Hanlon, published in Dublin in 1682, models at least part of the early life of O'Hanlon on a saint's life, with its portents and miraculous birth, and calls him a 'young St Patrick'.[36] In such stories the saint of hagiographical legend was removed from the ecclesiastical world in which he had first found fame and was placed in an alternative world of moral and entertaining reading.

Such stories were usually thought to belong to the young but in reality were read throughout one's life. After the world of the popular romance, often encountered while one was learning to read, the next stage in the life cycle at which one might encounter books was at school, where schoolbooks were part of the apparatus of formal learning. Even those of the middling sort who were not ardent book buyers would come into contact with schoolbooks. The account book of one merchant in Drogheda at the end of the seventeenth century suggests that he was not a frequent patron of the bookseller. Between 1698 and 1705 he bought only a work on gardening, a travel account of the new world and a Bible, apparently as a gift. In 1702 three of his children began school and by 1705 he was purchasing more books than he ever had before for the boys' education. Lilly's grammar and a Westminster grammar were followed by Evaldus Gallus's *Pueriles confabulatiunculae* and other books. In the two years between 1705 and 1707, when the account book ends, he had spent almost as much on books as he had during the previous ten years.[37]

Schoolbooks comprised a very wide range of works from simple horn-books, which were little more than printed sheets mounted between thin sheets of horn to protect them, intended to teach basic reading through to Latin grammars for the more sophisticated. Many of these works had long lives. Francis Seager's *School of virtue*, for instance was being imported from Bristol into the Munster towns in the 1590s, and in 1689 it was still being advertised in a Dublin almanac as a schoolbook being used in Dublin. Evaldus Gallus's *Pueriles confabulatiunculae*, also imported in the late sixteenth century, appeared in the same bookseller's advertisement and was being purchased at the beginning of the eighteenth century by the Drogheda merchant referred to above.[38] Some individuals could manage with only a few specialist books. Richard Cox in his autobiography described his education in Clonakilty in the early 1660s, claiming, 'it was an advantage to me that I had no book but a grammar, for by writing my lessons in the classic authors and by writing rhetoric, logic and part of physic I learnt to write fast and well and it also made a great impression in my mind of what I learned'.[39] Most scholars required at least a few basic textbooks, making the schoolbook trade a steady and profitable one.

Initially most schoolbooks had been imported from England and there are indications that some English printers may have been targeting the Irish schoolbook market in the late sixteenth century. John Hart's reading primer produced in London in 1570 claimed that if the method of spelling he exhorted was adopted 'the desirous Welsh and Irish [would be very much advanced] to the pronunciation of our speech which was never before this time presented to them'.[40] In the later seventeenth century, Irish editions of the standard school-books began to appear.[41] According to advertisement in a 1689 almanac:

> Whereas such chapmen who deal in books have been forced to send to England for all their histories and schoolbooks these are now to give them an account that the books undernamed may be had at the king's printing house on Ormond Quay or any of the booksellers in Dublin and all other schoolbooks and histories useful to this kingdom will be done as fast as possible and afford as cheap as can be had in London.[42]

Before the middle of the 1690s this market was largely the preserve of the king's printer but from 1697 as his power waned others began to move into the lucrative schoolbook trade. In 1698, for instance, two Dublin printers attempted to pirate a work on arithmetic by putting a different title page on it, which the guild of St Luke rapidly suppressed.[43]

Once one had moved out of the youthful stage of the life cycle there was a diverse range of books to which the early modern Irish reader could turn. Something of the range might be seen in the comment of Patrick Plunket, a student in the Irish college at Douai, who was implicated in a plot to smuggle Catholic books into Ireland in 1610. The mayor of Chester discovered the books, which Patrick claimed were 'certain books of history, philosophy and other science'.[44] While this was clearly untrue, Patrick's dissembling does suggest the range of books which a young man of the upper social rank would expect to encounter in an Irish house. Some of these were serious books while others provided entertainment as well as instruction. On the one hand books were intended to be practical. As one man claimed, when leaving his books to the earl of Ormond during the crisis of the 1640s, 'to serve your lordship and your house was a principal use I made of them'.[45] On the other hand there were works of literature which could be read mainly for pleasure. As Archdeacon William Hamilton noted in his life of James Bonnell, 'the pleasure of narrative would still engage our attention and prevent weariness, which few can escape when only books of reasoning and argument are before them'.[46] In the 1540s copies of Sir Thomas Wyatt's poetry were available in Dublin, and by the 1590s Sir John Harington's translation of *Orlando Furioso* was available in Galway.[47] Printers and booksellers had a vested interest in making the most unlikely material interesting to readers. One translation of a French philosophical work published in Dublin in 1687, written as a series of dialogues for those 'knowing readers, particularly of the female sex, that desire to be philosophers', stressed that it was 'for diversion and instruction' and 'these contemplations which are delivered not with the severe air of philosophy but so interspersed with pleasant illustrations and facetious instructive remarks that certainly he that once sets up on them will hardly lay the book aside till he has run quite through them, the whole is so very charming'.[48] The efforts of booksellers and others ensured that contemporaries had a range of books to which they could to turn for profit and pleasure according to their needs.

At the simplest there were books which conveyed factual information useful for many. One sort of practical book which circulated widely was the almanac, a compendium of miscellaneous information issued annually by some printers. From at least the beginning of the seventeenth century, almanacs were being imported into Ireland from England. According to the Bristol port books almanacs valued at wholesale rates at 1*d* a dozen were being imported into Cork in the early seventeenth century.[49] At the beginning of 1591 Lord Deputy Fitzwilliam recorded that he bought two new almanacs costing 7*d*, and in 1594 he paid 6*d* for two more almanacs, presumably imports.[50] In a few cases the origins of almanac imports may have extended more widely than just England. In 1650, for instance, one Dublin will bequeathed a 'Dutch almanac'.[51] The earliest surviving almanac published in Ireland is that for 1612 by William Farmer.[52] Since almanacs were cheap books, consulted frequently, they tended to fall apart from use and hence few copies have survived. Thus it is not certain if Farmer had previously published an Irish almanac, although he had published one in London in 1587 which may have been aimed at the Irish import trade.[53] How long Farmer's almanacs were published is not known. Only a fragment of a 1614 issue is known but it is conceivable that their life was short.[54] Certainly the printer John Franckton did not think the Irish market was large, and in a note from the printer on the verso of the title page to the 1612 almanac he apologised for not printing the important days in the calendar in red, 'the reason partly was that printing so small a number of them it would not countervail the charges'.[55] The small-scale Irish market for books in English at this point clearly could not absorb a work which relied on a large-scale circulation, and it seems Farmer's almanac did not last long. The next venture in 1636 by a Patrick True may well have been under the patronage of the Stationers since their arms are displayed prominently in the work.[56] It seems likely to have been a reprint of an English work since in the list of 'festival days' there is no mention of any specifically Irish saint. Most of the content is not specific in its place except for some of the calculations for latitudes, which were probably grafted on to the text of an English almanac.

Most extant Irish almanacs date from the years after 1660 but this may be as much an accident of survival as a reflection of production. The earliest is that of Ambrose White in 1665 printed by Nathaniel Thompson, who was operating William Bladen's press in Dublin. It was sold by Robert Howes. This may be significant since it seems highly likely that this was the almanac that resulted in accusations against Bladen for infringing the monopoly of the king's printer, John Crooke, to produce such books.[57] If so that might suggest that this almanac was a speculative venture that was an attempt to break into the market dominated by legal imports. It may be that Crooke, determined to reassert his authority in this field, was behind Michael Haward's almanac which appeared from Crooke's press the following year. It is not until the late 1670s that the Irish almanac trade managed to establish itself with a regular output of volumes. There are almanacs for 1678 and 1679 by A. Shepherd and Patrick Plunkett respectively and a group of three by John Bourke in the mid-1680s.

From the middle of the 1680s the appearance of John Whalley in Dublin served to invigorate and transform the almanac trade. Whalley, a rabid Whig and astrologer who was forced to flee Ireland briefly in 1689, turned out a succession of almanacs in the 1680s and 1690s which were overtly political, which previous Irish almanacs had not been.[58] Initially he used the king's printer to produce his works but by 1697 he had broken the connection with the king's printer and his almanac published in that year was printed and distributed by himself. It seems likely that these almanacs were available from the same people who acted as distributors for his patent medicines. Of the twenty-two agents listed in the 1697 almanac the majority, thirteen, described themselves as merchants but there was also a clothier, a bookseller, a postmaster, an innkeeper, a widow and a gentleman, and two were involved in the cloth trade. These were based in twenty-one towns in the commercialised part of the country in a arc from Derry to Cork and stretching as far west as

Galway and Loughrea. For areas which had few towns, such as Mayo, a pedlar was used to distribute almanacs.[59]

Almanacs seem to have been widely diffused across Irish society. At least part of the success of the almanac lay in its low cost. As John Mc Comb in his almanac for 1694 claimed, 'if every man in every county in Ireland would secure the sale of a hundred almanacs in each county the printer is willing to afford them at sixpence a piece with as much variety as can be expected in four sheets'.[60] In practice there was a wide range of editions and formats. At the luxury end of the market leather-bound versions might sell for as much as a shilling but at the lower end of the market a penny was more usual by the early part of the eighteenth century.[61]

Almanacs usually appeared in a fairly standard format. they contained information about road networks, markets and fairs, the times of sunrise and sunset throughout the year, lists of monarchs and law terms, ideas for agricultural improvement and handy medical hints. In addition Whalley's almanacs contained astrological predictions, usually of a highly political nature, for the coming year. Some of this information was contained in verse form with a short, easily memorised verse for each month of the year. Such verses often carried messages which were wider than the agricultural hints they were meant to convey. One verse for November in Patrick True's 1636 almanac, for example, proclaimed:

> Regard all thy life the 5 day of November
> And teach thy children ever the same day to remember
> God's mercy and pope's cruelty with one fatal blow
> The king and state most wickedly quite to overthrow.[62]

However, most messages were not political but social. The verse from Ambrose White's 1665 almanac, for instance, urged readers to 'relieve the poor', entertain one's neighbours, be moderate in one's drinking and, in the case of husbands, be faithful to one's wife.[63] Such messages of common morality might appeal to potential purchasers on all sides of the confessional divide in Ireland, and so almanacs, like popular romances, may have helped provide sets of common ideas that helped to shape local societies.

Despite the similarities between them, not all almanacs were uniform in format. As the late seventeenth-century almanac writer John Whalley observed in 1697, ''Tis not [one] swallow makes a summer, not one field of corn a harvest nor one sort of people that yearly for if it were so such as are sometimes imposed upon the people of Ireland would turn to so slender an account that the printers would soon grow weary of that labour'.[64] Printers and compilers of almanacs clearly tried to introduce new features into their work that would enhance their popularity and encourage sales. In one case, the three almanacs published by John Bourke in the 1680s, it is possible to see something of the attempts of an author to make his work more appealing.[65] Little is known of Bourke himself. His name might suggest that he was from a Gaelicised background. It is possible that he was related to Patrick Bourke, a 'teacher of mathematics', who petitioned Dublin corporation in 1687 to set up a school to teach mathematics to the young, and he is probably the same 'Patrick Bourke, gent' who became a freeman of the city in 1688.[66] It is also possible that Patrick and John are the same, since most almanac compilers had a mathematical background necessary for the astronomical calculations needed for an almanac. A name change to a more Irish name in the early years of James II's reign when Catholicism and Irish culture seemed in the ascendant is entirely probable. Bourke issued his first almanac in 1683. In many ways it was a rather crude production, clearly copied from English models. The calendar which marks the saints' days does not include Sts Patrick or Columcille, suggesting an English origin for this. Most of the content of the almanacs was standard: lists of regnal years, tables for the conversion of money, a monthly calendar with weather prognostications, lists of routeways, and schedules of markets and fairs. Bourke's innovation was to print on the page opposite the monthly calendar material which he thought might attract buyers. In the 1683 almanac he included a list of Irish lords deputy and lords lieutenant from 1169. This clearly was not attractive and in the following year he replaced this with medical and dietary advice for each month. This too seems not to have increased sales and in 1685 he included a history of Ireland from the coming of Christianity to 1172. This seems to be a history of Bourke's own devising, drawing on a range of scholarly and popular works by James Ware and Peter Walsh to construct, in a traditional manner, a succession list of kings with comments on their reigns. In this case it may be that Bourke, sensing a change in attitudes to the world of Gaelic Ireland, as Protestants began to acquire copies of Keating's history of early Ireland and poets celebrated the period, was trying to cash in on popular sentiment.[67] No further almanacs by Bourke survive and it is possible that despite his manoeuvrings he had failed to catch the mood of the market and was forced to suspend publication.

Practical works, such as almanacs, were perhaps not read systematically at all but merely consulted from time to time. Certainly surviving almanacs, usually from the luxury end of the market with leather bindings, were kept for long periods of time as suggested by the notes made at different times in the back of the volume. One copy of the 1683 almanac by John Bourke, for instance, has notes of debts and purchases up to 1724, although this is exceptional.[68] As such they were probably dipped into rather than read. While some material in an almanac, such as the prognostications and astronomical information, had to be updated for each new year, much else, such as the list of regnal years, dates of markets, medical advice and hints for agricultural improvement, had a longer lifespan. The useful life of an almanac may well have been five or ten years, after which it would have disintegrated and needed to be replaced. Over such a period sections of it might have been repeatedly consulted.

Almanacs certainly conveyed practical information but more specialist works were also available to meet the needs of farmers or craftsmen. Patrick Plunket in the 1690s, urging that Ireland should be improved economically, told his readers that each 'may excellently help himself out of several books of husbandry lately sent forth in England'.[69] Dublin printers, too, produced practical books to meet some of this market. In the area of agriculture Michael Haward's *The herdsman's mate or a guide for herdsmen* published in 1673 offered a handy pocket-sized compendium of cures for animal diseases. This was compiled as much from astrological learning as from practical experience although its author's intention in writing it was to prevent 'English-Irish lukewarm Protestants' from resorting to 'popish' cures for animal ills. In commerce too there were handbooks. In the 1690s one Dublin teacher of bookkeeping published a manual which he intended would be the first of a number on the subject. The significance of the work was quickly downplayed by a respondent who claimed that the sort of knowledge the work purported to convey was already well known in Dublin.[70] However, printed works could not meet the demands of many with specialist needs and so individuals created their own manuscript books which sometimes circulated alongside the printed ones. One settler in County Londonderry claimed among his losses in the rising of 1641 not only surveying instruments but 'my written hand book both of arithmetic and geometry'. Again in the late seventeenth century one Belfast mariner owned a manuscript handbook of mathematical material, notes on sailing, navigation and currents as well as doggerel verse which helped him to remember the constellations and planets, presumably for navigation purposes.[71]

For those higher in the social scale who had landed or mercantile interests, news of government decisions, London fashions or international relations which might affect trade was of prime importance. In the sixteenth and early seventeenth centuries that sort of information was supplied by letters, rumour, gossip, travellers and leaks from Dublin castle. The sixteenth-century Irish annals, for instance, show that information about events in Europe was spreading into Ireland. The Annals of Loch Cé record the battle of Flodden in 1516, the General Chapter of the Franciscans in Rome in 1517, the taking of Antwerp in 1585, the campaigns of the king of Persia against the Turks, and the execution of Mary, queen of Scots. This sort of material was not collected systematically and it probably represents what came to hand locally through the movements of clergy or merchants or through other casual means such as 'the folk who spread news and frequent ports'.[72]

From the middle of the seventeenth century Irish-produced newspapers began to appear for the first time. The earliest example of an Irish newspaper was Samuel Dancer's *Mercurius Hibernicus or Ireland's Intelligence*, which lasted for only fifteen numbers in 1663. It claimed 'from week to week to give account of all news or transactions which shall occur either at home or abroad which being a means to prevent the disquiet of people's spirits, continually agitated by fanatic lies'.[73] In practice the staple news which carried the paper throughout its short life was that leaking from the Court of Claims established under the act of settlement, which was probably the main reason that many purchased the paper. Following the demise of *Mercurius Hibernicus* there was a significant hiatus in the development of Irish newspapers, and it was not until the middle of the 1680s that new newsheets appeared and not until the early eighteenth century that the form developed in any significant way.[74]

What the print run or circulation of these early newspapers was is unknown but they may have had a wide geographical distribution based on the postal system. In one March issue of *Mercurius Hibernicus* a reward was advertised for a horse stolen in Dundonald, County Down, and later in the month a County Louth theft was advertised, which may indicate the sort of range of the paper's penetration.[75] In the 1680s *The Newsletter* contained an advertisement for a horse stolen at Maryborough, and its successor *The Dublin Intelligence* had advertisements from Waterford in 1693 and Raphoe in 1702, and the *Flying Post* of 1701 had an advertisement relating to Tuam.[76] The corporation of Kinsale subscribed to a news-sheet as early as 1685 but, thinking they received poor value for their money, cancelled the subscription. It was renewed soon after but cancelled again in 1702 as 'of no use and great expense'.[77] In the 1690s the agent on the Herbert estate at Castleisland in County Kerry was also considering whether he should subscribe to the new Dublin gazette at 20s a year.[78] By the early eighteenth century prices had fallen so that the twice-weekly *Dublin Post* could be had for 2s 2d a quarter.[79] On such evidence it does seem clear that the Dublin news-sheets of the late seventeenth century had a reach well outside the capital. While Dublin remained the main centre of news gathering, the emergence of the postal system and the commercialisation of print played a part in stimulating an ever increasing appetite for news and opinion fuelled by periodical political crises.

Such news-sheets were of limited value because of their erratic nature; they were fed by political crisis rather than by the demand for steady flows of news. That need was more usually met by news-sheets or manuscript gazettes, which originated in England during the 1620s, to which some subscribed or which were sent to them by friends in England or elsewhere.[80] In Munster in the early 1680s there was considerable enthusiasm for the acquisition of news-sheets in this way and a desire for news conveyed by these means. John Perceval in Cork, for instance, wrote to a contact in Dublin in 1683 asking him

to give Mr John Brown of the post office a new year's gift of two guineas and desire him or such as he shall recommend to send me the newsletters and gazettes as often as they come in and do you agree for how much per annum or per quarter to have it done. The town of Charleville have them and all pamphlets of a sheet of trials, speeches etc. for £5 10s per annum.[81]

Foreign news-sheets were of particular interest to merchants and those interested in political developments in Europe, and the growth of the resident Irish merchant community in the later seventeenth century was certainly an incentive to provide such news-sheets. The Dutch *Haarlem Gazette*, for example, was in Dublin in 1693, and in 1703 one of the Dublin newspapers advertised that 'at [the] printing house at [the] back of Dick's coffee house will be continually printed best and foreign news. Supplied with Leyden and Haarlem gazettes in English and other prints of consequence' probably supplied from London.[82] How efficient this supply was is unclear but at least some Dublin printers thought they had spotted a gap in the market. In January 1692 three Dublin booksellers, Andrew Crooke, Eliphal Dobson and Patrick Campbell, proposed to establish a monthly journal to be known as *The Present State of Europe and the Historical and Political Monthly Mercury*. The proposal consisted of a Dublin printing of the *Monthly Mercury* printed at The Hague and reprinted at London. The rationale of the publication was to

> give a monthly account of the most considerable events and transactions of Europe which lies scattered in the gazettes and news letters and are many times wholly omitted by them so that those who cannot have those different relations, or will not be at the expense, need no more than repair to this Mercury to satisfy their curiosity ... [about] nothing that is mean and trivial but with affairs of the greatest importance and which all men are concerned to know.

The news-sheet was intended to be by subscription, the undertakers declaring that they 'do intended to print but very few more than what they have subscriptions for'. If four hundred subscriptions were raised the five sheets would cost 8d an issue.[83] In fact by April they had raised under three hundred subscribers and the cost had risen to 12d an issue for non-subscribers. By November subscribers were cancelling their subscriptions, probably because the same material was available more cheaply elsewhere. By the end of the year the project was dead, although a brief attempt was made to revive it in 1704.[84]

Among the landed at the pinnacle of the social scale yet other types of books were deemed important to fulfil the social and political duties expected. A case in point comprises the sort of historical works which appeared in seventeenth-century Ireland. Sir James Perrot in his *Chronicle of Ireland* written at the beginning of the seventeenth century urged the case for a more considered reading of historical works since 'the monuments and mirrors of times past, the directions of things present and foresight of the future are no way better discerned than by diligent reading of histories well and judicially written'. Contemporary history was better than ancient history and more relevant. The reading of such history was essentially a practical exercise since 'the use of reading histories is twofold: either private for a man's particular knowledge and information or public for the application of it to the service of the state'.[85] History, most agreed, taught practical and moral lessons. In the 1570s the Protestant pamphleteer Barnaby Rich lamented the lack of learning in Ireland and in particular the lack of facilities to read histories 'that giveth light of understanding'. Such and exercise was necessary since

> there is nothing which may be either pleasure, profitable or necessary for man but is written in books wherein are reported the manners, conditions, government, counsels and affairs of every country: the gestes, acts, behaviours and manner of living of every people: the form of sundry commonwealths with their augmenting and decays and the occasions thereof: the precepts, exhortations, counsels and good persuasions comprehended in quick counsels and good persuasions comprehended in quick sentences. To conclude in books and histories are actually expressed the beauty of virtue and the loathsomeness of vice ... which knowledge and light cometh chiefly unto us by reading of histories.[86]

The theme of history as morality was taken up again by the clerk to the Munster council, Lodowick Bryskett, in the early seventeenth century when he observed that readers 'sometimes in reading of histories, which are mirrors or looking glasses for every man to see good or evil actions of all ages, the better to square his life to the rule of virtue by the examples of others', and at least one man in the later seventeenth century described one group of his books as 'history and other books of morality'.[87] Reading history was therefore a practical exercise which required time and the careful extracting of underlying meanings from what was read rather than a mere summary of arguments or events. The Irish lord deputy in the 1630s, Christopher Wandesford, instructed his son:

> read not histories for your delight only or for the vain glory of being able to discourse of them, but to be bettered by the instances that you find in them. For to what end are the examples of former times delivered unto us but that after ages may reject the vicious and gather up by imitation the virtuous example of those that lived before them.[88]

It was assumed, by at least some, that in the course of pamphlet debate the educated could draw on a stock of these sorts of examples to illustrate or prove particular positions. During his debate with the earl of Orrery in the 1660s, the Franciscan Peter Walsh urged his opponent to note that 'your own reading can furnish you with sufficient proofs that ordinarily the most unhappy states have been those that who have made the greatest show of knowledge to deceive under humane policy'.[89] Reading history could provide the grammar for the construction of ideas on how societies should work and in that sense shaped the political language of the elite. It could also provide warnings of dangers in store. During the early stages of the popish plot one anonymous correspondent of the duke of Ormond spilled out on paper his fears that Catholics were poised to take over Ireland and warned that 'the rest that is intended you may read the massacre in Paris [in] octavo printed 1655'. He also urged 'plain headed English Protestants' in Ireland to read the recently reprinted Pascal's *The mystery of Jesuitism discovered in certain letters* and Edward Coleman's *Mr Coleman's two letters to Monsieur l'Chaise, the French king's confessor* since in dealing with Catholics 'experience and history informs us' that they are untrustworthy.[90]

Even when the reading of history did not seem to be practical, printers could endeavour to make it so by packaging historical works with a more attractive purchase. The motive of the early seventeenth-century antiquarian Sir James Ware in writing his historical works about Ireland seems to have been a purely scholarly one. He declared as much in the prefaces to his works, and the early editions of these were published in Latin, suggesting an exclusively scholarly readership. When three Dublin printers, Andrew Crooke, Ephiphal Dobson and Mathew Gunn, reissued the works in English in 1705 they declared on the title page that the work was 'very useful for all persons who are desirous of being acquainted with the ancient and present state of that kingdom'. In order to bolster their claim that Ware's scholarly work had current relevance they included with the works a copy of the Roman calendar, a list of the mayor and corporation of the Dublin in 1705, a copy of the 'New rules' of 1675 which governed the elections to corporations, a list of chief governors of Ireland, a catalogue of the nobility of Ireland in 1704, a list of members of the house of Commons and Convocation, a list of the privy council, a list of the principal civil and military officers in Ireland and a description of the riding of the franchises of Dublin. All this undoubtedly proved useful for those not convinced that reading history brought its own reward.

However, history could be read in another way. As the godly chaplain to the earl of Cork, Steven Jerome, commented in 1624, those who blasphemed against God would be destroyed 'as histories and experience relate'.[91] As evidence for his proposition he cited two historical works, John Foxe's book of martyrs and Thomas Beard's *Theatre of God's judgement*. Both were godly works and not much evidenced in Ireland. John Foxe's work appears only in the collection of goods owned by the parish of St Catherine's in Dublin in the 1650s.[92] For the godly this providential reading of the past seems to have been common, at least in the early part of the seventeenth century. The forceful godly preacher Richard Olmstead hammered home the same message in a sermon of 1630, asking his audience to 'search all histories, chronicles and records in all ages of the church if ruin and desolation were not the ... recompense of this villainous and cursed idolatry'.[93] In the 1680s the Baptist Richard Lawrence, who certainly adhered to the view of reading history as a providential narrative, deployed examples from the past in his moral analysis of Ireland's economic position. While providing economic reasons for abstaining from swearing, drunkenness and fornication, he backed up his propositions with historical examples. Turning his analysis to the role of religion and rebellion, historical precedent on the disloyalty of Catholics (and Jesuits in particular) fed the argument yet further.[94]

Linked to the reading of histories was the reading of biography, which also was held to have a practical effect. According to William Hamilton, the archdeacon of Armagh and biographer of the godly Irish accomptant general James Bonnell, 'lives are usually read with greater pleasure and application than any other kind of writing and it must be owned that when rightly chosen they give us the most useful view of human nature and justest representation of virtue and vice with their different consequences and effects'. However, according to Hamilton, the sort of biographies people wished to read were the lives of those 'who have acted the most entangled and busy parts of life' and in particular soldiers and statesmen. It was to counter this trend that Hamilton turned to a religious subject to raise minds to what he regarded as a higher plane.[95] Hamilton, in fact, was following an older tradition of hagiography in creating a model life which others might hope to emulate: in short the first Church of Ireland saint's life.

If the reading of history and biography was a practical activity then the reading of law by non-professionals was equally important. For those who owned or leased land, a working knowledge of the law was important. Sensing a market opportunity, the Dublin printers produced legal guides for the landowner to help him run his estate. In the 1630s the Dublin presses reprinted two English works intended to guide landowners on how to keep manorial courts on their estates.[96] The ability to defend oneself in legal actions was too important to be left to the professionals. Thus the Kilkenny landowner Richard Shee left all his law books to his son Marcus, and his books of divinity, civil and canon law to his second son John, but enjoined Marcus 'to be kept at the law to be a better member of the commonwealth and to defend himself'.[97] Local gentry might be called upon to act as local government officials such as justice of the peace or county sheriff. For these offices a knowledge of the law was essential. As Richard Bolton observed in the dedication to his 1638 handbook for justices of the peace, 'it will be needful that the justice of the peace should well understand the duty of his place and neither exceed nor come short of the authority given him either by commission or by the statute laws of the realm'.[98] A case in point is John Swanley of Gloucestershire who by 1637 had settled in St John's parish in Wexford. According to his probate inventory he had books worth £10 among his goods which comprised a great Bible, two little Bibles, a great Latin Bible and a Latin dictionary. The remaining books were 'a great statute book and many other law books'.[99] Swanley, though not a lawyer, clearly had more than a passing interest in the law. Reading law, with its technical language and multifarious assumptions about a knowledge of statute law and precedent, was not an easy business.

Christopher Wandesford, both an government official and a Kilkenny land-owner, recommended that his son should be thoroughly acquainted with the laws 'in reading and digesting them', suggesting a slow careful reading, possibly with note taking.[100]

II

By the end of the seventeenth century printed books and more ephemeral printed items for both business and pleasure had become commonplace in Ireland. The dramatist Richard Steele, for instance, recalled that when he was growing up in Dublin the relation who was his guardian 'had a pretty large study of books'. It was Steele's task to dust the books each week and so he was obliged to take every book from its shelf. As he observed

> I thought there was no way to deceive the toil of my journey thro' the different abodes and habitations of these authors but by reading something in every one of them and in this manner to make my passage easy from the comely folio in the upper shelf or region, even through the crowd of duodecimos in the lower. By frequent exercise I became so great a proficient in this transitory application to books that I could hold open half a dozen small authors in my hand, grasping them with as secure a dexterity as a drawer doth his glasses and feasting my curious eye with all of them at the same instant. Through these methods the natural irresolution of my youth was much strengthened, and having no leisure, if I had the inclination, to make pertinent observations in writing I was thus confirmed a very early wanderer.[101]

The growth in the number of volumes in circulation had the potential to educate, entertain and inform. One preacher in the scholarly surroundings of the chapel of Trinity College, Dublin, in 1694 waxed eloquent about the new-found role of books in that world:

> In books we may freely talk with the most celebrated philosophers and compendiously reap the advantage of their studies and improvements ... by their means we may converse with mighty heroes whom in their lifetime we durst scarce perhaps salute with our eyes, we may be admitted confidants to statesmen ... thus by the assistance of books and learning we may acquire an intellectual omnipresence in all ages and to all places.

However, the preacher also warned that 'indefatigable reading brings in a vast stock of matter which is often without form and void like the first chaos till thinking and contemplation, like the seminal spirit, agitate the dull shape-less lump and work it up into figure and symmetry'.[102] Almost a hundred years earlier similar sentiments had been echoed by the Protestant polemicist Barnaby Rich. 'One of the diseases of this age', he declared, 'is the multitude of books that doth so overcharge the world that it is not able to digest the abundance of idle matter that is every day hatched and brought into the world that are as divers in their forms as their authors be in their faces'.[103] Many were excited by this same development and entered the world of print with enthusiasm. In one play of the 1680s written by John Wilson, the recorder of Derry, a character demands books, about which she claims, 'I can't sleep for thinking of them' and 'I should have broken my heart long ere this if 'twere not for them'.[104] Others were more modest. One Ulster Presbyterian doctor in the 1690s was proud of his 'small library', but it was 'well picked', having 'the marrow of all ancient and modern authors'.[105] While many in Ireland owned only one or two books, perhaps a Bible or a chapbook romance, and read them repeatedly, there were those who did read widely and with excitement, deeply engaged with what they read. The lord deputy's secretary in the 1630s, George Radcliffe, wrote to Bishop Bramhall of Derry of his excitement at the arrival in Dublin of a Cambridge-printed work of Arminian theology, adding, 'I am very desirous to read the book which I got but this evening and therefore, it being now past 9 o'clock I shall bid your lordship goodnight'.[106] Clearly Radcliffe in his enthusiasm for his new acquisition wanted to become acquainted with its contents as soon as possible. Similar reactions are betrayed by a poem prefixed to the 1624 Dublin printing of Richard Bellings's sixth book of *Arcadia*, which began: 'I read thy book on[e] night late'.[107] In the 1620s this sort of enthusiastic reading almost caused a major fire. Robert Blair, the minister of Bangor, spent one Saturday 'all day reading, meditating and writing until very late'. The heat from the fire which had been kept burning on the hearth ignited one of the rafters. Unaware of this, Blair kept reading and called for another candle, which was refused by the mistress of the house 'entreating me to go to bed'. He persisted in his demand for a candle to read and in fetching it the fire was discovered and extinguished, otherwise it would have spread to the town and 'no human skill nor power could have preserved the most part of that town'.[108]

Reading of all sorts of books in the course of the seventeenth century became a popular, practical and enjoyable activity. Part of the explanation for this shift was the rapid growth in the number of publications available in Dublin and, to a lesser extent, in Ireland generally. The uses to which this growing volume of books on all subjects was put was determined not by their apparent aim but by the way in which readers approached them. Private reading could be emotional and highly subjective but could leave few clues for the historian to uncover. Sir John Harrington, for instance, reported that in Galway in the 1590s a young lady was so enthusiastic about his newly published translation of *Orlando Furioso* that she read herself to sleep with it. The reason was that 'the verse I think so lively figured her fortune', she having been jilted by her lover as one of the characters in the text had been.[109] To some extent such reading of practical and pleasurable books was conditioned by the extent of one's reading and the inter relationship of texts which one read. For those who lived only in the world of the chapbook, reading might be a relatively simple matter but for those with larger libraries the range of referents was larger and readings more complex. The Catholic bishop of Ferns, Nicholas French, recorded at the beginning of his 1679 tract *The bleeding Iphigenia* how some years earlier he had read a printed account of the abjuration of Catholicism by Andrew Sall in 1674:

> as I was reading with great attention Sall's abjuration I called to mind that great red dragon whose tail drew the third part of the stars of heaven, and cast them to the earth (Apoc. cap 12). And then I said to myself, the tail of an infernal beast had cast this Sall to the earth out of a little heaven (*The state of religion*) wherein for a time he shined like a small star in virtue and learning.[110]

In this case the Bible provided a context for Bishop French's reading. In another case a later seventeenth-century reader of Sir John Temple's 1646 *History of the Irish rebellion*, probably a Henry Echlin in 1674, annotated his copy '2 Nalson page 8 of introduction suspicion of our author's partiality'.[111] Here is an indication that the reading of two historical works together provided a context for understanding each of them. Such readings were not simple. One could extract multiple meanings from almost any text regardless of its nature. For example Samuel Foley, the Church of Ireland bishop of Down and Connor, complained in the 1690s that people in his diocese were not reading the Bible for spiritual edification, as they should, but for stories of wars or fabulous occurrences such as 'the strength of Samson, the bigness of Goliath and the age of Methuselah'.[112] Such multiple readings were recognised and even encouraged. When William Swayne produced his translations of the life of St David and St Ciaran in Kilkenny in 1647 it was clearly intended for devotional purposes but he added the rider that 'I doubt not but that the translation of St David's life will be heartily embraced by the gentry and commonality of the ancient corporation of Knocktopher within the afore-mentioned diocese [Ossory], and to all both Irish and Welsh in general, brother Erinagh, brother Brenagh'.[113] There was a long-standing connection between Knocktopher and St David, the parish church there being dedicated to the saint since at least the fifteenth century.[114] Swayne seems to have envisaged that at least the community of Knocktopher would read the life of the saint not solely for religious reasons but out of a sense of local pride and an expression of Old English identity, like St David neither English nor Irish.

Again a work of political polemic such as Sir John Temple's *History of the Irish rebellion*, first published in 1646, could be read in many ways.[115] While it was certainly a political tract, and later regarded as a historical source by political commentators in the late seventeenth century, some people could read it in other ways. One man in Chester reading the work in May 1646, shortly after it had been published, declared it to be a piece of massacre literature, Sir John being 'largest' on 'cruelties'.[116] Reading a piece of massacre literature was rather different from scholarly reading of history. It was not subjected to the same critical appraisal nor was its readership confined to Protestants interested in the fate of their co-religionists. In 1652 Brian Kavanagh of Carlow deposed to Cromwellian commissioners that about four years earlier he had met James Butler of Tinnahinch in Carlow who told him

> that he had seen the copy of a printed book setting forth some murders acted in Ireland in which book the murder of the English at Graige is charged on him the said James by the Lady Butler ... but he the said James denied that he was guilty thereof and hoped to find all those who gave orders for it.[117]

From the description the work must be Temple's *Irish rebellion*, yet it was being read for its stories of murder by a Catholic and probably one involved in those murders. This reflects another reading of Temple. The appeal of the murder stories to a Catholic reader may have stemmed from their capacity to shock and titillate, and some of the later short abstracts of the depositions published without commentary may have been aimed at this popular market.[118] Temple's commentary on stories of ripped-up bellies, live burials, knocked-out brains and hangings are immediate and violent, dwelling lovingly on the details of the murders. The excitement could be prolonged and further enlivened by reading not just the text but the extracts from the depositions themselves conveniently printed as part of the text yet separated from it. By the early eighteenth century images of such murders had become part of the text. Moreover the stories of social inversion by which servants attacked their masters and 'Irish tenants and servants [made] a sacrifice of their English landlords' may well have appealed to an anarchic streak in some readers.[119] This did not exhaust the way that one could read Temple outside its primary function as a political tract. In the late seventeenth century the Baptist Richard Lawrence urged families to read Temple not as a political tale of the untrustworthiness of the Irish but rather as a moral story to prevent themselves falling into sin by compromising with the Irish and 'swallow down full cups of their superstition and close in with that religion [Catholicism]'.[120]

III

Books which had at least the potential to bring profit and pleasure grew dramatically in number in the course of the sixteenth and seventeenth centuries. What people read was related to a wide range of variables. Books were not simply the prerogative of the upper social orders but cheap romances and almanacs circulated widely at all levels of society. Some books, such as historical or legal works were certainly more common in the great house than in the countryside, and wealth meant that a larger library could be afforded by the upper social classes. Lending and borrowing might go some way to close this gap and the sociability associated with print, such as the coffee houses discussed in Chapter 1, helped to ensure that print was widely diffused. To some extent what one read was determined by one's point in the life cycle as much as by economic status. Schoolbooks and romances were at least as much the province of the young as of the poor. More important than the mere presence of print were the reading strategies for dealing with it. Texts could be read in many ways, often not approved of by either author or authority. Yet how one read, and since reading was an ephemeral activity the evidence is thin, was determined to some extent by the frame of referents available whether those were other books, life experiences or the opinions of friends. The ability of individuals to read news-sheets, history, law, almanacs or romances with agreed meanings within a group gave rise to a significant reshaping of Irish society. Almanacs spoke of the importance of neighbours and, whether they were Irish or settler, many had read the same romances and such stories provided commonalities. Other books, such as the Bible or catechisms, created other communities of interpretation around them. Such micro-societies were the stuff of everyday life in early modern Ireland, and to understand the world in which those people lived we need to understand their books.

NOTES

1 Bodl., Carte MS 219, ff. 216–17.

2 Bodl., Carte MS 219, f. 296.

3 Raymond Gillespie, 'The religion of the first duke of Ormond' in T.C. Barnard and Jane Fenlon (eds), *The dukes of Ormonde, 1610–1745* (Woodbridge, 2000), pp. 102–3, 106, 108.

4 H.M.C., *Calendar of the manuscripts of the marquess of Ormonde* (new series, 8 vols, London, 1902–20), vii, pp. 513–27.

5 Bodl., Carte MS 60, f. 288.

6 Bodl., Carte MS 36, f. 344.

7 Bodl., Carte MS 35, ff. 191, 292, 576.

8 Bodl., Carte MS 45, f. 238.

9 Bodl., Carte MS 50, f. 109.

10 Cheshire Record Office, Chester, DLT/B43.

11 P.R.O.N.I., D695/228, pp. 84–90; T.C. Barnard, 'What became of Waring? The making of an Ulster squire' in T.C. Barnard, *Irish Protestant ascents and descents, 1641–1770* (Dublin, 2003), p. 257.

12 Richard Head, *Hic et ubique or the humours of Dublin* (London, 1663), pp. 20, 21. The reference to 'the brethren' appears to be to the Baptists.

13 Francis de Sales, *An introduction to the devout life*, ed. Henry Dodwell (Dublin, 1673), sig. e5.

14 The location of the sheet is now unknown: see Tony Sweeney, *Ireland and the printed word, 1475–1700* (Dublin, 1997), p. 238, for the history of the sheet.

15 Gearóid Mac Niocaill (ed.), *Crown surveys of lands, 1540–41* (Dublin, 1992), p. 314.

16 Uáitéar MacGearailt, 'Togail Troí: an example of translation and editing in medieval Ireland' in *Studia Hibernica* no. 31 (2000–1), pp. 76–85.

17 Raymond Gillespie, 'The book trade in southern Ireland, 1590–1640' in Gerard Long (ed.), *Books beyond the pale: aspects of the provincial book trade in Ireland before 1850* (Dublin, 1996), pp. 3, 5, 13.

18 P.R.O., SP63/256/9i; Stephen Jerome, *Ireland's jubilee and joys io paen* (Dublin, 1624), p. 100.

19 T.C.D., MS 807, f. 50.

20 P.J. Corish (ed.), 'Bishop Wadding's notebook' in *Archivium Hibernicum* xxix (1970), p. 87.

21 Mac Niocaill (ed.), *Crown surveys of lands*, pp. 314, 356.

22 Margaret Spufford, *Small books and pleasant histories* (London, 1981), p. 74.

23 Quoted in Antonia McManus, *The Irish hedge school and its books, 1695–1831* (Dublin, 2002), p. 174.

24 Robert Craghead, *Advice to communicants* (Edinburgh, 1698), 'To the Christian reader'.

25 T.C.D., MS 1206, ff. 305–6.

26 Fred Henegan, 'Mummers of County Wexford' in *Irish Booklover* xvii (1929), pp. 59–61. The plays existed in nineteenth-century chapbook versions. For the subject generally see Alan Gailey, *Irish folk drama* (Cork, 1969).

27 T.C.D., MS 883/1, p. 196.

28 Alan J. Fletcher, *Drama, performance and polity in pre-Cromwellian Ireland* (Cork, 2000), pp. 132–3, 145–8, 192–3.

29 N.L.I., MS 16085, f. 113.

30 *Cal. Carew, Book of Howth*, p. 246.

31 F.N. Robinson (ed.), 'The Irish lives of Guy of Warwick and Bevis of Hampton' in *Zeitschrift für Celtische Philologie* vi (1908), pp. 9–104, 273–338, 556, 908.

32 Robinson (ed.), 'The Irish lives of Guy of Warwick', pp. 9–104, 273–338, 556, 908; David Greene, 'A Gaelic version of the "Seven wise masters"' in *Béaloideas* xiv (1944), pp. 219–36.

33 Mac Niocaill (ed.), *Crown surveys of lands*, p. 356.

34 Geoffrey Keating, *Foras feasa ar Éirinn*, eds David Comyn and P.S. Dinneen (4 vols, London, 1902–14), ii, pp. 326–7; Barnaby Rich, *A true and kind excuse written in defence of that book entitled* A new description of Ireland (London, 1612), p. 4.

35 *The history of the life and death of St Patrick* (London, 1685).

36 *The life and death of the incomparable and indefatigable tory Redmond O Hanlyn* (Dublin, 1682), pp. 3–4.

37 N.L.I., MS 9536.

38 Gillespie, 'Book trade', pp. 5–6, 6–7, 13; Dom Russell, *A new almanac for the year of our Lord 1689* (Dublin 1689), 'Advertisement' [N.L.I., microfilm p 4529].

39 Richard Caulfield (ed.), *Autobiography of the Rt Hon. Sir Richard Cox, bart* (London, 1860), p. 9.

40 Quoted in Frank Davies, *Teaching reading in early England* (London, 1973), p. 148.

41 E.R. McClintock Dix, 'Schoolbooks printed in Dublin from the earliest period to 1715' in *Publications of the Bibliographical Society of Ireland* iii (1926–27), pp. 5–10.

42 Russell, *A new almanac for ... 1689*, 'Advertisement' [N.L.I., microfilm p 4529].

43 N.L.I. MS 12123, p. 21.

44 *Cal. S. P. Ire., 1608–10*, p. 192.

45 Bodl., Carte MS 2, f. 266.

46 William Hamilton, *The exemplary life and character of James Bonnell, late accomptant general of Ireland* (Dublin, 1703), sig. a2.

47 L.M. Oliver, 'A booksellers account book, 1545' in *Harvard Library Bulletin* xvi (1968), pp. 150, 151; N. Mc Clure (ed.), *The letters and epigrams of Sir John Harington* (Philadelphia, 1930), p. 74.

48 *The discourse of the plurality of worlds* (Dublin, 1687), sigs A4–4v.

49 Gillespie, 'The book trade in southern Ireland', pp. 5, 13.

50 Northampton County Record Office, Fitzwilliam of Milton MSS, Irish no. 30, 33.

51 N.A., Dublin Prerogative will book, 1644–84, f. 12.

52 For a description see E.R. McClintock Dix, 'A Dublin almanac of 1612' in *Proceedings of the Royal Irish Academy* xxx sect. C (1913), pp. 327–30.

53 William Farmer, *The common almanac or calendar drawn forth for the year 1587 ...* (London, 1587).

54 Sweeney, *Ireland and the printed word*, p. 27.

55 *[William] Farmer 1612 his prognostical almanac* (Dublin, 1612).

56 For a description see E.R. McClintock Dix, 'An early Dublin almanac' in *Proceedings of the Royal Irish Academy* xxxiii sect. C (1916), pp. 225–9.

57 Mary Pollard, *A dictionary of members of the Dublin book trade, 1550–1800* (London, 2000), pp. 565.

58 Pollard, *Dictionary*, pp. 603–4.

59 John Whalley, *Advice from the stars or an almanac for the year of Christ 1697* (Dublin, [1697]).

60 John McComb, *A new almanac for the year of our Lord 1694* (Dublin, [1694]), sig. A1v.

61 George Benn, *A history of the town of Belfast* (Belfast, 1877), p. 148; John Whalley, *A treatise of eclipses* (Dublin, 1701), sig. a2.

62 Patrick True, *A new almanac and prognostication for the year ... 1636* (Dublin, [1635]), sig. C1v.

63 For a set of such verses from Ambrose White's almanac see Andrew Carpenter (ed.), *Verse in English from Tudor and Stuart Ireland* (Cork, 2003), pp. 402–4.

64 Whalley, *Advice from the stars or an almanac for the year of Christ 1697*, sig. B2v.

65 John Bourke, *Hiberniae Merlinus for the year of our Lord 1683* (Dublin, 1683); John Bourke, *Hiberniae Merlinus for the year of our Lord 1684* (Dublin, 1684); John Bourke, *Hiberniae Merlinus for the year of our Lord 1685* (Dublin, 1685).

66 J.T. and R. Gilbert (eds), *Calendar of the ancient records of Dublin* (19 vols, Dublin, 1889–1944), v, pp. 461–2, 470.

67 Bernadette Cunningham, *The world of Geoffrey Keating* (Dublin, 2000), pp. 190–2, 206–8, Bernadette Cunningham and Raymond Gillespie, 'Lost worlds: history and religion in the poetry of Dáibhí Ó Bruadair' in Pádraigin Riggs (ed.), *Dáibhí Ó Bruadair: his historical and literary context* (London, 2001), pp. 37–41. The 1680 portrait of Sir Neil O'Neill of Killileagh in native Irish costume by Michael Wright now in the Tate Britain Gallery, London, may be another indication of this trend.

68 The 1683 almanac is now in N.L.I. I 6551.

69 Patrick Kelly (ed.), 'The improvement of Ireland' in *Analecta Hibernica* no. 35 (1992), pp. 70–1. In one case, that of Samuel Waring in County Down, the notes which he made from one English improving work survive, P.R.O.N.I., D695/229, pp. 7–8.

70 S. A[mmonet] *The key of knowledge for all merchants* (Dublin, 1696); J. G[ibbon], *Reflections on a book published by Mr Ammonet* (Dublin, 1696).

71 T.C.D., MS 839, f. 22v; Scottish Record Office, GD 154/935.

72 W.M. Hennessy and B.MacCarthy (eds), *Annála Uladh, Annals of Ulster* (4 vols, Dublin, 1887–1901), iii, pp. 538–9.

73 *Mercurius Hibernicus*, no. 1, 13–20 Jan. 1663.

74 Robert Munter, *The history of the Irish newspaper, 1685–1760* (Cambridge, 1967), pp. 11–18.

75 *Mercurius Hibernicus*, no. 9, 10–17 March 1663; no. 11, 24–31 March 1663.

76 *The Newsletter*, 26 Dec. 1685; *The Dublin Intelligence*, 18–22 April 1693, 9–13 June 1702; *Flying Post*, 17 Nov. 1701.

77 Michael Mulcahy (ed.), *Calendar of Kinsale documents* (2 vols, Kinsale, 1988–89), i, p. 86, ii, p. 12.

78 N.L.W., Powis Castle correspondence, no. 723.

79 *Dublin Post*, 21 Nov. 1702.

80 For examples, *Cal. S. P. Ire., 1663–5*, pp. 9, 176, 182, 683, 231; *Cal. S. P. Ire., 1666–9*, pp. 195, 338, 371, 460, 690, 723, 737; *Cal. S. P. Ire., 1669–70*, pp. 22, 27, 28, 29, 68, 131.

81 B.L., Add. MS 47024, f. 52.

82 Wouter Troost (ed.), 'Letters from Bartholomew van Homrigh to General Ginkle' in *Analecta Hibernica* no. 33 (1986), pp. 87, 110; *The Flying Post*, 29 June 1702.

83 *The Present State of Europe and the Historical Monthly Mercury*, Jan., 1692; April 1692.

84 *The Present State of Europe*, Nov., 1692; *The Present State of Europe or the Historical and Political Monthly Mercury ... for the Month of February 1703*, Feb., 1704.

85 Sir James Perrot, *The chronicle of Ireland, 1584–1608*, ed. Herbert Wood (Dublin, 1933), p. 3.

86 Barnaby Rich, *Alarme to England* (London, 1578), sig. Diiiv.

87 Lodowick Bryskett, *A discourse of civil life* (London, 1606), p. 17; B.L., Add MS 19865, f. 77.

88 Thomas Comber (ed.), *A book of instructions written by the Rt Hon. Sir Christopher Wandesford* (Cambridge, 1777), p. 18.

89 [Peter Walsh], *The Irish colours folded* (London, 1662), p. 22.

90 Bodl., Carte MS 118, ff. 189v, 190.

91 Jerome, *Ireland's jubilee*, p. 20.

92 R.C.B., P117/5/1, pp. 6, 14.

93 Richard Olmsted, *Sion's tears leading to joy* (Dublin, 1630), p. 7.

94 Richard Lawrence, *The interest of Ireland in its trade and wealth stated* (Dublin, 1682).

95 Hamilton, *The life and character of James Bonnell*, sigs a1–2.

96 For examples see John Wilkinson, *A treatise collected out of the statutes of this kingdom ... together with an easy and plain method of keeping a court leet* (Dublin, 1630); Jonas Adames, *The order of keeping a court leet and court baron with the charges appertaining to the same* (Dublin, 1634).

97 John Ainsworth (ed.), 'Power O'Shee papers' in *Analecta Hibernica* no. 20 (1958), p. 228.

98 Richard Bolton, *A justice of the peace for Ireland* (Dublin, 1638), 'epistle dedicatory'.

99 Gloucestershire Record Office, Diocesan inventories, 1637, no. 7. For his will made in Wexford, Diocesan wills, 1637, no. 78.

100 Comber (ed.), *A book of instructions*, pp. 69.

101 *The Guardian: volume the first* (London, 1767), pp. 257–8.

102 St George Ashe, *A sermon preached in Trinity College chapel before the University of Dublin, January the 9th 1693/4* (Dublin, 1694), p. 12.

103 Barnaby Rich, *A new description of Ireland* (London, 1610), sig. A4.

104 James Maidment and W.H. Logan (eds), *The dramatic works of John Wilson* (Edinburgh and London, 1874), pp. 309, 325.

105 BL, Sloane MS 4036, f. 106, Sloane MS 4037, f. 25.

106 Edward Berwick (ed.), *The Rawdon papers* (London, 1819), p. 23.

107 Carpenter (ed.), *Verse in English from Tudor and Stuart Ireland*, p. 165.

108 Thomas McCrie (ed.), *The life of Mr Robert Blair* (Edinburgh, 1848, pp. 59–60.

109 McClure (ed.), *The letters and epigrams of Sir John Harington*, p. 74.

110 Nicholas French, *The bleeding Ipigenia; Unkind deserter and The sale and settlement of Ireland*, ed. S.H. B[indon] (Dublin, 1848), p. 11.

111 Copy of John Temple, *History of the ... Irish rebellion* (London, 1646) now T.C.D., RR ll 64.

112 Samuel Foley, *An exhortation to the inhabitants of Down and Connor concerning the education of their children* (Dublin, 1695), pp. 19–20.

113 [William Swayne], *The lives of the glorious Saint David, bishop of Menevia, patron of Wales and master of many Irish saints and also Saint Kieran, the first born saint of Ireland, first bishop and principal patron of the diocese of Ossory* (Waterford, 1647).

114 P.F Moran (ed.), *Spicilegium Ossoriense* (3 vols, Dublin, 1874–84) i, p. 9.

115 For a more detailed discussion of how Temple's work was read see Raymond Gillespie, 'Temple's fate: reading the *Irish rebellion* in seventeenth-century Ireland' in Ciarán Brady and Jane Ohlmeyer (eds), *British interventions in early modern Ireland* (Cambridge, 2005), pp. 315–33.

116 H.M.C., *Report on the manuscripts of the earl of Egmont* (2 vols, London, 1905–9), i, p. 292.

117 T.C.D., MS 812, f. 118v.

118 For example *An abstract of some of those barbarous cruel massacres of the Protestants and English in some parts of Ireland* (London, 1662).

119 Temple, *Irish Rebellion*, pt 1, p. 40.

120 Lawrence, *The interest of Ireland*, pt ii, p. 84.

Appendix

Book production in
seventeenth-century Ireland

The first two tables in this appendix are based on the CD Rom version of the *English short title catalogue, 1473–1800* (3rd edn, London, 2003). They count items of output and in that sense distort the workings of the trade since a single-sheet proclamation is regarded in the same way as a folio work. Some duplication is removed since texts, such as proclamations, which have only minor variants are here regarded as only one item. In the case of Table 2 official publications are defined as material related to the day-to-day working of government, including that of the church. It includes proclamations, individual statutes and visitation articles. Collections of statutes and other reference works as a result of government action are included in the 'other' category. Reprints include both older Irish works and contemporary English publications.

Table 1 The output of the Irish presses, 1601–1700

	Dublin	Cork	Waterford	Kilkenny	Belfast
1601–5	12				
1606–10	12				
1611–15	8				
1616–20	14				
1621–25	56				
1626–30	29				
1631–35	51				
1636–40	51				
1641–45	102		9		
1646–50	30	7	2	39	
1651–55	67	1	1		
1656–60	64	2			
1661–65	211	2			
1666–70	132	1			
1671–75	98	1			
1676–80	162	1			
1681–85	229	0			
1686–90	250	1			
1691–5	279	2			1
1696–1700	305	0			14

Table 2 Analysis by book type of the output of the Dublin presses, 1601–1700

	Official	*Reprints*	*Others*
1601–5	11	0	1
1606–10	9	2	0
1611–15	4	0	4
1616–20	7	1	6
1621–25	34	2	20
1626–30	19	2	8
1631–35	26	4	21
1636–40	26	8	17
1641–45	82	4	16
1646–50	13	2	15
1651–55	59	2	6
1656–60	37	0	27
1661–65	151	5	55
1666–70	87	17	28
1671–75	47	24	27
1676–80	65	66	31
1681–85	47	106	76
1686–90	74	111	65
1691–95	129	42	108
1696–1700	130	73	102

Table 3 Imports of books by Dublin booksellers, 1680–87 in cwts.

	1680	*1681*	*1682*	*1683*	*1684*	*1685*	*1687*
Patrick Campbell	1.50	11.50	14.75	14.50	13.70	7.00	2.00
Andrew/Mary Crooke	–	3.00	1.25	–	–	2.50	–
Eliphal Dobson	12.00	11.75	19.75	18.00	10.75	13.25	2.75
John Forster	3.00	7.00	–	–	3.50	–	–
Samuel Helsham	18.00	3.50	9.20	24.25	8.50	11.25	–
Joseph Howes	11.50	6.00	9.00	16.70	9.25	17.00	1.00
James Malone	22.50	9.75	2.00	7.25	–	10.50	11.25
William Mendy	22.50	2.00	–	–	–	–	–
John North	6.00	10.50	16.50	12.25	5.50	8.00	11.75
William Norman	–	–	1.50	14.50	–	–	8.00
Joseph Ray	3.00	1.00	–	–	–	–	–
Robert Thornton	–	15.00	2.25	11.25	5.00	9.50	–
Joseph Wilde	8.00	1.00	–	–	5.00	–	–
William Winter	–	6.50	–	–	–	–	–

Sources: P.R.O., E190/1342/10; E190/1343/3; E190/1344/6; E190/1345/16; E190/1346/1,12; E190/1349/11.

Bibliography

PRIMARY SOURCES

Manuscripts

ABERYSTWYTH

National Library of Wales
Powis castle deeds
MS 9108D   Col John Jones correspondence

ANTWERP

Plantin-Moretus Museum
Plantin-Moretus archive

ARMAGH

Armagh Public Library
Dopping correspondence
Catalogue of second Viscount Conway's library, c. 1630

BELFAST

Presbyterian Historical Society
PA 48   Notebook of John Kennedy
Diary of John Cook
Carnmoney session book
Larne session book
Public Record Office of Northern Ireland
D265   Antrim papers
D671   Downshire papers
D1614/3   Account book of Andrew Rowan
D695   Waring papers
D929   Adair papers
D1460/1   Autobiography of James Trail

D1759   Minutes of Ulster presbyteries

D2977   Antrim papers

D3078   Kildare papers

Mic1/5   Thomas Haslam's commonplace book

Mic 1P/3   First Antrim presbyterian register

Union Theological College

MS Robert Chambers 'Explanation of the Shorter Catechism'

CAMBRIDGE

Cambridge University Library

Add MS 711

CHESTER

Cheshire Record Office

DLT/B43   Biography of Lord Deputy Wentworth

Chester City Archive

QSE   Quarter sessions examinations

DUBLIN

Dublin City Archives

MS C1/J/2/4 Tholsel court records

MS MR/35   City treasurer's book

Marsh's Library

Z3. 2.6

National Archives

Chancery Bills

Prerogative will book, Dublin

M2817   St John Seymour's notes from Commonwealth records

RC   Record Commissioners transcripts

National Library of Ireland

MS 642   Contemporary translation of David Rothe's *Analecta sacra*

MS 1793

MS 2554   Ormond inventories

MS 4201   Youghal sermons, 1674–83

MS 4715   Notebook of Joseph Carleton

MS 7861   Inventory of Castleisland

Bibliography

MS 9536   Account book of a Drogheda merchant

MS 11048

MS 12123   Sexton notebook, Limerick

MS 16085

MS 19465

MS G11

Representative Church Body Library

MS 25   Catalogue of the library of Henry Jones, bishop of Meath

MS C12   Records of the cathedral of Cloyne

MS P117   Records of St Catherine's parish, Dublin

MS P118   Records of St Michael's parish, Dublin

MS P326   Records of St Werburgh's parish, Dublin

MS P327   Records of St Bride's parish, Dublin

MS P351

MS P804   Records of Clones parish, Co. Monaghan

Royal Irish Academy

23 L 19

Society of Friends Historical Library

MS MM II A1   Dublin men's monthly meeting, 1677–84

MS MM II F1   Dublin testimonies of condemnation

MS MM IV A1   Moate men's monthly meeting, 1680–1731

Trinity College, Dublin

MS 287   Ambrose Ussher's notebook

MS 357   List of Luke Challoner's books

MS 562   Visitation notes of Dives Downes, bishop of Cork

MS 676   Sir Charles Calthorpe's commonplace book

MS 750   Archbishop King correspondence

MS 803–839 Depositions relating to the 1641 rising

MS 865

MS 883   Molyneux papers

MS 1050   Jonathan Swift's autobiography

MS 1178

MS 1181

MS 1206   Crofton Croker notes

MS 1354

MS 1375   Collection of poems in Irish, 1696–98

MS 1383   Keating's *Foras feasa*, 1704

MS 1490   Archbishop King's library catalogue

MS 1995–2008   Archbishop King correspondence

MS 2160   Booklists from Trinity College, Dublin

Ms 2467   Dopping papers

MS 2929

MS 4468   Prayers of Jane Bingham of Castlebar

MUN   College muniments

EDINBURGH

Scottish Record Office

E72   Port books

GD 154   Agnew of Lochnaw muniments

GLOUCESTER

Gloucestershire Record Office

Diocesan inventories

Diocesan wills

KILKENNY

Corporation Archives

CRO/3   Liber Albus, corporation minutes 1656–1687

LEEDS

Leeds City Library

Temple Newsham papers, Irish port books

LONDON

British Library

Add MS 4312

Add MS 4756   Entry book of the 1622 commissioners of enquiry

Add MS 4787

Add MS 4821

Add MS 11687   Tholsel court records, 1638–39

Add MS 19865   Sexton papers

Add MS 31885   Papers of Thomas Arthur of Limerick

Bibliography

Add MS 41769   Tour of Ireland by James Verdon, 1699

Add MS 46957   Egmont MS

Add MS 47024   Egmont MS

Add Charter 13340   Inventory of Geashill, Co. Laois

Cotton MS Julius C III

Cotton MS Titus X B

Egerton MS 136

Egerton MS 196

Egerton MS 1627   Diary of Philip Maddox, 1680–7

Harley MS 697   Council book for Munster, 1601–21

Harley MS 3298

Harley MS 4279   Petition book for the midland plantations

Royal MS 17 A xviii   'A key to controversies' by Robert Marshall

Sloane MS 1008   Borlase correspondence

Sloane Ms 3567

Corporation of London Records Office

Court of Orphans inventories

Public Record Office (The National Archives)

CUST   Customs returns

E190   Port Books

PROB4   Prerogative Court of Canterbury, engrossed inventories

SP20

SP63   Irish State Papers

NORTHAMPTON

Northampton County Record Office

Fitzwilliam of Milton MSS

OXFORD

Bodleian Library

Carte MSS

Rawlinson B 480   Catalogue of Limerick cathedral library

Smith MS 45   Correspondence with Narcissus Marsh

SHEFFIELD

Sheffield Archives

Wentworth Woodhouse papers, Strafford Letter books

WASHINGTON

Folger Library

MS V.a. 125 Viscount Dungarvan's commonplace book

MS G. a. 10

Contemporary writings

An abstract of some of those barbarous cruel massacres of the Protestants and English in some parts of Ireland (London, 1662).

An account of the public affairs in Ireland since the discovery of the late plot (London, 1679).

An account of the present miserable state of the affairs of Ireland (London, 1689).

An act of the lord mayor, sheriffs, commons and citizens of the city of Dublin, 14 May 1681 (Dublin, 1681).

Adames, Jonas, *The order of keeping a court leet and court baron with the charges appertaining to the same* (Dublin, 1634).

An agreement and resolutions of the ministers of Christ associated with the city of Dublin and the province of Leinster (Dublin, 1659).

A[mmonet], S., *The key of knowledge for all merchants* (Dublin, 1696).

Ashe, St George, *A sermon preached in Trinity College chapel before the University of Dublin, January the 9th 1693/4* (Dublin, 1694).

Barnwall, Robert, *Syntomotaxia del second part de roy Henrie le sixt* (London, 1601).

Barry, James, *A reviving cordial for a sin-sick, despairing soul in time of temptation* (2nd edn, Edinburgh, 1722).

[Bedell, William], *The ABC or the institutes of a Christian* (Dublin, 1630).

Bernard, Nicholas, *The penitent death of a woeful sinner* (Dublin, 1641).

——, *The whole proceedings of the seige of Drogheda in Ireland* (London, 1642).

Beveridge, William, *A sermon concerning the excellency and usefulness of the common prayer* (Dublin, 1698).

Blake, Richard, *Richard Blake his speech in the House of Commons at the grand committee for the bills against paper petitions* (London, 1641).

Bolton, Richard, *A justice of the peace for Ireland* (Dublin, 1638).

Bourke, John, *Hiberniae Merlinus for the year of our Lord 1683* (Dublin, 1683).

——, *Hiberniae Merlinus for the year of our Lord 1684* (Dublin, 1684).

——, *Hiberniae Merlinus for the year of our Lord 1685* (Dublin, 1685).

[Boyle], Michael, *Rules and orders to be used and observed in the high court of Chancery in Ireland* (Dublin, 1685).

Boyle, Roger, earl of Orrery, *The Irish colours displayed* ([London, 1662])

——, *Poems of the festivals of the church* (Cork, 1681)

[Boyse, Joseph], *Some impartial reflections on D[r] Manby's considerations etc.* (Dublin, 1687).

——, *Remarks on a late discourse of William, lord bishop of Derry* (Dublin, 1694).

——, *A vindication of the remarks of the bishop of Derry's discourse* (Dublin, 1695).

——, *Family hymns for morning and evening worship* (Dublin, 1707).

——, *Sermons preached on several subjects* (2 vols, Dublin, 1708).

——, *The works of the Rev. and learned Joseph Boyse* (2 vols, London, 1728).

Browne, Peter, *A letter in answer to a book entitled Christianity not mysterious* (Dublin, 1697).

Bryskett, Lodowick, *A discourse of civil life* (London, 1606).

Carolan, Neal, *Motives of conversion to the Catholic faith as it is practised in the reformed Church of England* (Dublin, 1688).

Christian thoughts for every day of the month (n.p., 1698).

The church catechism explained and proved by apt texts of scripture (Dublin, 1699).

C[omerford], P[atrick], *The inquisition of a sermon* (Waterford, 1644).

Coote, Edward, *The English schoolmaster* (42nd edn, Dublin, 1684).

Cox, Richard, *Hibernia Anglicana or the history of Ireland* (2 vols, London, 1689–90).

Craghead, Robert, *An answer to a late book entitled a discourse concerning the inventions of men in the worship of God* (Edinburgh, 1694).

——, *Advice to communicants* (Edinburgh, 1698).

de Sales, Francis, *An introduction to the devout life*, ed. Henry Dodwell (Dublin, 1673).

Eyres, Joseph, *The church sleeper awakened* (London, 1659).

Farmer, William, *The common almanac or calendar drawn forth for the year 1587 ...* (London, 1587).

——, *Farmer 1612 his prognostical almanac* (Dublin, 1612).

Fitzsimons, Thomas, *The primer more ample and in a new order* (Rouen, 1684).

Foley, Samuel, *An exhortation to the inhabitants of Down and Connor concerning the education of their children* (Dublin, 1695).

[Foley, Samuel], *A catalogue of the books of the Rt Rev. father in God, Samuel Foley, late lord bishop of Down and Connor* (Dublin, 1695).

Folkingham, William, *Feudigraphia: the synopsis or epitome of surveying methodised* (London, 1610).

G[ibbon], J., *Reflections on a book published by Mr Ammonet* (Dublin, 1696).

Gilbert, Claudius, *The libertine schooled* (London, 1657).

Gostellow, Walter, *Charls Stuart and Oliver Cromwell united* (London, 1654).

[Greatrix, Valentine], *A brief account of Mr Valentine Greatrix ... written by himself* (London, 1666).

Hall, Thomas, *A plain and easy explication of the assembly's Shorter cathechism* (Edinburgh, 1692).

Hamilton, William, *The exemplary life and character of James Bonnell, late accomptant general of Ireland* (London, 1703).

Head, Richard, *Hic et ubique or the humours of Dublin* (London, 1663).

The history of the life and death of St Patrick (London, 1685).

The works of the reverend and learned Ezekiel Hopkins, lord bishop of Londonderry (London, 1710).

Huddleston, John, *A short and plain way to the faith and church* (Dublin, 1688).

Instructions for the collection of customs and imported excise in the kingdom of Ireland (Dublin, 1677).

Instructions for the collection of inland excise with directions how to keep their books and make up their abstracts (Dublin, 1677).

Instructions for gaugers of excise with the form of their pocket book and vouchers (Dublin, 1677).

Ireland's lamentation: being a short but perfect, full and true account of the situation, natural constitution and produce of Ireland (London, 1689).

Jerome, Steven, *Ireland's jubilee and joys io paen* (Dublin, 1624).

——, *The soul's sentinel ringing an alarm against impiety and impenitency* (Dublin, 1631).

Jones, Henry, *A sermon on antichrist preached at Christ Church, Dublin* (Dublin, 1676).

King, William, *An answer to the considerations which obliged Peter Manby...* (Dublin, 1687).

——, *A discourse concerning the inventions of men in the worship of God* (Dublin, 1694).

——, *An admonition to the dissenting inhabitants of the diocese of Derry* (Dublin, 1694).

——, *State of the Protestants of Ireland* (Dublin, 1744).

Kirkpatrick, James, *An historical essay upon the loyalty of the presbyterians* ([Belfast], 1713).

Lawrence, Richard, *The interest of Ireland in its trade and wealth stated* (Dublin, 1682).

L'Estrange, Roger, *Considerations upon a printed sheet entitled the speech of the late Lord Russell to the sheriffs together with the paper delivered by him to them at the place of his execution on July 21 1683* (London, 1683).

A letter from a Protestant in Ireland to a member of the House of Commons in England (n.p., 1643).

The life and death of the incomparable and indefatigable tory Redmond O Hanlyn (Dublin, 1682).

Lord Chief Justice Scroggs, his speech in the King's bench the first day of this present Michaelmas term (Dublin, 1679).

Lye, Thomas, *A plain and familiar method of instructing the younger sort* (Dublin, 1683).

McComb, John, *A new almanac for the year of our Lord 1694* (Dublin, [1694]).

Manby, Peter, *The considerations which obliged ... to embrace the Catholic religion* (Dublin, 1687.

Mercer, William, *A welcome in a poem to his excellency John, Lord Robartes* (Dublin, 1669).

——, *The moderate cavalier or the soldiers description of Ireland* (Cork, 1675).

Merrick, John, *A brief abstract of all the English statutes which are now in force within the realm of Ireland* (Dublin, 1625).

Moryson, Fynes, *An itinerary written by Fynes Moryson, gent.* (London, 1617).

Murcot, John, *Saving faith and pride of life inconsistent* (London, 1656).

Musarum lacryamyra (Dublin, 1630).

A narrative of the proceedings of the seven general synods of the northern presbyterians in Ireland by the ministers of the presbytery of Antrim (n.p., 1717).

N[ary], C[ornelius], *The New Testament of our Lord and Saviour Jesus Christ* ([Dublin], 1718).

No pamphlets but a detestation of against all such pamphlets as are printed concerning the Irish rebellion (London, 1642).

Olmstead, Richard, *A treatise on the union betwixt Christ and the church* (Dublin, 1627).

——, *Sion's tears tending to joy* (Dublin, 1630).

[Orpen, Richard], *The London master or the Jew detected* (Dublin, 1694).

Parr, Richard, *The life of the most reverend father in God James Ussher* (London, 1686).

Pollard, Thomas, *The necessity and advantages of family prayer in two sermons preached in St Peter's, Dublin* (Dublin, 1696).

A representation of the present state of religion ... drawn up and agreed by both houses of convocation in Ireland (Dublin, 1712).

Rich, Barnaby, *Alarm to England* (London, 1578).

——, *A short survey of Ireland* (London, 1609).

——, *A new description of Ireland* (London, 1610).

——, *A true and kind excuse written in defence of that book entitled* A new description of Ireland (London, 1612).

Richardson, John, *The great folly, superstition and idolatry of pilgrimage in Ireland* (Dublin, 1727).

Rogers, John, *Ohel or Beth Shemesh* (London, 1653).

Rules and instructions for the sodality of the immaculate conception of the most glorious Virgin Mary, mother of God, ([Dublin], 1703).

Rules and orders to be observed in the proceedings of causes in the high court of Chancery (Dublin, 1659).

Russell, Dom, *A new almanac for the year of our Lord 1689* (Dublin, 1689).

Rust, George, *A sermon preached at Newtown[ards] the 23 of October 1663 at the funeral of the Honourable Hugh, earl of Mount Alexander* (Dublin, 1664).

Sall, Andrew, *A sermon preached in Christ Church in Dublin* (Dublin, 1674).

Scroggs, Benjamin *A sermon preached before the religious societies in the city of Dublin on the 29th of September 1695* (Dublin, 1695).

Sheridan, William, *St Paul's confession of faith or a brief account of his religion* (Dublin, 1685).

Short view of the methods made use of in Ireland for the subversion and destruction of the Protestant religion and interests in that kingdom (London, 1689).

Sherlock, William, *A sermon preached at the Temple church, December 30 1694* (Dublin, 1695).

Sibthorpe, Christopher, *A reply to an answer which a popish adversary made in two chapters contained in the first part of that book which is entitled A friendly advertisement* (Dublin, 1625).

——, *A surreplication to the rejoinder of a popish adversary* (Dublin, 1627).

The soldier's best exercise (Dublin, 1696).

[Stevens, Steven], *Exceeding happy news from Ireland* (London, 1642).

Stockdale, William, *The great cry of oppression* ([Dublin], 1683).

[Swayne, William], *The lives of the glorious Saint David, bishop of Menevia, patron of Wales and master of many Irish saints and also Saint Kieran, the first born saint of Ireland, first bishop and principal patron of the diocese of Ossory* (Waterford, 1647).

Taylor, Jeremy, *A discourse of confirmation for the use of the clergy and instruction of the people of Ireland* (Dublin, 1663).

Teate, Faithful, *The soldier's commission, charge and reward* (London, 1658).

——, *A discourse grounded on Prov. 12.5, 'The thoughts of the righteous are right'* (Dublin, 1666).

Temple, John, *History of the ... Irish rebellion* (London, 1646).

Tennison, Richard, *A sermon preached at the primary visitation of ... the archbishop of Armagh* (Dublin, 1679).

Tisdall, William, *The conduct of the dissenters in Ireland* (Dublin, 1712).

Toland, John, *An apology for Mr Toland in a letter from himself to a member of the House of Commons in Ireland* (Dublin, 1697).

True, Patrick, *A new almanac and prognostication for the year ... 1636* (Dublin, [1635]).

Upon the arrival of his excellency Henry, earl of Clarendon and his entering upon the government of Ireland (Dublin, 1686)

[Wadding, Luke], *A small garland of pious and godly songs* (Ghent, 1684).

W[alsh], P[eter], *The Irish colours folded* (London, 1662).

——, *The history and vindication of the loyal formulary or Irish remonstrance* (n.p., 1674).

[Ware, Robert], *The second part of foxes and firebrands* (Dublin, 1683).

——, *The hunting of the Romish fox and the quenching of sectarian firebrands* (Dublin, 1683).

W[aring], T[homas], *A brief narration of the plotting, beginning and carrying on that execrable rebellion and butchery in Ireland* (London, 1658).

Wetenhall, Edward, *Collyrium: a sense of the destructive ignorance and saving knowledge preached in Christ Church Dublin, August 4 1672* (Dublin, 1672).

——, *Gifts and offices in the public worship of God* (Dublin, 1679).

——, *A plain and practical discourse of the form of godliness visible in the present age* (Dublin, 1683).

Whalley, John, *Advice from the stars or an almanac for the year of Christ 1697* (Dublin, [1697]).

——, *A treatise of eclipses* (Dublin, 1701).

——, *Ptolemy's Quadrapartite or four books concerning the influence of the stars* (Dublin, 1701).

Wilkinson, John, *A treatise collected out of the statutes of this kingdom ... together with and easy and plain method of keeping a court leet* (Dublin, 1630).

Wilson, John, *To his excellency, Richard earl of Arran ... lord deputy of Ireland: a poem* (Dublin, 1684).

Wolveridge, James, *Speculum matricis or the expert midwives handmaid* (London, 1671).

Bibliography

Contemporary newspapers

The Dublin Intelligence

Dublin Post

The Flying Post

The Guardian

Mercurius Hibernicus

The Newsletter

The Present State of Europe and Historical Monthly (1692)

The Present State of Europe or the Historical and Political Monthly Mercury (1704).

Printed editions

Acts of the privy council of England (London, 1890–).

Ainsworth, John (ed.), 'Abstracts of seventeenth-century Irish wills in the prerogative court of Canterbury' in *Journal of the Royal Society of Antiquaries of Ireland* lxxviii (1948).

—— (ed.), 'Doneraile papers' in *Analecta Hibernica* no. 20 (1958).

—— (ed.), 'Dillon papers' in *Analecta Hibernica* no. 20 (1958).

—— (ed.), 'Power O'Shee papers' in *Analecta Hibernica* no. 20 (1958).

—— (ed.), *The Inchiquin manuscripts* (Dublin, 1961).

Anselment, Raymond (ed.), *The remembrances of Elizabeth Freke* (Cambridge, 2001).

Appleby, John (ed.), *A calendar of material relating to Ireland in the High Court of Admiralty examinations, 1536–1640* (Dublin, 1992).

Berwick, Edward (ed.), *The Rawdon papers* (London, 1819).

Bradley, John (ed.), *Treasures of Kilkenny: charters and civic records of Kilkenny city* (Kilkenny, 2003).

Brady, Ciarán (ed.), *A viceroy's vindication?: Sir Henry Sidney's memoir of his service in Ireland, 1556–78* (Cork, 2002).

Brady, W.M. (ed.), *State papers concerning the Irish church in the time of Queen Elizabeth* (London, 1868).

Buchan, Hanna (ed.), *The poems of Thomas Pestell* (Oxford, 1940).

Calendar of State Papers preserved in the Public Record Office, domestic series, 1547–1695 (81 vols, London, 1856–1972).

Calendar of State Papers relating to Ireland, 1509–1670 (24 vols, London, 1860–1912).

Calendar of the Carew manuscripts preserved in the archiepiscopal library at Lambeth, 1515–1624 (London, 1867–73).

Campion, Edmund, *Two bokes of the histories of Ireland*, ed. A.F. Vossen (Assen, 1963).

Canny, Nicholas (ed.), 'Rowland White's "Discors touching Ireland, c. 1569"' in *Irish Historical Studies* xx (1976–77).

—— (ed.), 'Rowland White's "The dysorders of the Irishery"' in *Studia Hibernica* no. 19 (1979).

Carney, James (ed.), *Poems on the O'Reillys* (Dublin, 1950).

Carney, Maura (ed.), 'Agreement between Ó Domhnaill and Tadhg Ó Conchobhair concerning Sligo castle (23 June 1539)' in *Irish Historical Studies* iii (1942–43).

Carpenter, Andrew (ed.), *Verse in English from Tudor and Stuart Ireland* (Cork, 2003).

Carrigan, William (ed.), 'Catholic episcopal wills' in *Archivium Hibernicum* iv (1918).

Caulfield, Richard (ed.), *The autobiography of the Rt Hon. Sir Richard Cox, bart* (London, 1860).

——, (ed.) *The council book of the corporation of Cork* (Guildford, 1876).

——, (ed.), *The council book of the corporation of Youghal* (Guildford, 1878).

Clark, Andrew (ed.), *The life and times of Anthony Wood, antiquary of Oxford, 1632–95* (4 vols, Oxford, 1891–95).

Comber, Thomas (ed.), *A book of instructions written by the Right Hon. Sir Christopher Wandesford* (Cambridge, 1777).

Connolly, Philomena (ed.), *Statute rolls of the Irish parliament, Richard III–Henry VIII* (Dublin, 2002).

Corish, P.J. (ed.), 'Bishop Wadding's notebook' in *Archivium Hibernicum* xxix (1970).

Croker, T. Crofton (ed.), *The tour of M. de la Boullaye Le Gouez in Ireland, 1644* (London, 1837).

Curtis, Edmund (ed.), *Calendar of Ormond deeds* (6 vols, Dublin, 1932–43).

Dunton, John, *The Dublin scuffle*, ed. Andrew Carpenter (Dublin, 2000).

—— , *Teague land or a merry ramble to the wild Irish (1698)*, ed. Andrew Carpenter (Dublin, 2003).

[Edmundson, William], *A journal of the life, travels, sufferings of William Edmundson* (Dublin, 1820).

Elrington, C.R. and Todd, J.H. (eds), *The whole works of the most reverend James Ussher* (17 vols, Dublin, 1847–64).

Fenning, Hugh, 'The library of Bishop William Daton of Ossory, 1698' in *Collectanea Hibernica* no. 20 (1978).

Fraser, J., Grosjean, Paul and O'Keeffe, J.G. (eds), *Irish texts* (4 vols, London, 1931–4).

Freeman, A.M. (ed.), *Annála Connacht* (Dublin, 1944).

French, Nicholas, *The bleeding Ipigenia; Unkind deserter and The sale and settlement of Ireland* ed. S.H.B[indon] (Dublin, 1848).

Gent, Thomas, *The life of Mr Thomas Gent, printer of York, by himself* (London, 1832).

Gilbert, J.T. (ed.), *Facsimiles of the national manuscripts of Ireland* (4 vols, Dublin, 1874–84).

—— (ed.), *A contemporary history of affairs in Ireland* (3 vols, Dublin, 1879).

—— (ed.), *History of the Irish confederation and the war in Ireland* (7 vols, Dublin, 1882–91).

Gilbert J.T. and R. (eds), *Calendar of the ancient records of Dublin* (19 vols, Dublin, 1889–1944).

Gillespie, Raymond (ed.), *The proctor's accounts of Peter Lewis. 1564–1565* (Dublin, 1996).

—— (ed.), 'Borrowing books from Christ Church cathedral, Dublin, 1607' in *Long Room* no. 43 (1998).

——, (ed.), 'Rev Dr John Yarner's notebook: religion in Restoration Dublin' in *Archivium Hibernicum* lii (1998).

Gogarty, Thomas (ed.), *The council book of the corporation of Drogheda* (Drogheda, 1915).

Goodbody, Olive C. (ed.), 'Inventories of five Dublin Quaker merchants in the late seventeenth century' in *Irish Ancestor* x (1978).

Greene, David (ed.), *Duanaire Mhéig Uidhir* (Dublin, 1972).

Grosart, A.B. (ed.), *Lismore papers* (10 vols, London, 1886–88)

Hainsworth, D.R. (ed.), *The commercial papers of Christopher Lowther* (Durham, 1977).

Hand, G.J. and Treadwell, V.W. (eds), 'His majesty's directions for ordering and settling the courts within his kingdom of Ireland, 1622' in *Analecta Hibernica* no. 26 (1970).

Hanly, John (ed.), *The letters of Saint Oliver Plunkett* (Dublin, 1979).

Hardiman, James (ed.), 'Ancient Irish deeds and writings' in *Transactions of the Royal Irish Academy* xv (1826).

Harington, John, *Short view of the state of Ireland written in 1605* ed. W.D. Macray (Oxford, 1879).

Hennessy, W.M. and MacCarthy, B. (eds), *Annála Uladh, Annals of Ulster* (4 vols, Dublin, 1887–1901).

Hennessy, W.M. (ed.), *The Annals of Loch Cé* (2 vols, London, 1871).

Hill, George (ed.), *The Montgomery manuscripts* (Belfast, 1869).

Historical Manuscripts Commission, *Salisbury (Cecil) MSS at Hatfield House* (24 vols, London, 1883–1976).

——, *Report on the manuscripts of the marquess of Ormonde* (old series, 3 vols, London 1895–1909; new series, 8 vols, London, 1902–20).

——, *Report on the manuscripts of the duke of Buccleuch and Queensberry* (3 vols, London, 1899–1926).

——, *Report on the manuscripts of the earl of Egmont* (2 vols, London, 1905–9)

——, *Report on the Franciscan manuscripts* (London, 1906).

——, *Report on the Laing manuscripts* (2 vols, London, 1914–25).

——, *Report on the manuscripts of the marquess of Downshire* (5 vols, London, 1924–).

——, *Report on the manuscripts of Lord L'Isle and Dudley* (6 vols, London, 1925–66).

——, *Report on the manuscripts of the late R.R. Hastings* (4 vols, London, 1928–47).

Hogan, Edmund (ed.), *Ibernia Ignatiana* (Dublin, 1880)

Hooker, John, *The life and times of Sir Peter Carew*, ed. John Maclean (London, 1857).

Hore, H.F. and Graves, James (eds), *The social state of the southern and eastern counties of Ireland in the sixteenth century* (Dublin, 1870).

Jackson, Charles (ed.), *The autobiography of Mrs Alice Thornton* (Durham, 1875).

Jackson, W.A. (ed.), *Records of the court of the Stationers' Company, 1602 to 1640* (London, 1957).

Jennings, Brendan (ed.), *Wadding papers, 1614–38* (Dublin, 1953).

—— (ed.), 'Ecclesiastical appointments in Ireland, August 1643–December 1649' in *Collectanea Hibernica* no. 2 (1959).

Journals of the House of Commons of the kingdom of Ireland (19 vols, Dublin, 1796–1800).

Journals of the House of Lords [of Ireland] (8 vols, Dublin, 1779–1800).

Keating, Geoffrey, *Foras feasa ar Éirinn*, eds David Comyn and P.S. Dinneen (4 vols, London, 1902–14).

Kelly, James (ed.), *Gallows speeches from eighteenth-century Ireland* (Dublin, 2000).

Kelly, Patrick (ed.), 'The improvement of Ireland' in *Analecta Hibernica* no. 35 (1992).

Kew, Graham (ed.), 'The Irish sections of Fynes Moryson's unpublished *Itinerary*' in *Analecta Hibernica* no. 37 (1998).

King, C.S. (ed.), *A great archbishop of Dublin* (Dublin, 1908).

Kleine, Jean (ed.), *The Southwell–Sibthorpe commonplace books* (Binghamton, 1997).

Knott, Eleanor (ed.), *The bardic poems of Tadhg Dall Ó hUiginn* (2 vols, London, 1922–26).

Laing, David (ed.), *The Bannatyne miscellany: iii* (Edinburgh, 1885).

Lansdowne, marquis of (ed.), *The Petty papers* (2 vols, London, 1927).

——, (ed.) *Petty–Southwell correspondence* (London, 1928).

Lindley, Keith and Scott, David (eds), *The journal of Thomas Juxon, 1644–1647* (Cambridge, 1999).

McCamick, William, *A further impartial account of the actions of the Inniskillen men*, ed. W.T. Latimer (Belfast, 1896).

McClure, N. (ed.), *The letters and epigrams of Sir John Harington* (Philadelphia, 1930).

Mhag Craith, Cuthbert (ed.), *Dán na mBráthar Mionúir* (2 vols, Dublin, 1967–80).

McCrie, Thomas (ed.), *The life of Mr Robert Blair* (Edinburgh, 1848).

MacDonnell, Hector (ed.), 'A seventeenth-century inventory from Dunluce castle, Co. Antrim' in *Journal of the Royal Society of Antiquaries of Ireland* cxxiii (1992).

McKelvie, Colin (ed.), 'Jeremy Taylor's recommendations for a library of Anglican theology' in *Irish Booklover* iv (1978–80).

McKenna, Lambert (ed.), *Iomarbhágh na bhfileadh* (2 vols, London, 1918).

MacLysaght, Edward (ed.), 'Report on documents relating to the wardenship of Galway' in *Analecta Hibernica* no. 14 (1944).

—— (ed.), 'O'Grady papers' in *Analecta Hibernica* no. 15 (1945).

—— (ed.), *Calendar of the Orrery papers* (Dublin, 1941).

McNeill, Charles (ed.), 'Lord Chancellor Gerrard's notes of his report on Ireland' in *Analecta Hibernica* no. 2 (1931).

Mac Niocaill, Gearóid (ed.), 'Cairt o Mhaolmhordha Ó Raighilligh, 1558' in *Breifne* i no. 2 (1959).

—— (ed.), 'Seven Irish documents from the Inchiquin archives' in *Analecta Hibernica* no. 26 (1970).

—— (ed.), *Crown surveys of lands, 1540–41* (Dublin, 1992).

Mahaffey, J.P. (ed.), *The particular book of Trinity College, Dublin* (London, 1904).

Maidment, James and Logan, W.H. (eds), *The dramatic works of John Wilson* (Edinburgh and London, 1874).

Maxwell, Constantia (ed.), *Irish history from contemporary sources, 1509–1610* (London, 1923).

Miller, Liam and Power, Eileen (eds), *Holinshed's Irish chronicle* (Dublin, 1979).

Millett, Benignus, 'Calendar of vol 1 of the collection *Scritture riferite nei congressi, Irlanda* in Propaganda archives' in *Collectanea Hibernica* nos 6–7 (1963–64).

——, 'Maurice MacBrien, bishop of Emly, and the confiscation of his baggage, March 1578' in *Collectanea Hibernica* no. 35 (1992–93).

——, 'Irish Franciscans ask *Propaganda* to give them books for their pastoral ministry in Ireland, 1689–96' in *Collectanea Hibernica* nos 44–5 (2002–3)

[Molyneux, Thomas], 'Sir Thomas Molyneux' in *Dublin University Magazine* xviii (July–December 1841).

Moody, T.W. (ed.), 'The revised articles of the Ulster plantation, 1610' in *Bulletin of the Institute of Historical Research* xii (1935).

Moran, P.F. (ed.), *Spicilegium Ossoriense* (3 vols, Dublin, 1874–84).

Morgan, Hiram (ed.), '"Lawes of Irelande": a tract by Sir John Davies' in *Irish Jurist* n.s. xxviii–xxx (1993–95).

Mulcahy, Michael (ed.), *Calendar of Kinsale documents* (2 vols, Kinsale, 1988–89).

Murphy, Denis (ed.), *The annals of Clonmacnoise* (Dublin, 1896).

Murray, L.P. (ed.), 'Archbishop Cromer's register' in *Journal of the County Louth Archaeological Society* viii (1933–6).

—— (ed.), 'The will of James Hussey of Smarmore, Co. Louth "priest", 1635' in *Journal of the County Louth Archaeological Society* viii (1933–36).

Ní Chróinín, Áine (ed.), *Beatha Chríost* (Dublin, n.d.).

Ó Cuív, Brian (ed.), *Párliament na mBan* (Dublin, 1952).

—— (ed.), *Aibidil Gaoidheilge agus caiticiosma* (Dublin, 1994).

Ó Dálaigh, Brian (ed.), 'An inventory of the contents of Bunratty castle and the will of Henry, fifth earl of Thomond' in *North Munster Antiquarian Journal* xxxvi (1995).

O'Doherty, J.F. (ed.), *The 'Catechismus' of Theobald Stapleton* (Dublin, 1945).

O'Donovan, John (ed.), 'Covenant between Mageoghegan and the Fox' in *The miscellany of the Irish Archaeologcal Society, i* (Dublin, 1846).

—— (ed.), *The annals of the kingdom of Ireland by the Four Masters* (7 vols, Dublin, 1851).

—— (ed.), 'Original letters in the Irish and Latin languages by Shane O'Neill' in *Ulster Journal of Archaeology* 1st ser., v (1857).

—— (ed.), 'The Irish correspondence of James Fitz Maurice [earl] of Desmond' in *Journal of the Royal Society of Antiquaries of Ireland* ii (1859).

Ó Maonaigh, Cainneach (ed.), *Seanmónta chúige Uladh* (Dublin, 1965).

Ó Raghallaigh, Tomás (ed.), 'Seanchus Búrcach' in *Journal of the Galway Archaeolgical and Historical Society* xii (1926–27).

O'Rahilly, Cecile (ed.), *Five seventeenth-century political poems* (Dublin, 1952).

O'Sullivan, William (ed.), 'Correspondence of David Rothe and James Ussher, 1619–23' in *Collectanea Hibernica* nos 36–7 (1994–95).

Perrot, James, *The chronicle of Ireland, 1584–1608*, ed. Herbert Wood (Dublin, 1933).

Pender, Séamus (ed.), *Council books of the corporation of Waterford* (Dublin, 1964).

Piers, Henry, *A chorographical description of the county of Westmeath* (reprint Tara, 1981).

Robinson, F.N. (ed.), 'The Irish lives of Guy of Warwick and Bevis of Hampton' in *Zeitschrift für Celtische Philologie* vi (1908).

Russell, Charles (ed.), 'On an agreement in Irish between Gerald, ninth earl of Kildare and the Mac Ranald' in *Proceedings of the Royal Irish Academy* x (1866–69).

'A seventeenth-century Anglo-Irish library' in *Irish Book Lover* xxx (1946–48).

Shuckburgh, E.S. (ed.), *Two biographies of William Bedell* (Cambridge, 1902).

Spenser, Edmund, *A view of the present state of Ireland*, ed. W.L. Renwick (Oxford, 1970).

Steele, R.R. (ed.), *Tudor and Stuart proclamations* (2 vols, Oxford, 1910)

Stokes, G.T. (ed.), *The memoirs of Mistress Anne Fowke, née Geale* (Dublin, 1892).

Thomas, Patrick (ed.), *The collected works of Katherine Philips* (3 vols, Stump Cross, 1992).

Todd, J.H. (ed.), 'On some ancient Irish deeds' in *Proceedings of the Royal Irish Academy* vii (1858).

Troost, Wouter (ed.), 'Letters from Bartholomew van Homrigh to General Ginkle' in *Analecta Hibernica* no. 33 (1986).

29th Report of the deputy keeper of the public records of Ireland (Dublin, 1897).

White, J.D. (ed.), 'Extracts from original wills' in *Journal of the Royal Society of Antiquaries of Ireland* v (1858–59).

Williams, Harold (ed.), *The poems of Jonathan Swift* (2nd edn, 3 vols, Oxford, 1958).

Williams, N.J.A. (ed.), *Pairlement Chloinne Tomáis* (Dublin, 1981).

Young, R.M. (ed.), *The town book of the corporation of Belfast* (Belfast, 1892).

SECONDARY SOURCES

Adams, J.R.R., *The printed word and the common man: popular culture in Ulster, 1700–1900* (Belfast, 1987).

Armory, Hugh and Hall, David (eds), *A history of the book in America i: the colonial book in the Atlantic world* (Cambridge, 2000).

Armstrong, E.R.C., *Irish seal matrices and seals* (Dublin, 1913).

Bannister, Saxe, *Some revelations in Irish history* (London, 1870).

Barnard, John and McKenzie, D.F. (eds), *The Cambridge history of the book in Britain: iv 1557–1695* (Cambridge, 2002).

Barnard, Toby, 'Learning, the learned and literacy in Ireland, 1660–1760' in T.C. Barnard, Dáibhí Ó Cróinín and Katharine Simms (eds), *'A miracle of learning': studies in manuscripts and Irish learning* (Aldershot, 1998).

——, 'Libraries and glazed bookcases in eighteenth-century Ireland' in *Eighteenth–Ninteenth Century Irish Fiction Newsletter* no. 14 (Feb. 1999).

——, *Irish Protestant ascents and descents, 1641–1770* (Dublin, 2003).

——, *The new anatomy of Ireland: the Irish Protestants, 1649–1770* (London, 2003).

——, *Making the grand figure: lives and possessions in Ireland, 1641–1770* (London, 2004).

Benn, George, *A history of the town of Belfast* (London, 1877).

Birrell, T.A., 'Reading as pastime: the place of light literature in some gentlemen's libraries of the seventeenth century' in Robin Myers and Michael Harris (eds), *Property of a gentleman: the formation, organisation and disposal of the private library, 1620–1920* (Winchester, 1991).

Blagden, Cyprian, *The Stationers' Company: a history, 1403–1959* (London, 1960).

Boran, Elizabethanne, 'Luke Challoner's library' in *Long Room* no. 37 (1992).

——, 'The libraries of Luke Challoner and James Ussher, 1595–1608' in Helga Robinson-Hammerstein (ed.), *European universities in the age of Reformation and Counter Reformation* (Dublin, 1998).

——, 'The function of the library in the early seventeenth century' in Vincent Kinane and Anne Walsh (eds), *Essays on the history of Trinity College library, Dublin* (Dublin, 2000).

——, 'Reading theology within the community of believers: James Ussher's "Directions"' in Bernadette Cunningham and Máire Kennedy (eds), *The experience of reading: Irish historical perspectives* (Dublin, 1999).

Boyarin, Jonathan (ed.), *The ethnography of reading* (Berkeley, 1993).

Breeze, Andrew, 'The charter of Christ' in *Celtica* xix (1987).

Bruford, Alan, *Gaelic folk tales and medieval romances* (Dublin 1969).

Burke, W.P., *History of Clonmel* (Waterford, 1907).

Caball, Marc, 'Providence and exile in seventeenth-century Ireland' in *Irish Historical Studies* xxix (1994–95).

Cains, Anthony, 'The Long Room survey of sixteenth and seventeenth-century books' in Vincent Kinane and Anne Walsh (eds), *Essays on the history of Trinity College library, Dublin* (Dublin, 2000).

Capp, Bernard, *Astrology and the popular press: English almanacs, 1500–1800* (London, 1979).

Carey, Vincent, '"Neither good English nor good Irish": bi-lingualism and identity formation in sixteenth-century Ireland' in Hiram Morgan (ed.), *Political ideology in Ireland, 1541–1641* (Dublin, 1999).

Cavallo, Guiglielmo and Chartier, Roger (eds), *A history of reading in the west* (Cambridge, 1999).

Chartier, Roger, *The cultural use of print in early modern France* (Princeton, 1987).

—— (ed.), *The culture of print* (Cambridge, 1989).

——, *The order of books* (Cambridge, 1994).

Clanchy, M.T., *From memory to written record: England, 1066–1307* (2nd edn, Oxford, 1993).

Clark, Charles, *The public prints: the newspaper in Anglo-American culture, 1665–1740* (Oxford, 1994).

Clark, Peter, 'The ownership of books in England, 1560–1640: the example of some Kentish townsfolk' in Laurence Stone (ed.), *Schooling and society* (London, 1976).

Conlan, J.P., 'Some notes on the "Disputatio apologetica"' in *Publications of the Bibliographical Society of Ireland* vi (1955).

Connolly, Seán, *Religion, law and power: the making of Protestant Ireland, 1660–1760* (Oxford, 1992).

Cosgrove, Art (ed.), *A new history of Ireland ii: medieval Ireland, 1169–1534* (Oxford, 1987).

Cowan, Brian, 'The rise of the coffee house reconsidered' in *Historical Journal* xlvii (2004).

Craig, Maurice, *Irish bookbindings, 1600–1800* (London, 1954).

Cressy, David, *Literacy and the social order* (Cambridge, 1980).

Cronin, Anne, 'Printed sources of Keating's *Foras feasa*' in *Eigse* iv (1943–44).

Cunningham, Bernadette, *The world of Geoffrey Keating* (Dublin, 2000).

—— and Gillespie, Raymond, *Stories from Gaelic Ireland: microhistories from the sixteenth-century Irish annals* (Dublin, 2003).

——, 'Lost worlds: history and religion in the poetry of Dáibhí Ó Bruadair' in Pádraigín Riggs (ed.), *Dáibhí Ó Bruadair: his historical and literary context* (Dublin, 2001).

Darnton, Robert, *The kiss of Lamourette: reflections in cultural history* (New York, 1989).

Davies, Frank, *Teaching reading in early England* (London, 1973).

Davis, Natalie Zemon, 'Beyond the market: books as gifts in sixteenth-century France' in *Transactions of the Royal Historical Society* 5th ser., xxxiii (1983).

Dix, E.R.McC., *Catalogue of early Dublin printed books, 1601–1700* (5 pts in 2 vols, Dublin, 1912).

——, 'A Dublin almanac of 1612' in *Proceedings of the Royal Irish Academy* xxx sect. C (1913).

——, 'An early Dublin almanac' in *Proceedings of the Royal Irish Academy* xxxiii sect. C (1916).

——, 'Schoolbooks printed in Dublin from the earliest period to 1715' in *Publications of the Bibliographical Society of Ireland* iii (1926–27).

——, *Printing in Dublin prior to 1601* (2nd edn, New York, 1971).

Donovan, Brian and Edwards, David (eds), *British sources for Irish history, 1485–1641* (Dublin, 1998).

Drennan, A.S., 'On the identification of the first Belfast printed book' in *The Library* 7th ser., i (2000).

Eisenstein, Elizabeth and Johns, Adrian, 'A.H.R. forum: how revolutionary was the print revolution' in *American Historical Review* cvii (2002).

English short title catalogue, 1473–1800 (CD Rom, 3rd edn, London, 2003)

Estabrook, Carl, *Urbane and rustic England: cultural ties and the social spheres in the provinces, 1660–1780* (Manchester, 1998).

Evans, Edward, *A historical and bibliographical account of almanacs and directories published in Ireland from the sixteenth century* (Dublin, 1897).

Fagan, Patrick, *Dublin's turbulent priest: Cornelius Nary* (Dublin, 1991).

Febvre, Lucien and Martin, Henri-Jean, *The coming of the book: the impact of printing, 1450–1800* (London, 1976).

Fletcher, Alan J., *Drama, performance and polity in pre-Cromwellian Ireland* (Cork, 2000).

Bibliography

Foster, R. F., *Modern Ireland, 1600–1972* (London, 1988).

Fox, Adam, *Oral and literate culture in England, 1500–1700* (Oxford, 2000).

Gailey, Alan, *Irish folk drama* (Cork, 1969).

Gillespie, Raymond, *Colonial Ulster: the settlement of east Ulster, 1600–41* (Cork, 1985).

——, 'Irish printing in the early seventeenth century' in *Irish Economic and Social History* xv (1988)

——, 'Landed society and the interregnum in Ireland and Scotland' in Rosalind Mitchison and Peter Roebuck (eds), *Economy and society in Scotland and Ireland, 1500–1939* (Edinburgh, 1988).

——, 'A question of survival: the O'Farrells and Longford in the seventeenth century' in Raymond Gillespie and Gerard Moran (eds), *Longford: essays in county history* (Dublin, 1991).

——, *The transformation of the Irish economy* (Dundalk, 1991).

——, 'Church, state and education in early modern Ireland' in Maurice O'Connell (ed.), *O'Connell: education, church and state* (Dublin 1992).

——, 'Destabilising Ulster, 1641–2' in Brian Mac Cuarta (ed.), *Ulster 1641: aspects of the rising* (Belfast, 1993).

——, 'Faith, family and fortune: the structures of everyday life in early modern Cavan' in Raymond Gillespie (ed.), *Cavan: essays on the history of an Irish county* (Dublin, 1995).

——, 'The circulation of print in seventeenth-century Ireland' in *Studia Hibernica* no. 29 (1995–97).

——, 'The book trade in southern Ireland, 1590–1640' in Gerard Long (ed.), *Books beyond the pale: aspects of the provincial book trade in Ireland before 1850* (Dublin, 1996).

——, 'Dublin, 1600–1700: a city and its hinterlands' in Peter Clark and Bernard Lepetit (eds), *Capital cities and their hinterlands in early modern Europe* (Aldershot, 1996).

——, '"Into another intensity": prayer in Irish nonconformity, 1650–1700' in Kevin Herlihy (ed.), *The religion of Irish dissent, 1650–1800* (Dublin, 1996).

——, *Devoted people: belief and religion in early modern Ireland* (Manchester, 1997).

——, '"A good and godly exercise": singing the word in Irish dissent, 1660–1701' in Kevin Herlihy (ed.), *Propagating the word of Irish dissent, 1650–1800* (Dublin, 1998)

——, 'Political ideas and their social contexts in seventeenth-century Ireland' in Jane Ohlmeyer (ed.), *Political thought in seventeenth-century Ireland* (Cambridge, 2000).

——, 'The religion of the first duke of Ormond' in T.C. Barnard and Jane Fenlon (eds), *The dukes of Ormonde, 1610–1745* (Woodbridge, 2000).

——, 'The social thought of Richard Bellings' in Micheál Ó Siochrú (ed.), *Kingdoms in crisis: Ireland in the 1640s* (Dublin, 2001).

——, 'The reformed preacher: Irish Protestant preaching, 1660–1700' in Alan J. Fletcher and Raymond Gillespie (eds), *Irish preaching, 700–1700* (Dublin, 2001).

——, 'Negotiating order in seventeenth-century Ireland' in M.J. Braddick and John Walter (eds), *Negotiating power in early modern society* (Cambridge, 2001).

——, 'The religion of the Protestant laity in early modern Ireland' in Brendan Bradshaw and Dáire Keogh (eds), *Christianity in Ireland: revisiting the story* (Dublin, 2002).

——, 'Irish print and Protestant identity: William King's pamphlet wars, 1687–1697' in Vincent Carey and Ute Lotz-Heumann (eds), *Taking sides: colonial and confessional mentalities in early modern Ireland* (Dublin 2003).

——, 'Temple's fate: reading the *Irish rebellion* in seventeenth-century Ireland' in Ciarán Brady and Jane Ohlmeyer (eds), *British interventions in early modern Ireland* (Cambridge, 2005).

Gilmont, Jean–François (ed.), *The Reformation and the book* (Aldershot, 1990).

Gilmore, William, *Reading becomes a necessity of life: material and cultural life in rural New England, 1780–1835* (Knoxville, 1989).

Goody, Jack (ed.), *Literacy in traditional societies* (Cambridge, 1968).

——, *The logic of writing and the organisation of society* (Cambridge, 1986).

Greaves, Richard, *God's other children: Protestant nonconformists and the emergence of denominational churches in Ireland* (Stanford, 1997).

Greene, David, 'A Gaelic version of the "Seven wise masters"' in *Béaloideas* xiv (1944).

Green, Ian, '"The necessary knowledge of the precepts of religion": catechisms and catechising in Ireland, 1560–1800' in Alan Ford, James McGuire and Kenneth Milne (eds), *As by law established: the Church of Ireland since the Reformation* (Dublin, 1995).

——, *Print and Protestantism in early modern England* (Oxford, 2000).

Greg, W.W., *A companion to Arber* (Oxford, 1967).

Halasz, Alexandra, *The market place of print: pamphlets and the public sphere in early modern England* (Cambridge, 1997).

Hall, David, *Cultures of print: essays in the history of the book* (Amherst, 1996).

Hellinga, Lotte and Trapp, J.B. (eds), *The Cambridge history of the book in Britain: iii 1400–1557* (Cambridge, 1999).

Henegan, Fred, 'Mummers of County Wexford' in *Irish Booklover* xvii (1929).

Hore, H.F., *History of the town and county of Wexford* (6 vols, London, 1900–11).

Hunter, R.J., 'John Gwillam and the Dublin book trade in 1614' in *Long Room* no. 36 (1991).

——, 'Chester and the Irish book trade, 1681' in *Irish Economic and Social History* xv (1988).

James, F.G., *Lords of the ascendancy* (Dublin, 1995).

Jardine, Lisa and Grafton, Anthony, '"Studied for action": how Gabriel Harvey read his Livy' in *Past and Present* no. 129 (1990).

Johns, Adrian, *The nature of the book: print and knowledge in the making* (Chicago, 1998).

Jones, Philip Henry and Rees, Eiluned (eds), *A nation and its books: a history of the book in Wales* (Aberystwyth, 1998).

Kilroy, Phil, *Protestant dissent and controversy in Ireland, 1660–1714* (Cork, 1994).

Kinane, Vincent, 'Some red morocco bindings by Christopher Chapman in the Worth Library, Dublin' in *Long Room* no. 42 (1997).

Lennon, Colm, *Richard Stanihurst: the Dubliner, 1547–1618* (Dublin, 1981).

Love, Harold, *Scribal publication in seventeenth-century England* (Oxford, 1993)

McCann, Wesley, 'An unrecorded edition of John Taylor's *Verbum sepiterum*' in *Linen Hall Review* vi no. 2 (1989).

——, 'Patrick Neill and the origins of Belfast printing' in Peter Isaac (ed.), *Six centuries of the provincial book trade in Britain* (Winchester, 1990).

McCarthy, Muriel, 'An eighteenth-century Dublin bibliophile' in *Irish Arts Review* iii no. 4 (Winter 1986).

Mac Craith, Mícheál, *Lorg na hasachta ar na dánta grá* (Dublin, 1989).

McDonnell, Joseph, *Five hundred years of the art of the book in Ireland* (Dublin and London, 1997).

Mac Gearailt, Uáitéar, 'Togail Troí: an example of translation and editing in medieval Ireland' in *Studia Hibernica* no. 31 (2000–1).

McKenzie, D.F., *Bibliography and the sociology of texts* (Cambridge, 1999).

McKitterick, David, *Print, manuscript and the search for order, 1450–1830* (Cambridge, 2003).

McManus, Antonia, *The Irish hedge school and its books, 1695–1831* (Dublin, 2002).

Mandlebrote, Scott, 'John Baskett, the Dublin booksellers and the printing of the Bible' in A. Hunt, G. Mandlebrote and A. Shell (eds), *The book trade and its customers* (Winchester, 1997).

Mann, A.J., *The Scottish book trade, 1500–1720* (East Linton, 2000)

Mant, Richard, *History of the Church of Ireland from the Restoration to the union of the Churches of England and Ireland* (London, 1840).

Matteson, Robert, 'Francis le Janu's letter to William King' in *Long Room* nos 16–17 (1978).

——, 'Archbishop King and the conception of his library' in *The Library* 6th ser., xiii (1991).

Miller, John, 'Thomas Sheridan (1646–1712) and his "Narrative"' in *Irish Historical Studies* xx (1976–77).

Molyneux, Capel, *An account of the family and descendants of Thomas Molyneux* (Evesham, 1820).

Moody, T.W., Martin, F.X. and Byrne, F.J. (eds), *A new history of Ireland iii: early modern Ireland* (Oxford, 1976).

Moore, Catherine, 'The library catalogues of the eighth and ninth earls of Kildare', unpublished M.Phil. thesis, Trinity College, Dublin, 1998.

Munter, Robert, *The history of the Irish newspaper, 1685–1760* (Cambridge, 1967).

——, *A dictionary of the print trade in Ireland, 1550–1775* (New York, 1988).

Ní Mhurchadha, Maighréad, 'Contending neighbours: society in Fingal, 1603–60', unpublished Ph.D. thesis, N.U.I. Maynooth, 2002.

Ó Caiside, Seamus, 'Cork printing in the seventeenth century' in *Irish Book Lover* xxi (1933).

Ó Ciosáin, Niall, *Print and popular culture in Ireland, 1750–1850* (Basingstoke, 1997).

Ó Clabaigh, Colmán, *The Franciscans in Ireland, 1400–1534* (Dublin, 2002).

O'Connor, Thomas, 'Custom, authority and tolerance in Irish political thought: David Rothe's *Analecta sacra et mira* (1616)' in *Irish Theological Quarterly* lxiv (2000).

Ó Dúshláine, Tadhg, *An Eoraip agus litríocht na Gaeilge, 1600–1650* (Dublin, 1987).

Olden, Michael, 'Counter Reformation problems: Munster' in *Irish Ecclesiastical record* 5th ser., civ (July–Dec. 1965).

Oliver, L.M., 'A bookseller's account book' in *Harvard Library Bulletin* xvi (1968).

Ó Macháin, Pádraig, 'The early modern Irish prosodic tracts and the editing of bardic verse' in H.L.C. Tristram (ed.), *Metrik and medienwechsel/metricks and media* (Tübingen, 1991).

Ó Siochrú, Micheál, *Confederate Ireland, 1642–1649: a constitutional and political analysis* (Dublin, 1999).

Palmer, Patricia, *Language and conquest in early modern Ireland* (Cambridge, 2001).

Patterson, Annabel, *Censorship and interpretation: the conditions of reading and writing in early modern England* (Madison, 1982).

Perceval-Maxwell, Michael, 'The Anglesea–Ormond–Castlehaven dispute, 1680–1682: taking sides about Ireland in England' in Vincent Carey and Ute Lotz-Heumann (eds), *Taking sides: colonial and confessional mentalities in early modern Ireland* (Dublin, 2003).

Phillips, James, *Printing and bookselling in Dublin, 1670–1800* (Dublin, 1998).

Plomer, H.R., 'Some notes on the Latin and Irish stocks of the Company of Stationers' in *The Library* 2nd ser., viii (1907).

——, *A dictionary of booksellers and printers who were at work in England, Scotland and Ireland from 1641 to 1667* (London, 1907).

——, *A dictionary of the printers and booksellers who were at work in England, Scotland and Ireland from 1668 to 1775* (Oxford, 1922).

Pollard, Mary, 'Print costs c. 1620' in *Long Room* no. 10 (1974).

——, 'Paper making in Ireland in 1590' in *Irish Booklore* iii (1976–77).

——, 'Control of the press through the king's printers patent, 1600–1800' in *Irish Booklore* iv (1980).

——, *Dublin's trade in books, 1550–1800* (Oxford, 1989).

——, *A dictionary of members of the Dublin book trade 1550–1800* (London, 2000).

Quinn, David, 'Government printing and the publication of the Irish statutes in the sixteenth century' in *Proceedings of the Royal Irish Academy* xlix sect. C (1941).

——, 'Information about Dublin printers, 1556–1573 in English financial records' in *Irish Booklover* xxviii (1942).

——, *The Elizabethans and the Irish* (Ithaca, 1966).

——, 'Edward Walsh's *The office and deuty in fightyng for our country* (1545)' in *Irish Booklore* iii (1976–77).

——, 'John Denton requests William Kearney to print books for use in Down c. 1588: a sidelight on printing in Ireland' in *Irish Booklore* iii (1976–77).

Raven, James, Small, Helen, and Tadmor, Naomi (eds), *The practice and representation of reading in England* (Cambridge, 1996).

Raymond, Joad, *Pamphlets and pamphleteering in early modern Britain* (Cambridge, 2003)

Reeves, William, *The book of Common Prayer according to the use of the Church of Ireland: its history and sanction* (Dublin, 1871).

Reid, J.S., *History of the Presbyterian church in Ireland* (3 vols, Belfast, 1867).

Roberts, R.J., 'The Latin stock (1616–1627) and its library contacts' in Robin Myers, Michael Harris and Giles Mandelbrote (eds), *Libraries and the book trade* (Delaware, 2000).

Robinson, J.L., 'Churchwarden's accounts 1484–1566, St Werburgh's church, Dublin' in

Journal of the Royal Society of Antiquaries of Ireland xliv (1914).

Roebuck, Peter, 'The Irish registry of deeds: a comparative study' in *Irish Historical Studies* xviii (1972–73).

Rogers, Charles 'Notes in the history of Sir Jerome Alexander' in *Transactions of the Royal Historical Society* n.s. ii (1873).

Roy, Ian, 'The libraries of Edward, second Viscount Conway and others: an inventory and valuation of 1643' in *Bulletin of the Institute of Historical Research* xli (1968).

Royal Irish Academy, *Dictionary of the Irish language based mainly on Old and Middle Irish materials* (Dublin, 1983).

Savage-Armstrong, G.F., *A genealogical history of the Savage family in Ulster* (London, 1906).

Sessions, W.K., *The first printers in Waterford, Cork and Kilkenny pre-1700* (York, 1990).

——, *Further Irish studies in early printing history* (York, 1994).

Shiels, Hugh, *Narrative singing in Ireland* (Dublin, 1993).

Simms, J.G., 'Land owned by Catholics in Ireland in 1688' in *Irish Historical Studies* vii (1950–51).

Simms, Katharine, 'Literacy and the Irish bards' in Huw Pryce (ed.), *Literacy in medieval Celtic societies* (Cambridge, 1998).

Spufford, Margaret, *Small books and pleasant histories: popular fiction and its readership in seventeenth-century England* (London, 1981).

——, *The world of rural dissent, 1520–1725* (Cambridge, 1995).

Stevenson, A., 'Shirley's publishers: the partnership of Cooke and Crooke' in *The Library* 4th ser., xxv (1945).

Stewart, R., 'The king's printer' in *The Library* 3rd ser., xvii (1926–27).

Stock, Brian, *The implications of literacy: written languages and models of interpretation in the eleventh and twelfth centuries* (Princeton, 1983).

Sweeney, Tony, *Ireland and the printed word, 1475–1700* (Dublin, 1997).

Thomas, Keith, 'The meaning of literacy in early modern England' in Gerd Baumann (ed.), *The written word: literacy in transition* (Oxford, 1986).

Tilley, Charles, *The formation of national states in western Europe* (Princeton, 1975).

Wallace, P.F. and Ó Floinn, Raghnall (eds), *Treasures of the National Museum of Ireland: Irish antiquities* (Dublin, 2002).

Walsh, Paul, *Irish men of learning* (Dublin, 1947).

——, *Irish chiefs and leaders* (Dublin, 1960).

Watt, Tessa, *Cheap print and popular piety, 1550–1640* (Cambridge, 1991).

Williams, Nicholas, *I bprionta í leabhar: na Protastúin agus prós na Gaeilge, 1567–1724* (Dublin, 1986).

Wood, Herbert, 'The public records of Ireland before and after 1922' in *Transactions of the Royal Historical Society* 4th ser. xiii (1930).

Woolfe, D.R., *Reading history in early modern England* (Cambridge, 2002).

Zimmermann, George Denis, *The Irish storyteller* (Dublin, 2001).

Index